The Titans
of Takeover

The Titans of Takeover

Robert Slater

Prentice-Hall, Inc.
Englewood Cliffs, New Jersey 07632

Library of Congress Cataloging-in-Publication Data

Slater, Robert (date)
    The titans of takeover.

    Bibliography: p.
    Includes index.
    1. Consolidation and merger of corporations—
United States.   2. Capitalists and financiers—
HD2785.S44   1987   338.8'3'0973   86-25364
ISBN 0-13-922055-0

Editorial/production supervision
  and interior design: Sophie Papanikolaou
Cover design: Lundgren Graphics, Ltd.
Manufacturing buyer: Carol Bystrom

The publisher offers discounts on this book when ordered
in bulk quantities. For more information, write:

        Special Sales/College Marketing
        Prentice-Hall, Inc.
        College Technical and Reference Division
        Englewood Cliffs, NJ 07632

Printed in the United States of America

10 9 8 7 6 5 4 3 2 1

ISBN 0-13-922055-0   025

Prentice-Hall International (UK) Limited, *London*
Prentice-Hall of Australia Pty. Limited, *Sydney*
Prentice-Hall Canada Inc., *Toronto*
Prentice-Hall Hispanoamericana, S.A., *Mexico*
Prentice-Hall of India Private Limited, *New Delhi*
Prentice-Hall of Japan, Inc., *Tokyo*
Prentice-Hall of Southeast Asia Pte. Ltd., *Singapore*
Editora Prentice-Hall do Brasil, Ltda., *Rio de Janeiro*

Contents

Acknowledgments

Five or ten years ago it would have been impossible to have the kind of cooperation I enjoyed from the key figures in this narrative. But as the public thirst for information about the major personalities in the takeover game has increased, so has the willingness of these personalities to share a part of their professional careers in more open fashion.

Throughout my research for this book I was constantly impressed—and pleased—that the movers and shakers of the takeover game thought it important to tell their stories. They had obviously learned that cultivating a public image was important. Making money wasn't enough: they wanted to be understood, and, if possible, liked.

Not everyone thought it crucial to tell his tale. A good deal of secrecy remains on the subject of modern takeovers, and perhaps that is understandable. Revealing too many tricks of the trade might just wreck the next deal.

I wish to express my gratitude to the numerous people who took time away from peering at their stock quotations to explain the ins and outs of the takeover phenomenon; and to those who helped in the gathering of material for the book. I especially want to thank: Ivan Boesky, Richard Cheney, Joseph Flom, Ronald Freeman, Gail Golden, John Greenwald, John Guenther, Jay Higgins, Carl Icahn, Sharon Kalin, Al Kingsley, Martin Lipton, Katherine McMillan, Tim Metz, Roger Miller, David Nachman, Ed Navotny, Joseph Perella, Monica Prihoda, Judith Resnik, Allan Sloan, Fred Ungeheurer, and Michael Zimmerman, and others who asked not to be identified.

Acknowledgments

I benefited greatly from all manner of help, moral and otherwise, from my friends and colleagues at Time-Life. I thank one and all.

Martin Lipton and Fred Ungeheurer kindly agreed to read the manuscript and I wish to thank them for taking so much of their valuable time in helping to improve it.

My children, Miriam, Adam, and Rachel, once again exhibited great patience and tolerance for their father who, while only a few feet from them most of the time, was permitted to seclude himself in his study at home to write this book. I thank them.

Finally, a word of thanks to my wife, Elinor. With the eye of a professional editor, which she is, she constantly pointed out ways to clarify and improve the text—for that and much more I thank her.

Few authors could have an editor as encouraging and supportive as Jeff Krames. His enthusiasm for the subject of this book and his advice and guidance at key points during the writing were significant factors in the final product. I am most indebted to him. My thanks are due as well to my production editor, Sophie Papanikolaou, who, with patience and diligence, made a major contribution to this book.

I dedicate this book to the businessmen in my family: my late father, Joseph Slater; my brother Jack Slater; my brother-in-law, Judd Winick; and my late father-in-law, Nathan Resnik. Without knowing it, they provided me with a fascination for the business world, a fascination which admittedly was latent for long periods. It pleases me to have written a book on a subject with which they have been so deeply associated.

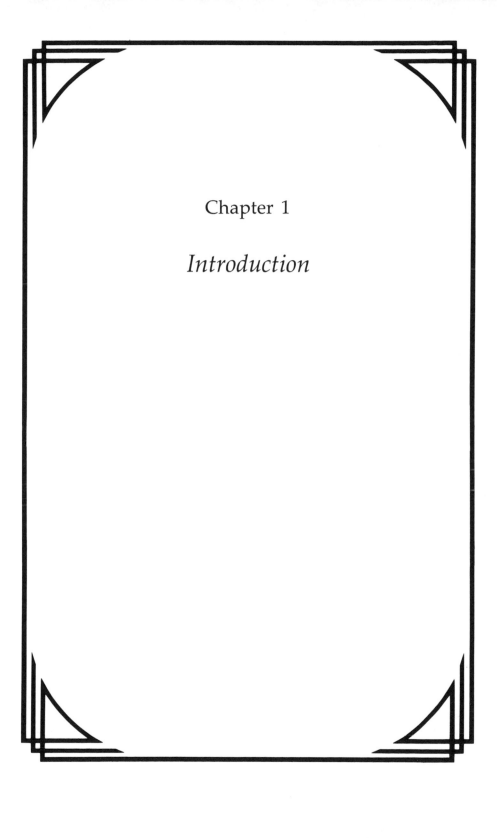

Chapter 1

Introduction

By the early 1980s their names began to appear in the press more frequently. Their photographs adorned the covers of the business magazines, and the national news magazines as well. Men like T. Boone Pickens, Carl Icahn and Saul Steinberg—corporate raiders, they were called. Joe Perella and Bruce Wasserstein, Eric Gleacher, and Michael Milken: investment bankers with a specialty called mergers and acquisitions—M&A, to anyone in the trade. Ivan Boesky: the press liked to call him the king of the arbitragers when few outside of Wall Street knew what arbitragers did. Joseph Flom and Martin Lipton—lawyers who were experts in M&A. Corporate executives got into the news too for chasing other companies: Bill Agee and Mary Cunningham—dubbed by the media the king and queen of Bendix. Suddenly, the public at large was interested in the goings on of American businessmen, particularly when they were involved in dramatic takeover fights. Names like Harry Gray of United Technologies, Hugh Liedtke of Pennzoil, Ted Turner of Turner Broadcasting showed up in the news. They all had one thing in common—they were part of the takeover game.

It was a game that had been played before, one American business merging with a second. In a sense, it began with the Trusts and Monopolies at the turn of the twentieth century, and it continued into the twenties and the sixties when the great conglomerates swept over American business. Yet this time there was a difference, a major one. This time all America was watching intently.

Americans watched the drama of the takeover game unfold day by day, hour by hour. Watched the personalities who were no longer back-page news but were now America's heroes, villains, larger-than-life figures whose antics kept the nation enthralled. In the past, the corporate giants of America ran the takeover show: they decided whether they wanted to merge with another business. No smaller company could even contemplate taking over one of the giants. The dominance of the large corporations in American business was as sacrosanct as the profit motive and free enterprise itself. While their activities certainly produced news, that news focused on the conglomerates. Now, all of American business became the subject of public interest.

In the second half of the 1970s traditions were breaking down, rules were changing, corporate life as America knew it for so many decades was undergoing a radical shift. All that had once seemed inviolate was now up for grabs. Those who had been considered the strong and impregnable now appeared weak and open to attack. With these changes new opportunities arose, and exploiting them were a whole new set of actors—actors who a decade earlier could not have dreamed of becoming part of the takeover game, who would not have dared to confront the corporate behemoths. These were the corporate raiders, men of means who were the first to discover the opportunities in the takeover field. They saw before others did that some companies, among them the largest on the corporate landscape, could be had for a bargain; some companies were really anomolies: their behavior on the stock market was unimpressive; yet they contained assets making them worth a good deal more than what "the Street" was paying. These companies were therefore ripe for a takeover, and a clever businessman, even if his company's assets were smaller than the target's, even if he might have thought twice in the past about engaging in a hostile takeover, could profit handsomely.

In challenging the establishment, these raiders aroused great public interest—especially because suddenly the stakes were large. Players in the takeover game could reap millions of dollars—if they played skillfully. Wanting to knock over a corporation and knowing how to accomplish the deed were, of course, two very distinct matters. An executive skilled in managing a company, in selling a product, commonly had little or no experience in acquiring other firms, big or little. He needed advice—the best advice he could get. To chase after larger corporate prey was a monumental task, perhaps the single most important task that an executive would ever face. To make sure he got the best advice, the executive was prepared to pay dearly. Enter the investment banker who handles M&A, that man of mystery on Wall Street with his talent for sizing up companies, for getting his hands on cash quickly, for knowing when to strike a deal and how to do it—enter the dealmaker. For his efforts, he would rake in fees in the millions of dollars and become, along with a handful of colleagues in this tiny group of financial wizards, a new pop star of the business world. A decade earlier, investment bankers were largely unknown. But by the mid-1980s hardly anyone interested in the takeover game had not heard of the big names.

Others played the takeover game as well. Attorneys became active players, but only a select few who had mastered the intricacies were able to advise how to topple a company; or how to defend against a takeover. Two names stood above the rest, Joseph Flom and Martin Lipton. Though Joe had acquired the reputation of being "Mr. Takeover" and Marty "Mr. Defense," each was equally comfortable on the other side of the takeover fence. Another set of players were the professionals on the stock market, the arbitragers; they sought to take advantage of stock run-ups which resulted from takeover situations. Often the decisions they would make while playing the takeover game would determine the outcome. Hence, they were crucial actors.

Raiders, investment bankers, attorneys, and arbitragers—these are the personalities in the takeover game. They are the main subject of this book. In these pages, I have focused on some of these personalities, going beyond the daily news stories to discuss what these people do and what they are like, and in that way narrating some of the major events of the modern takeover game.

The new-wave takeover plays have been part of a revolution in American business.

Mergers have always been part of American corporate life. Indeed there were twice as many mergers in 1969 (6,107) as in 1985 (roughly 3,000). The difference in the late 1970s and early 1980s was that the takeovers were more likely to be hostile, and their total dollar volume was far higher. In 1969, for example, only $23.7 billion of transactions had taken place; but by 1981 the figure had grown nearly fourfold, to $82.6 billion. In the decade between 1974 and 1984—the critical one for the modern takeover game—American corporations spent the record-breaking sum of $398 billion on mergers and acquisitions in some 23,000 transactions. The revolution was impacting on the corporate giants: there were many more giant-sized mergers than in the past. The very first billion-dollar merger actually occurred way back in 1901 with the formation of U.S. Steel out of the combination of the Carnegie Steel Corporation and its opponents, but until the 1980s transactions on such a large scale were rare. In the 1970s things started to change: in 1975 there was only one takeover transaction worth $500 million or more; but in 1980 there were fifteen. In 1975, only fourteen transactions of $100 million or more occurred; but only five years later, there would be fifty-five. During the 1960s, the typical acquirer was twenty times larger than his target. But that was clearly changing. Between 1980 and 1985, sixty-two *Fortune* 500 corporations were taken over by other companies. Prior to the 1980s investment bankers and takeover attorneys felt at ease in assuring $2 billion firms that they were safe from a hostile takeover. But that too was changing, and companies worth $5 and $6 billion no longer seemed immune.

The years 1983 and 1984 produced the peak in modern takeovers both in terms of the size and the number of transactions. The number of mergers and acquisitions in 1983 reached 2,533, the highest figure in nine years, worth some $73.5 billion. The following year topped that, with 2,543 such deals worth $122 billion. Some of the largest deals were completed in 1984. Apart from the $13.2 billion Chevron-Gulf merger, there was the $10.1 billion Texaco-Getty deal and the $5.7 billion merger of Mobil and Superior Oil.

The pace did not slow in 1985, as the 3,000 transactions which took place were worth a record-breaking $200 billion. The takeover game hit nearly every industry. Moreover, some of the biggest names in corporate warfare made the headlines in 1985, in sharp contrast with the takeover situation in the early 1980s when billion-dollar mergers occurred only in the oil patch. In 1985, Capital Cities Communications purchased the American Broadcasting Company in March for $3.5 billion; Phillip Morris, the cigarette maker, acquired General Foods in September, for $5.7 billion; and General Electric took over RCA, the parent of NBC, in December, for $6 billion.

What had happened to bring about this earthquake?

What had happened was simple. A man named Ronald Reagan entered the White House on January 20, 1981.

He was a Republican and he believed in the unshackling of Big Business. He insisted that the floodgates be opened. Until he was elected President, America had done a good job of keeping those floodgates closed to Big Business. Closed to anything big. In corporate America bigness had come to be synonymous with bad. Bigness meant trust and monopolies. Bigness meant a stifling of competition, the temptation to fix prices, to get stodgy and inefficient. America had had its share of bigness in earlier days—when Standard Oil controlled 84 percent of American oil marketing; when U.S. Steel was an amalgam of 148 companies, dwarfing all others; when American Tobacco knew almost no competition. But weren't these dynamos the key factors in building America? Weren't they the engines of economic progress? Yes, but they were too large, too large to harness, too large to keep from doing damage to society, from doing damage to those sacred gods of American capitalism—competition and pluralism.

But Ronald Reagan had a sacred god—not competition or pluralism, but rather American business per se. Once a dominant force around the world, American business had been suffering—from foreign competition, from foreign corporate giants which did not have to wrestle with antitrust limitations or worry about growing too big. And so the foreign giants had grown efficient, and American business had slipped into lethargy. The new American president planned to change all that. The place to start was in antitrust enforcement. That enforcement had been anchored for years in one of America's most immovable objects, the Clayton Antitrust Act of 1914, legislation adopted to deny robber barons dominion over the American economy. Yet conditions were vastly different then from what they would become in the 1970s and 1980s. In the early part of the twentieth century, America was the world's major industrial power, hardly affected by foreign competition, a situation that still prevailed even when the law was amended in 1950. As late as 1966 antitrust enforcement remained the conventional wisdom in Washington. The United States Supreme Court had in that year upheld an enforcement action against the merger of two supermarket chains because the court believed their combined share of only 8 percent of the Los Angeles market was potentially anticompetitive.

Once the new administration took over, the hard-nosed antitrust atmosphere would go by the boards. Something had to be done to protect American firms from the growing competition. By 1980 the primary rivals of U.S. corporate giants such as IBM and General Motors were foreign firms, particularly Japanese ones. It was time for Washington to develop a more benign attitude toward the size of American businesses. With the arrival of Ronald Reagan to the White House, that was precisely what happened. "Bigness," Attorney General William French Smith would say in an oft-quoted speech before the District of Columbia Bar in 1981, "does not necessarily mean badness. Efficient firms should not be hobbled under the guise of antitrust enforcement."[1] The administration soon put that into practice. A nine-year government effort to break up Kellogg Co., General Mills, and General Foods was dropped. Antitrust suits against AT&T and IBM ended. Most importantly, when the large-scale takeover wars began in the 1980s, rather than serve as referee and halt the big companies from consolidating, Washington acted like a cheerleader. Du Pont and Conoco; Chevron and Gulf; Texaco and Getty: none of these deals could have been contemplated in the past. By the early 1980s, as the investment bankers would say, they were do-able.

Do-able, but did that automatically mean American businesses would feel an urge to merge? The handcuffs had been removed. But would there be a sudden rush to embrace? The existing anomolies on the stock market certainly made it seem all but inevitable. Consider, for example, the situation at Conoco, a major energy producer. When the energy crisis hit the United States in 1973, the value of Conoco's oil, coal, natural gas, and uranium reserves was $2.6 billion. By 1981, inflation had pushed the value up to $14 billion. In the summer of 1981, Conoco had assets that included domestic oil reserves of almost 400 million barrels. The company's shares on the stock market should have been trading at $160 a share (its book value), but were only at $50. Domestic oil was selling for $30 a barrel and the cost of drilling was between $11 and $15 a barrel. Whoever purchased Conoco would be getting oil at $4.50 to $9 a barrel. This would make it far more inexpensive to buy the company than to drill for oil! Buying the company meant acquiring manufacturing facilities, a research arm, resource reserves—it was much better than beginning from scratch. Even if one thought of starting up a new venture, high inflation rates made it very expensive. Those rates were sending investors scurrying from the stock market, driving the prices of shares down. What resulted were under-valued companies (particularly ones with fixed assets like natural resources), which suddenly looked particularly attractive to a corporate raider.

A number of factors came together in the 1960s to fuel the last great merger movement: lax accounting rules, the new availability of paper (as opposed to cash), and a booming stock market. So too did the law, encouraging a corporation to engage in takeovers by rewarding it with liberal tax concessions. A relatively liberal antitrust atmosphere prevailed as well. The whole field of mergers was largely unregulated, and only toward the end of the decade with the enactment of the Williams Act (in 1968) did Washington take the first cautious steps to serve as a watchdog. By the end of the 1960s accounting rules tightened up, the antitrust mood toughened, and many states adopted legislation to curb takeovers: in all, 38 states set up laws, all of which were eventually declared unconstitutional. Meanwhile, the market went into a tailspin; money was no longer available for the merger movement. And so a dry spell occurred between 1970 and 1973.

Then in the mid-1970s a variety of factors boosted a fresh merger wave, which we chronicle in these pages. Suddenly cash was available, as were bargains. Finance men came to see the new legislation in Washington, not as a curb to hostile takeovers but rather as a road map. Other conditions suggested an upsurge in takeover interest. As the Government loosened its hold on the financial market, more money became available for raiders to use. Unlike the paper offers of the 1960s, there was a revival of cash offers. Federal deregulation in such industries as banking, the airlines, and broadcasting also spurred takeovers. Deregulation encouraged companies to grow: if federal rules permitted one to own more television stations, the instinct of corporate executives was to search out ways to acquire those stations.

All of this would seem to presage a certain wildness in the takeover game of the 1980s. But corporation executives had learned some important lessons from the conglomerates of the 1960s. These mammoth companies had bought up smaller firms in unrelated enterprises on the assumption that a good manager could manage anything. That assumption proved false. By the 1980s an executive interested in a takeover saw the virtue of remaining in his field of expertise, staying with the same technology, the know-how, keeping the comparative advantage his company had always enjoyed. Hence, corporate executives asked themselves, "Is this company a good fit?" Only if it was, did they jump in and seek a merger. In that respect, the merger wave of the 1980s bears far more resemblance to the period earlier in the century when such dynamos as Carnegie, Morgan, and Rockefeller were busy rationalizing the steel, railroad, and oil industries than to the conglomerate age of the 1960s. There was one interesting twist in the 1980s takeover movement. A new motive surfaced. Some takeover artists got into the game not for the purpose of expansion or diversification but in order to liquidate a firm and make a quick profit. These were the "bust-up" artists who had discovered that sometimes the sum was worth less than the parts.

With conditions ripening for a new merger wave, this one in the 1980s would have seemed generally similar to those of the past—save for the occurrence of an event in 1974 which would rock Wall Street out of its conservative foundations. It happened when International Nickel Co., of Toronto, Canada, represented by perhaps the most old-line of the Wall Street investment banking houses, Morgan Stanley, went after ESB, Inc., a battery maker in Philadelphia—in a hostile takeover bid. The raid was successful and had tongues wagging. The event stood out all the more because of the virtual absence of merger activity in recent years. This was hardly the first hostile takeover—there had been many during the active period of the 1960s. But this unfriendly deal was one with a big difference.

It was one of the first involving important, blue-chip companies. And, equally as important, it marked the first time that a conservative investment banking firm had decided to get involved in a hostile takeover involving major firms. The fact that Morgan Stanley, one of the country's most important investment banks, had been willing to take part in what had seemed an unseemly action removed the stigma for the major financial institutions on the Street, and soon it became acceptable for them to be associated with unfriendly mergers. If Morgan Stanley could do it, why couldn't other investment banking firms join in and grab a piece of the action?

Mergers and acquisitions had never had a high priority among these houses. They were preoccupied with selling new stock and bond issues. But International Nickel sent a signal throughout the Street. M&A suddenly looked like something worth pursuing. It was not illegal, it was highly profitable, and the money seemed to be there waiting to be picked up off the ground. In time, it would be the investment bankers who would come up with one of the main facilitators of takeovers: the use of high-yield, low-rated bonds—known in the trade as "junk bonds"—to finance the mergers. By the late 1970s major corporations that had avoided unfriendly mergers like the plague suddenly became attracted to the idea. Soon, hostile takeovers became acceptable even to *Fortune* 500 companies. The investment bankers were responsible as well for another phenomenon of the takeover game: leveraged buyouts. While the notion of such buyouts had existed before—where the company's management bought out the stockholders and then took the company private—it gained great popularity in the 1980s. Its main function in that decade was to keep management in power—and, not coincidentally, to keep hostile raiders away.

I asked Joseph Flom, the man most associated with the founding of the modern takeover movement, what he thought were its underlying causes:

> It was the size of the deals; the fact that major companies were willing to treat this as a legitimate corporate tool and not say, "I'll be read out of the club if I get involved." They had gotten rid of fixed commission rates. The market was in the doldrums. This was the investment banking houses' big source of revenue and this encouraged them to go out and merchandise takeovers which gave it additional life. Takeovers also provided almost the only liquidity in a very dormant market.
>
> (Earlier) we were able to identify the aggressors. And there were only one or two aggressors we represented. Everybody else was purely defensive. The acquisitions were totally different in the 1980s in that in the 1960s they were balance-sheet oriented, or financially oriented. People would take two and two and make it five because everybody was analyzing business based on historical earnings and you could distort them. The takeovers which started in 1974 were cash takeovers; they started primarily for business fit. The takeover movement in

the 1980s is different again in the sense that the big deals have been fueled by the availability of money, huge amounts of money, both from the banks, high-yield bonds, and so forth. And you had people taking over companies which were worth more dead than alive; but more dead by a wide margin, or where by restructuring them after you took them over you could change the dynamics very significantly. In a lot of these takeovers you buy it and sell off a lot of the divisions and you end up with a core business that's worth a heck of a lot more than what you had before.[2]

With merger mania afoot, the raiders, investment bankers, arbitragers, and lawyers were able to pick the money off the ground. And as they did, they aroused an increasing amount of public interest. It was not surprising: these were figures who inspired both love and hate, who fearlessly overcame great obstacles, who had a creative energy which allowed them to invent new rules. These were figures who by virtue of their ability to wield great power and to amass large fortunes had become in effect the pop heroes of what I would call the new Age of Money in America. This was an age which began in earnest after World War II and came to full life in the 1970s and 1980s—an age when making money seemed the main pursuit of mankind, at least in the United States. The men who did it best understandably deserved a special status and a reverence which ordinary mortals would never be given. They would become the objects of intense public interest.

The modern raiders, unlike their cousins in the past, actually looked for public attention. Prior to the advent of the raiders, someone picking off another company wanted as little publicity as possible. The publicity might generate lawsuits against him: it might tip his competitors off to what he was doing. He would be content to propose a price for the company he wanted and hope that he could keep the public from focusing on his bid. Focusing on his plans to take over a company might lead to unpleasant disclosures about his own firm that might keep the deal from going through. But along came T. Boone Pickens and the others: they were not afraid of publicity; they rather enjoyed basking in the bright lights: they wanted to be liked, wanted to send a message across America. They saw themselves, some of them at least, as philosophers and idealogues in a brand-new cause: the awakening of the stockholder. They used the public relations resources available to them and spoke up loud and clear.

The raiders were not always understood, they were not always accepted as men of benevolence. Labeled pirates, accused of hit-and-run tactics, dismissed as fortune hunters, the raiders were a new breed of American businessmen. For years, no one imagined that one person could take on a whole company. But these raiders did just that. By the 1980s they had become the scourge of American corporate life. Envied, despised, resisted, they emerged on the scene with tornado force, and few were able to prevent their menacing moves. Routinely men of impressive wealth—or at least men who could get their hands on vast sums—they prowled Wall Street for a ripe corporate catch. When they spotted an undervalued corporation—the kind we have been discussing earlier—they went after it. They would try to build up a large enough stake to make themselves a serious threat. Then they would strike, making a tender offer that, if accepted by management, would earn stockholders a healthy premium.

Management, by virtue of the offer, would almost always be caught on the horns of a nasty dilemma. On the one hand, it did not want to be taken over by a corporate raider. That could mean management's replacement. On the other, the management could not pass up a chance for its stockholders to earn a huge premium offered by the raider. Management could choose to drive the raider away or give in to him. At the outset of the modern takeover game, in the early 1980s, raiders seemed almost unbeatable. They were able pretty much to write their own ticket, earning millions of dollars as target firms paid heavily to ward them off. Essentially, a firm would offer to buy back at a premium the shares the raider had acquired. The raider, in turn, would agree not to pursue the company. Eventually, managements grew tired of the ordeal imposed on them by corporate raiders and they began to erect defenses that would make the target firm unattractive to buy—and thus keep the raider at bay.

What motivated the raiders? Some, like T. Boone Pickens and Carl Icahn, contend that their motives are the purest: they are playing the takeover game to help their fellow man, the lowly stockholder. Pickens calls himself the "champion of the small shareholder." Others frankly admit they have no such altruistic strain. "Takeovers," said corporate raider Sir James Goldsmith, "are for the public good, but that's not why I do it. I do it to make money." That unabashed acknowledgement endears the raiders to precious few. Still, Irwin Jacobs, a Minneapolis-based raider, insisted, "We're really not a bunch of big bad wolves. . . . People say, 'Kill the raiders, they're no good for the economy.' Well, not too long ago I told Carl (Icahn) and Boone (Pickens) that we all ought to go on strike for six months. If you took all the merger speculation out of the market, you wouldn't have a market."[3]

Corporate raider, chief executive officer, or whoever wanted to play an active role in the takeover game would automatically hone in on Wall Street or midtown Manhattan to do the dealmaking. That was where the major investment banking houses were; that was where the law firms dealing with takeovers were located. "You're talking about spending lots of dough," noted Jay Higgins, formerly head of the mergers and acquisitions department and now co-head of corporate finance at Salomon Brothers. "It's one of the most significant events in a CEO's life, so I think it's rational, almost predictable that the guy is going to talk to the people in the business world that he trusts the most. Maybe one hundred years ago it was the parish priest or the rabbi. Now it's your lawyer and your banker."[4] This was indeed a change for the investment banking houses. For many years takeover counseling had been only a sideline service provided by some of the old-line houses like Goldman Sachs, Morgan Stanley, Lehman Brothers, or First Boston. After 1974, after the watershed International Nickel takeover, newcomers came to the fore: Salomon Brothers; Kidder, Peabody; and Merrill Lynch White Weld.

Lodged in the mergers and acquisitions departments of these firms were the dealmakers, the men who could raise the money for a merger, devise tactics to prevent a hostile takeover, advise and act quickly and professionally. A chief executive officer of a company might believe that he could handle a takeover on his own, might believe that a trusted lawyer with whom he had worked might get him through a deal, but investment bankers could easily demonstrate that the CEO would have been better off turning to one of them. They were the specialists, the financial equivalent of the brain surgeon. "Wall Street," observed Jay Higgins, "was the most logical place for them to come—not only for the financing, but because we talked to all the corporations. A CEO knows his own company, knows his major competitors, a few other people, but it's not like here at Salomon or any of our major (competitors) where we're dealing with people all the time one way or another, one issue or another. That's why Wall Street is the natural place to go, as distinct from your regional lawyer who may know everyone in Minneapolis but doesn't know many of the issues and may not have been through it as many times as somebody else."[5]

Whether a CEO was probing to take over another company or bracing against attack from some aggressor, his career often was on the line, as were those of many other senior executives in the company. Naturally, the CEO wanted the best advice he could get. And so he was quite prepared to pay for it. Hence, for these takeover efforts, the investment bankers were paid incredibly large sums, millions of dollars often for only a few weeks or months of work. The first large fee—$14 million—was given to Morgan Stanley in December 1979 when Belridge Oil Co., represented by Morgan Stanley, was sold to Shell Oil Co. for $3.65 billion. Fees for a completed deal could run as high as 1.5 percent of the takeover price. Usually the investment banker and the corporation would agree on a minimum figure; the banker was compensated increasingly as his achievements grew. For each $1 per share, for example, paid above a certain price, the investment banker would get a higher fee. The highest fees went to investment bankers representing acquired firms. One of the largest merger fees was the $28 million Salomon Brothers charged Gulf in 1984. First Boston received $6 million for rescuing Pullman in April 1980—or $1,500 per man-hour. The $45 million fee that the investment banking firm of Kohlberg, Kravis,

Roberts & Co. was reportedly to receive for arranging the leveraged buyout of Beatrice Co. in the spring of 1986 would be a record.

In 1981, Morgan Stanley led the way in merger fees with $40 million. In 1984, it was Goldman Sachs with $63 million; then in 1985, again it was Morgan Stanley with $82 million; First Boston was second at $72 million. As merger activity increased in the 1980s, so did the merger fees: $144.6 million was paid for the top fifty deals in 1981, and $588 million in 1985.

For a while corporations paid without blinking an eye. Then, as the press began to focus increasingly on takeovers in the 1980s, the spotlight fell on these merger fees. Questions were asked. Did the fees really have to be so high? Were the investment bankers in fact worth all that much money? Critics intimated that the investment bankers were far from neutral agents in the takeover game, that they in fact did their best to whip up business for themselves by goading clients into doing deals. Nonsense, shot back the bankers. That left the impression that CEOs were just so much putty in the hands of the bankers, that they were not their own men. "We are agents, not principals," said an angry Jay Higgins. "It's not our money, for Chrissakes."[6] Some investment bankers tried to roll with the punches. A few even suggested that all the publicity about their fees was healthy, it helped them draw in more customers. If a corporation saw that a certain investment bank received more fees for doing takeover work than another one, the CEO would presumably gravitate toward the more successful bank.

Despite the controversy over the fees, or perhaps because of it, investment bankers became the leading players in the takeover game. This was hardly surprising. They were the professionals, the men who knew the rules of the game better than anyone. They had invented most of them, had tried them out in one takeover or another. They were the best spokesman, the best analysts of what the takeover game was all about. A corporate executive would win headlines for a month, only to vanish when a takeover episode was over. But the investment bankers stayed around. What was more, they cultivated the idea that they were a small, elitist fraternity whose membership was greatly prized. The few in the select circle knew one another, spoke often, and seemed to enjoy one another's company—though they were rivals for the largest sweepstakes in the American business world.

A whole lexicon has developed to explain the moves and countermoves in the modern takeover game. That lexicon was created in large part by the investment banking community. The bankers came up with the ploys, then attached names to them. Soon the terms became part of the vocabulary of American businessmen. In earlier days gentlemen bankers would not speak of doing a "deal"; that expression seemed too slangy, not to mention ungentlemenly. But today the utterances of a business executive are sprinkled with the new takeover slang words: white knight, golden parachute, poison pill, or that great tongue-twister, the front-end-loaded two-tier tender offer.

The more I came to know investment bankers, the more I realized their delight in cultivating their own special language. Like a secret hand-shake or a special code, that language performed several important functions. It made one feel he belonged to a tiny, elite society. It also gave the appearance—so terribly important to anyone dealing with such high stakes—that the goal was not merely to make more and more money, but also to enjoy the struggle, to win for the sake of winning in much the same way that little children do when they play their own games. Finally, as investment bankers realized that the public wanted to know more about their game, they sensed there was gain to be realized from that as well: not monetary gain but a more personal kind. In the past, no one outside of Wall Street knew a Jay Higgins, a Joe Perella, a Bruce Wasserstein, or a Marty Siegel. Suddenly, their names appeared in print, their photographs were on the covers of business and news magazines. Some of them actually enjoyed the publicity. One way of assuring that one would continue to get publicity was to speak as simply and clearly as possible. Nothing was to be gained from confusing the public. What one did—and no one did it better than the investment bankers—was to come up with a whole new language that would serve as a guide book through the thicket of corporate takeovers. In this way, the public would come to know what the takeover game was all about. It would also get to know who its brightest stars were.

Some of the new language recalls the days of chivalry; it is distinctly military and macho in character. There was that heroic figure, for example, who came into the takeover game in order to keep a corporate raider from succeeding. It would have been far too simple for the investment bankers to call him—a friendly buyer. Entering the fray to save the day for the company, he was the modern-day parallel of the sword-carrying fellow arriving at the castle dramatically mounted on a horse—hence he was known as a white knight.

When General Cable made a hostile offer to buy Microdot, the industrial-fastener company built by Rudolph Eberstadt Jr., Eberstadt was furious. "We would have been more willing to merge with the garbage collector than with General Cable," he said.[7] The Securities and Exchange Commission required a ten-day waiting period before a raider could begin buying a target's shares, giving Eberstadt a chance to canvas for a friendly buyer. Eberstadt found his white knight in Northwest Industries, a diversified industrial conglomerate, which topped General Cable's bid of $17 a share. If the Microdot executive had not been able to find a white knight, he might have had to settle for second-best, in this case another company making an uninvited offer to buy the besieged firm. Depending on the terms this new company offered, it would be regarded as hero or villain. Hence, it has been dubbed a gray knight. Other cute names entered the vocabulary as well: golden parachutes and bear hugs; poison pills and scorched-earth defenses; Pac-Man strategies and show-stoppers, just to mention a few.

The chances of a target company's remaining independent after a tender offer were at first small. A raider who could come up with the cash to make a tender offer that carried a nice premium was in great shape. Corporations gave little thought to a takeover: it carried the same degree of probability as a plane crash. CEOs were convinced that it could not happen to them. And so they did not bother erecting real defenses. The raider could virtually stroll in and present his challenge. Executives themselves realized this but seemed impotent to do much about it. In a Louis Harris poll in the summer of 1984 70 percent of the executives polled said that the acquiring firm had the advantage, while only 19 percent thought the takeover target was in better shape in a takeover battle.[8] Searching for a white knight, a dubious proposition at best, and in fact not a real solution to saving one's company, was the main choice open to a CEO in the early days of the modern takeover game. Another choice—at best a remote hope—was to find some legal barrier such as an antitrust problem which would remove the raider with one sudden blow. That legal barrier became known as a show-stopper.

Eventually defense tactics were devised; a company could come up with ways to make itself unattractive to a potential corporate raider. Few CEOs felt good about employing them but there seemed little choice. If they didn't employ defensive devices, raiders would continue to walk all over them. And so one began to hear more and more of steps being taken by corporations that would make things more difficult for a raider. Some firms would stagger their directors' terms in such a way that an acquiring firm could not pack the board quickly. Another step was to require a supermajority vote of stockholders to approve a merger. These devices were called shark repellents. Then in the 1980s came a more potent device—the poison pill. It made an unfriendly takeover bid so expensive that very few raiders would exhibit interest in an unfriendly bid. The pill usually came in the form of a dividend of rights to buy the raider's stock at a bargain price.

The defensive tactics could get even wilder. Depending on its degree of desperation, a target company could employ a scorched-earth policy, such as scheduling all of its debts to come due immediately after a takeover; or it could sell its crown jewel, the firm's most profitable subsidiary. Carter-Hawley Hale, the California department store chain, managed in the spring of 1984 to fend off the Limited, a fast-growing group of women's specialty stores, by resorting to the "crown jewel" strategy. The Limited had sought a $1.1 billion takeover, but Carter-Hawley Hale kept it at bay by offering its profitable Waldenbooks chain—its crown jewel—to another firm, General Cinema, a group of movie theaters. Another defensive ploy, as tricky as it was brilliant, was the Pac-Man strategy in which a firm would bite back by trying to take over a would-be buyer. This was the maneuver employed by Martin-Marietta in its defense against a raid by Bill Agee's Bendix in the summer and fall of 1982.

The raider was not without devices as well. There was the bear hug, an offer so generous that a board of directors could not refuse it without facing the ire of stockholders. One such bear hug was Carl Icahn's offer to purchase Phillips Petroleum in February 1985. Phillips managed to avoid Icahn's clutches by offering him a financial deal he could not refuse. There was also the front-end-loaded two-tier tender offer. Here, a raider made clear that he would offer one price for the initial block of stock he would buy and then a second, lower price for the remaining stock to be bought. Realizing they would do better by selling their stock early rather than late, stockholders would flock to sell, creating the likelihood that control would fall quickly into the raider's hands.

The takeover game, as played by the corporate raiders, began with someone trying to buy enough shares to give the impression that he was a serious candidate for taking over a firm. Once the raider decided that he wanted to invest in a company, there was no way to keep him from accumulating shares. If a defensive measure was to serve as a deterrent, it would have to be erected before the raider began to prey. The better the defense, the less likely the raider was to decide to buy up the shares. In the absence of a good defense, the company could only sit back and watch. Once the raider acquired 5 percent of a company's shares, the Securities and Exchange Commission required him to divulge his holdings. Inevitably, the value of the company's shares would rise when it became known that a corporate raid was under way. As the battle for control of the company intensified, the raider and management became locked in a struggle for the support of the stockholders. Often there were expensive mailings and full-page ads in newspapers; often the raider called press conferences to explain who he was and what he was doing. If a stockholder experienced a sense of helplessness, dismay, and outright confusion, that was all very understandable. Once the company was "in play," the stockholders become all-important. Many of them would want a sale, any sale, hoping for that big, fat premium that came with it. So a CEO who fended off a raider might be able to do only by turning to a white knight. White knights were not automatically to be found. They had to be convinced the company was worth being taken over. After all, until the target company's investment banker called to find out if the outsider wanted to become a white knight, the outsider had more than likely not given the matter any thought at all.

If the white knight decided to engage in a friendly merger with the target company, his bid, higher than the raider's, would automatically squeeze the raider out of the picture. When that happened, the raider lost his chance to gain control of the firm, and everyone supposedly breathed a sigh of relief. But was the corporate raider all that disappointed? Not really. In fact, he probably had little desire to take over the firm in the first place. He, too, had been playing a game, in which he would profit immensely by threatening a takeover. What the raider usually hoped for—and what he often managed to get for himself and for stockholders—was an impressive jump in value of the company's stock while his takeover bid was in the works. One example was Gulf Oil: when T. Boone Pickens began to pursue Gulf in October 1983, Gulf's stock had been at $41 a share. But when Chevron agreed to acquire the company the following March, it had risen to $80 a share. As a result of friendly takeovers like Chevron-Gulf, the raider was the recipient of a windfall: he automatically reaped a large profit on his shares when the sale to the friendly party went through. Pickens and his partners emerged with a $760 million profit on the Gulf deal.

The act of acquiring shares and then threatening a takeover with the hope of reaping that windfall before actually acquiring the firm has been labeled greenmail. Corporate raiders vigorously deny that they have engaged in such a nefarious practice. Many of them insist that they really wanted to buy the companies all along, but when the target firm offered to buy out their shares at such an obvious premium in exchange for a stand-still agreement (the raider would promise not to seek another takeover within ten to twenty years), they could not refuse such an offer. After watching the way the raiders worked, after eyeing the enormous profits they made from these buy-backs, few could believe they really ever wanted to take over the firms in the first place. Yet that was precisely what happened to Carl Icahn, who wound up as Chairman of TWA in the winter of 1986. He had been stalking the company for the previous six months, building up larger and larger amounts of TWA's shares. Everyone assumed he would at one stage take his millions and run. But he did not. And he wound up with the whole company. But he has been the exception.

Merger mania in the 1980s sparked a fresh debate about the value of these consolidations. As the corporate raiders and the investment bankers attracted more and more attention, the public began to ask questions about the mergers themselves. Were they good for the economy? Were they good for society at large? Should they be encouraged? Or curbed? And if limits should be placed on them, just how much? And by whom? Many of these questions were being addressed for the first time in the mid-1980s as the merger mania became an object of great media attention.

The advocates of mergers were greatly aided by the warm support coming out of Washington. Antitrust was unfashionable, big was no longer bad. Let the marketplace do its thing. Let's stay out of the game. Thus spoke the Reagan Administration. The economists and the media offered their voices endorsing the craze. Mergers, said these advocates, increased business efficiency while doing nothing to eliminate competition. Mergers meant economies of scale, less administrative overhead, the arrival of fresh leadership to tired companies. Raw materials could be ordered in large quantities and new technologies employed—all at savings that would lower production costs. Those smaller costs would mean better products at cheaper prices. Thus, the larger the firm, the greater its chance for holding its own against the giant foreign rivals that had been benefiting for years from liberal antitrust policies. Bruce Wasserstein, an investment banker at First Boston, summed up neatly the positive effects of mergers:

> One of the key advantages of takeovers, whether friendly or aggressive, is creating a fluidity in the economic system. Takeovers also create a vehicle for people to realize on their investments. They give an out, a chance to cash in on ideas, and thereby give entrepreneurs motivation for starting companies when, for example, the going public market is shut down, or the public market does not give full value to the economic assets and benefits that are in a company. Also, mergers have a disciplining effect on the market. With our economy, we should be very concerned about avoiding indefinite preservation of a fixed status quo— we need a responsive and dynamic economy.[9]

For every pro-takeover argument there seemed to be a corresponding negative one. The naysayers believed strongly that mergers added nothing productive to the economy, neither new jobs nor new factories. A point in their favor: during the past decade two-thirds of all new jobs in America were created by businesses with fewer than one hundred workers. What were produced as a result of takeovers were larger and larger corporations which, they insisted, would only become excessively bureaucratic and sluggish. The larger they became, the less incentive these companies had— said the critics—to compete or push hard. Economic growth was thus slowed. So, too, was initiative. Indeed, the critics noted that some of the most creative and innovative firms in America had been the smaller ones: Apple Computer, Genentech, and New York Air. Rather than spend all that money on trying to gobble one another up, why not invest the millions in research or in modernizing existing plants?

Add to this the uncertainty and unpleasantness surrounding job loss. A takeover could mean that some employees would benefit from job promotions and new financial benefits. But invariably mergers caused job losses. One survey of senior executives in 1985 indicated that almost half of those polled had sought other positions within one year after a merger.[10] A similar survey four years earlier had showed that only 20 percent had left after the first year.

The critics also pointed to a number of research studies which indicated that many mergers simply did not work in the long run, they were not profitable. With some conglomerates divesting themselves of unprofitable subsidiaries, the dissenters eagerly noted that one could now draw conclusions about whether past combinations (those of the 1960s, principally) worked. And in fact, said the critics, many did not. Arthur Burck, a specialist in corporate mergers, acquisitions, and reorganizations, estimated that since 1953 some 50,000 corporate acquisitions and mergers had occurred in the United States. "Most were cases of huge companies taking over small ones. My guess is that more than half of the companies acquired by the giants were weakened, damaged, or destroyed."[11] But such judgments could not yet be applied to the latest merger mania.

Chapter 2

A Fellow Named Bill, A Girl Named Mary

William Agee and Mary Cunningham. Courtesy David
Drapkin/*Time* Magazine.

I toyed with the idea of writing this book without dwelling on the Bendix Affair. Few subjects have been documented so painstakingly. Four books have been written about it, not to mention countless magazine and newspaper articles. Why go over it again? So I casually asked a few members of the Takeover Fraternity what they thought of the Bendix story. "It has everything," insisted one such person, "corporate greed, power plays, and, best of all, sex. There's never been anything like it since." Another chimed in: "The main actors were playing chicken with the lives of 50,000 people. It was the takeover equivalent of a nuclear war." As I chatted with more takeover types and particularly with more Bendix Players, I began to sense that what happened there, in the late summer and early fall of 1982, was a watershed for the modern takeover phenomenon. Glossing over Bendix while trying to tell the story of the Takeover Game of the 1980s, I came to understand, was like attempting to recount Shakespeare's *Hamlet* to someone without once mentioning the main character. It simply could not be done.

My friend was right: there has never been anything like it since. I wouldn't find another takeover tale as bizarre as this one. Therein may lie its true significance. When it was all over, it was as if everyone awoke from a nightmare and collectively asserted, "Fascinating to watch, exciting to be part of, but, gee fellows, we really got carried away!"

Carried away, indeed. The main actors performed in what *Time* magazine termed a "Merger Theater of the Absurd"[1]—defying what normally passes for sound business judgment, taking near-suicidal risks, wasting billions of dollars investing the time and energy of scores of corporate executives, attorneys, investment bankers, judges, and stockholders in a grand parody of American business. Often the Bendix Affair sounded like a screenplay for a movie called *The Corporate Jungle.*

And then there were the Players. (By the way, Takeover participants relish being known as players—as if they were quarterbacks throwing touchdown passes, or pitchers putting fastballs past a batter while 80,000 cheering souls look on. More than once it seemed to me that they want the same respect and adulation as that ultimate American hero, the athlete.) The two main players in the Bendix Takeover were a fellow named Bill Agee and a girl called Mary Cunningham.

Bill Agee. Boy Wonder, they called him. The Wunderkind of American business. At the tender age of 31, when others were still negotiating the first few rungs of the executive ladder, there was Agee already chief financial officer of the fast-growing Boise Cascade Corporation. Just seven years later, in 1976, he would be elevated to the presidency of Bendix— youngest man ever to run one of the Top 100 corporations. With those credentials, the sky seemed the limit. Ambitious, too. The Governorship of Idaho? Or perhaps a seat in the United States Senate? Reach higher, his admirers encouraged. Bill Agee had a cabinet post coming to him, or even the Vice Presidency. Why not? It all seemed within grasp.

Then along came Mary.

Mary Cunningham. Long blond hair. Tall and graceful. Willowy, they called her in the press. Bright. Great credentials, too: Magna Cum Laude and a Phi Beta Kappa from Wellesley; graduate of the Harvard Business School. And ambitious. Superambitious.

At first she was attracted by investment banking. A good meal ticket into the corporate world, she thought, gaming her life at an early age. But out of the blue came that chance in a million. The chance to work as Bill Agee's right-hand whatever. The title was executive assistant. Nothing but a go-fer, some of the guys at Bendix had warned her. Agee insisted she would be in on the Big Deals. She thought about her dreams: Mary Cunningham, Chairperson of Major American Corporation Whichever. Shouldn't she get into the investment banking groove right away? But to say no to the Wunderkind of American business? To pass up being "mentored" by the chairman of Bendix? Why, it would be like a child prodigy casting aside the opportunity to study under a Mozart or a Beethoven. So, in June 1979, Mary went to work for Bill. The two main players in the Bendix Affair were in place.

The takeover would begin only three years later. It would be major news. Takeovers that occurred B.B.—Before Bendix—aroused scant attention. They were routinely relegated to the business pages. No great drama there, no excitement. Or so it seemed. By the time of the Bendix Affair the press had gotten a sniff of the takeover story. The deals were getting bigger, more complicated. Larger companies were becoming involved. And by the time of Bendix, the press had introduced its readers to the greatest corporate scandal of recent time. The scandal focused on Bill and Mary. Were they or weren't they lovers? They said no. That made it all the more intriguing. By the time of the Bendix Affair, Americans were losing interest in the question of Who Shot J.R. Real life was so much more interesting.

With such an arcane screenplay, with such intriguing players, Bendix indeed proved a critical moment in the modern takeover game. For the first time the nation took a collective peek behind the scenes of these Mega Deals and their Mega Players. For the first time a public debate began on what to do about this merger mania. Nearly everyone agreed—even the players themselves—that the words Bendix and Fiasco had become interchangeable. How bizarre indeed it all was: just as the players and observers were becoming familiar with the rules of the modern takeover game, the actors involved in Bendix seemed to be twisting them out of shape. It was almost as if someone had informed Bill Agee and the others that now that the chess board had been built, the players put in place, the rules devised, it was perfectly OK to go off the board in some wild frenzy of irrationality. In this "anything goes" kind of atmosphere, the Bill and Mary tale seemed to be just one more piece of the action.

The tale played a pivotal role in the Bendix takeover story. The storm which swirled around the Bill and Mary relationship certainly made it more difficult for Agee to function. He might argue differently; he might assert that with Mary at his side, with Mary as his chief adviser, he was able to make the necessary decisions. Nonetheless, in countless ways, the Bill and Mary scandal would return to haunt Agee as some kind of recurring nightmare; it would weaken him at key moments; it would bemuse nearly everyone who dealt with him during that period. He and Mary became larger than life—America's most visible corporate couple, according to *Time* magazine,[2] the most intriguing couple of 1982, according to *People*.[3] They put up a bold fight, hoping the storm would subside, but it never did. And when the Bendix Takeover moved inexorably to its incredible finale, and the critics of the Wildest Takeover There Ever Was hunted for scapegoats, inevitably they focused on the Bill and Mary tale.

The story had its beginnings in June 1979. It was then that Bill Agee had chosen Mary, fresh out of the Harvard Business School, as his executive assistant. Agee had lost trust in a number of his senior executives. Finding Mary a skilled businesswoman who could size up people and situations well, he gradually gave her more and more power. Agee's marriage was breaking up, and he and Mary were in each other's company a great deal. But, other than finding that they were "kindred spirits," in Mary's words, she insisted that no sparks went off. While nothing should have seemed more natural than for a corporation chairman and his executive assistant to spend a lot of time together, the surface appearance of their arriving at work, lunching, jetting around the country, and leaving the office together led tongues to wag. After Agee promoted Mary—a mere one year after she joined Bendix—to Vice President for Corporate and Public Affairs in June 1980 and then, three months later, to Vice President for Strategic Planning, the tongues were going a mile a minute. The gossip at the Bendix water coolers had it that she had come from nowhere and now, having just turned 29, had control over the strategic planning of the entire company. Even if she had come out of the Harvard Business School, wasn't that a rather meteoric rise to power? The gossip mongers thought so. Indeed, Mary's star had risen swiftly; in June 1980 she had become the youngest female corporate vice president among the *Fortune* 500 companies.

Bendix soon witnessed a series of power plays aimed at bringing the Wunderkind Agee down. What better way than to attack what appeared a sure-fire Achilles heel, the lady on the rise. The attack got under way in the late summer of 1980, when anonymous letters began reaching the Bendix board. They urged board members to investigate the relationship between Agee and Cunningham. Letters went to Detroit newspaper editors as well.

But the editors chose not to report the story, apparently sensing there was too little to go on. Then on Labor Day came the news that Agee had divorced his wife. (Mary had been separated from her husband since 1979.) The gossip at Bendix reached a new height. Some dozen or so anonymous letters had by now arrived. Agee was told that one board member had privately asked in anger whether he was having a midlife crisis, whether he had lost his judgment. A fling on the side could be condoned. But elevating Mary Cunningham to such lofty posts was simply not in keeping with acceptable corporate norms.

Hearing all this, Agee cautioned his executive assistant to stay calm; they would weather the rumors, there was no need for her to resign, as she had thought of doing. By mid-September Agee was still hoping that the fuss would die down. But it would not. Each day brought a new challenge, a new test for the two of them. Neither one was holding up very well. However much he offered comfort, Mary had difficulty keeping back the tears. Agee sensed the terrible choice he confronted: he could speak about Mary candidly in public and hope this would convince people to stop thinking they were having an affair. Or he could continue to keep silent on the issue in the hope that it would somehow go away. He had just won board approval for Mary's latest promotion as Vice President for Strategic Planning, and of course he would announce it to the world at the Bendix meeting coming up in the next days. Perhaps that was the time to go public. It was an agonizing decision.

Once a year Bill Agee gathered the six hundred executives of Bendix together for what amounted to a no-holds-barred press conference with the boss. The risks to the Bendix overlord were palpably obvious. Never mind, thought Agee. He radiated a quiet confidence preparing himself for this year's meeting. He could handle anything they threw at him. And certainly the audience would melt when it heard what he had to say about his favorite topic, The Strategy. It would be his turn to be Knute Rockne and Winston Churchill rolled into one. There was nothing complex about it: Bendix was going to move away from its traditional business lines in auto components and industrial manufacturing into the exciting, profitable world of high tech. Agee would sell off those parts of Bendix that it made no sense to keep and, with the cash, make a bold bid to acquire a company that would fit The Strategy.

Not surprisingly, The Strategy was not uppermost in the minds of Bendix executives as they began to assemble in the Civic Center Auditorium across the road from Bendix that September day. More pressing matters concerned them. Agee was only too well aware of that. He had asked a few lieutenants, including Mary Cunningham, to poll the executives so he would know what was on their minds. They wanted to know if the rumors about layoffs were true; whether Agee was going to take a cabinet post in Washington after the election; and, most important, what was going on between Agee and the person who was just taking a seat in a middle row of the auditorium.

Mary Cunningham had wanted to be as inconspicuous as possible during the meeting. Even invisible. Just as Agee had been debating with himself how to handle The Topic, Mary had also argued back and forth with herself about the best tactics. What would Bill do? Taking her seat, she realized that she still had no idea. She noticed that a lot of executives appeared in a festive mood. Why not? The meeting was a break in the routine, a kind of holiday from the regular drag. Besides, thought Mary, Bill was special, he had a charisma, and the executives probably looked forward to seeing him in action.

Now he was moving behind the podium. He began by calling the past year "difficult and interesting and paradoxical." No argument there, Mary thought. Especially the past few weeks. Quickly, Agee touched on the two hundred employees who would soon be out of work ("We will be as humane as we know how"), then on to a denial that he would be moving to Washington to join either a Reagan or Carter administration. A few more comments on other matters. Finally he got around to The Subject. There was no way to avoid it. He knew that now. Reporters were out there in the crowd. It would almost certainly come up in the question period. That would put him on the defensive. This way, raising the issue himself, he could confront it head-on. It seemed wise—at the time.

"I've been told by many people, and I know that it is buzzing around, that Mary Cunningham's rise in this company is very unusual and that it has something to do with a personal relationship that we have." Mary's nervousness grew. One part of her wanted Bill to lace into the organizers of the smear campaign. Another part thought: lay off, let it die. If it only would. But Agee was off and running. "Sure, it's unusual. Her rise in this company is unusual because she's a very unusual and a very talented individual. But her rapid promotions are totally justified." This was followed by a few more nice sentences about Mary's contribution. Then came the two sentences that would return to haunt the pair: "At the same time," Agee intoned, clearly not aware what impact his next few phrases would have on listeners, "I tell you it is true that we are very, very close friends, and she's a very close friend of my family. But that has absolutely nothing to do with the way that I and others in this company and on the board evaluate her performance."

The reaction was immediate and merciless. "So, how long have you been sleeping with the boss?" a short, rotund reporter asked Mary as she rose hastily from her seat. Another reporter, this one from the *Detroit Free Press*, had followed rumblings about Bill and Mary for a month, but, lacking a real peg, he had sat on the story. Until now. Agee, uttering those few explosive sentences, had supplied the peg. The headline the next day was splashed on page one, "Bendix Boss Slaps Down Office Gossip, Female

Exec's Rise Not Due to Friendship, Agee Tells Staff." The reporter understood how damaging Agee's phrases sounded. He wrote in the second paragraph: "It was an unusual moment in corporate America—a chief executive giving rumors the status of company concerns that needed to be discussed openly with subordinates."[4] In the coming days, Agee tried to contain the storm of criticism and to shield Mary from it all. He could not. Members of the Bendix board, shaking their heads in despair, insisted that Agee get rid of Mary. Two weeks after his now-famous remarks, she resigned from Bendix.

The turmoil which developed after the executives' meeting was traumatic for Mary. Agee, too, took Mary's resignation hard. He withdrew into a kind of personal cocoon for a long period, wondering all along why he had not seen the scandal coming and why he had been unable to keep it from getting out of hand.

In February of 1981 Mary became Vice President for Strategic Planning and Project Development with Joseph E. Seagram & Sons, the American subsidiary of the Seagram Company Ltd., largest producer and distributor of alcoholic beverages in the world. She formulated a new company strategy for its wine business and was then promoted to Executive Vice President, Planning, for the Seagram Wine Companies. In time, she and Bill Agee did become romantically entwined, and they were married in a Roman Catholic ceremony in June of 1982 in San Francisco.

Bill Agee was the third generation of Agees to grow up in Idaho. His family was originally Huguenot. Bill was the only son; he had a sister two years older, another twelve years younger. At the age of 15, Bill was learning how to milk cows and clean barns on the family dairy farm in Meridian, not far from Boise. His father taught him to be honest. And how to crunch out numbers. While at Meridian High School, Bill was a superachiever: senior class president; member of the tennis, basketball and track teams; sports editor of the school newspaper. The yearbook needed three pages to describe his accomplishments. No wonder his classmates voted him "hard worker." Upon graduation Bill went off to Stanford University, but he didn't stay there for long.

He was back in Idaho after only one year. His mind was set on getting married (to Diane Weaver), but marriage would increase his living expenses in Palo Alto. He had no wish to take the money from his parents. So he enrolled in Boise Junior College in his sophomore year—and he married Diane. After doing so well in high school, Bill found to his chagrin that he had a hard time in college; still, after picking up an associate in arts degree from Boise Junior, he graduated with highest honors and a bachelor of science degree in business from the University of Idaho. His first daughter was born on the day he graduated. His goal was to become president of a large corporation. Though he found work as controller of the Idaho Title

Company and became a Certified Public Accountant, he felt he needed something more before he could get on the fast track.

There was no better way to do that than study at the Harvard Business School. But when the opportunity arose, he wavered. After all, he had a job, a wife, and a child. Why risk such security on graduate school? His recruiter—the same one, as it turned out, who would recruit Mary Cunningham for the school—was persuasive. And Bill earned his MBA in 1963. With his knack for numbers, a winning personality, and that CPA certificate, he had no trouble landing a good job quickly at the Boise Cascade Corporation, a small lumber firm whose bosses dreamed of making it a giant of the forest industry. Agee impressed his superiors and gradually became a company spokesman and a leading candidate to take over the whole firm.

Then, in May of 1972, came the Bendix offer. Agee couldn't turn it down. He was made Executive Vice President, a director, and a member of the four-person office of the chief executive. Known to many for its washing machines, Bendix, based in Southfield, Michigan, had once been a specialist in the supply of parts, particularly brakes, to the auto industry; but then the firm expanded into such other fields as machine tools, aluminum siding, lumber and other wood products. It was also involved in aerospace and military weapons components and systems. Bendix Chairman Mike Blumenthal was so eager to make sure Agee would not be tempted away from the company that he made him President on December 1, 1976.

Then lightning struck. President-elect Jimmy Carter chose Blumenthal to be the new Secretary of the Treasury, leaving the post of Bendix chairman suddenly vacant. The job fell to Agee without much ado. He took over on January 1, 1977, just four days before his 39th birthday. Though there were the usual questions about whether Bendix should diversify so much, Agee was a firm believer in Bendix The Conglomerate. He would have no trouble stripping away unwanted assets, looking for better ones to take their place. Bendix, before Agee, enjoyed the reputation of being a well-run firm. Agee built on that record, as Bendix profits kept on growing an average of 10 percent a year. While a recession had been damaging to two of its main businesses, automobile parts and machine tools, Agee guided Bendix to prosperous days, selling off operations, making some wise investments, and streamlining his management. When his competitors were taking a nosedive in 1981, for example, Bendix revenues climbed to $4.4 billion and profits leaped 136 percent to $453 million. A remarkable record for The Boy Wonder.

Mary Cunningham's roots were in New England. She had been born on September 1, 1951, in Falmouth, Maine. Her father's family had built up a solid construction business there. Misfortune struck the family when

Mary's uncle—her father's brother—was killed in a car crash. This induced her father to drink heavily; by the time Mary was five her parents were divorced, and she had almost no contact with her father after that. Feeling guilty that she had caused the divorce, Mary vowed to be "so good that it would make up for this terrible thing (she had) done."[5] The family— Mary's mother, Mary, her two brothers and a sister—moved to Hanover, New Hampshire, and Mary became close with Father Bill, the pastor of the Roman Catholic parish there; he became her surrogate father. A religious streak ran through her, and she thought at times of becoming a nun. If not that, perhaps she would run an orphanage.

Finally she decided to become a lawyer. She studied logic and philosophy at Wellesley College. Then, at Notre Dame's law school in South Bend, Indiana, she became engaged to Bo Gray, a black New York City banking executive. She sensed that South Bend would not accept an interracial couple. After one term she moved to New York City, where she married Bo in December 1974. She took a job as a paralegal, and a colleague told her that she was a "born negotiator" and should embark on a business career. She liked the idea and soon was working as a trainee at Chase Manhattan, where her husband was a second vice president. She became a corporate lending officer and assistant treasurer, but, noticing Harvard MBAs going faster and farther than she, Mary enrolled in the fall of 1977 in the Harvard Graduate School of Business.

She found the place at first intimidating; for the first two and a half months she did not say a word in classes. By her second year, though, she was piling up awards. Job offers came her way with ease, including one to join the corporate finance department at Morgan Stanley. Then came the offer from Agee. She debated whether to go with Morgan or Bendix. If she joined Morgan, Agee said, she would merely be doing the paperwork on deals; if she went with Bendix, she would be designing the deals herself. That prospect, plus the chance to have Bill Agee as her mentor, led her to Bendix.

"I suspect Shakespeare had something like this case in mind when he said, 'A pox on both your houses,'" observed a federal judge during the Bendix Takeover.[6] Of course, Shakespeare had never heard of Pac-Man defenses or front-end-loaded two-tier offers or shark repellents. But he knew what it meant to go too far, knew what hubris was all about, knew that sometimes men could act in suicidal fashion without being able to restrain themselves. But, in knowing all that, Shakespeare might well have agreed with the federal judge and thought a pox the most deserving gift for the Players in the Bendix Affair.

What else did they deserve? Under ordinary circumstances, a corporate raider—whether a T. Boone Pickens, a Carl Icahn, or whoever—would be willing to gamble to get his hands on another firm; but never would he risk his own company. This is what makes the Bendix Takeover so unusual. Both Bendix and Martin Marietta, acting like two scorpions in a bottle, were prepared to take the game to the brink, placing their own companies at total risk in what was called the ultimate Pac-Man defense. Many who watched in horror sensed there was very little one could do to halt the process of mutual self-destruction.

How did it all begin?

It began with what Agee and Cunningham had called The Strategy: getting hold of a major high-tech firm. By the spring of 1982 Bendix had the cash to do the prowling. $500 million in the kitty. At first it looked like RCA would be the target. Agee had quietly purchased 7 percent of RCA's stock, and word was out that he had his eye on grabbing the whole prize. Agee never conceded such; but no matter. RCA had a secret weapon: Bill Agee. Or, more specifically, his personal vulnerability on the Bill and Mary issue. It was Marty Lipton, the supershrewd takeover lawyer, who got the bright idea to put out a news release hinting at Mr. Agee's Achilles heel. "He has not demonstrated the ability to manage his own affairs, let alone someone else's," the release said. Neat—and lethal. Agee never made a try for RCA.

With that episode behind them, Agee and Cunningham began to focus seriously on Martin Marietta. It had always been on their "hit list" of possible acquisitions. Mary had made the firm her number one choice. Martin was a true high-tech firm, heavily into aerospace and defense technology. It was building the Pershing and the MX missiles; it was engaged in the space shuttle program. Since its stock had plunged from $50 in early 1981 to $35 in 1982, Martin looked like a bargain. Turning to his investment banker, Jay Higgins, at Salomon Brothers, Bill instructed him in April to begin purchasing Martin Marietta shares for Bendix. Higgins, like most of his colleagues in the mergers and acquisitions part of investment banking, keeps possible deals close to his chest. In his personal codebook, Bendix had become Earth, Marietta, Fire. Earth, Higgins was convinced, could consume Fire.

In the next few months, Higgins quietly acted; by the end of July Bendix owned 4.5 percent of Martin—1.6 million shares. Agee had paid an average of $27.05 a share. When Bendix's share reached 5 percent, it would have to make its investment public. Agee was prepared to move slowly, but then a strange thing happened: Martin Marietta's stock began to soar in August, going from $24 a share on the 13th to $33 a share just eleven days later. Agee passed the word to his coterie of advisers. Let's go. It was hard to keep a secret, though. After taping a Barbara Walters interview in August, Mary Cunningham blurted out to ABC crew members to watch the newspapers soon.

Marty Siegel had been doing some watching, and he didn't like what he saw. Marty was the 34-year-old whiz-kid investment banker who had been advising Martin Marietta on how to avoid a takeover. That was Marty's bread and butter. A lover of statistics, as are all the Players in the Takeover Game, Marty would boast to potential clients that on the average only one in five takeover attempts were thwarted, but Marty had managed to put a stop to one in three. This was Marty Siegel who kept a reddish-brown tarantula in sight of clients. Everyone knew about Marty's little pet, which he kept frozen in a clear glass paperweight on his desk. Some grateful client had given it to him as a thank-you. The message Marty was trying to communicate by keeping the little fellow around seemed pretty clear: don't mess with Marty Siegel!

One key to his success was a set of powerful antennae. Lately, Siegel had been getting signals he didn't like. Someone over at Salomon Brothers was buying up stock for someone in Martin Marietta, a Marty Siegel client for some time. Then Martin's treasurer phoned Marty: the aerospace industry was awash with rumors that Bendix had cast a takeover spell on Martin Marietta. Had this been a few years later, the people at Martin Marietta would have done less worrying. Like many other companies they would have swallowed some "poison pills" designed to make them less attractive to a takeover, thus in all likelihood removing any real threat. But this was August 1982, and no one (except Marty Lipton) knew about pills in those days.

That left Bendix free to attack. As Agee watched Martin's stock leap in late August, he advanced his timetable. By August 24 he was distributing to his board an eleven-page memo deceptively entitled, "Acquisition of Georgia." Georgia, Agee explained to his board, stood for Martin Marietta. Slightly smaller than Bendix, Martin was Number 130 on the *Fortune* list in 1982 with annual sales of $3.2 billion and $2.5 billion in assets; Bendix, ranked 86 that year, had $4.3 billion in sales and $3.2 billion in assets. The board was sympathetic with Agee's Strategy of grabbing off a high-tech firm like Martin. Besides, Bendix President Al Mcdonald, who used to be Jimmy Carter's chief of staff, was close to Martin Marietta board member Griffin Bell, the former Attorney General. Don Rumsfeld was friendly with another Marietta director, Mel Laird. Rumsfeld summed up the board's favorable attitude when he called the proposed marriage "a brilliant strategic fit." Rumsfeld felt obliged to ask one question. Might Martin resist the Bendix offer? Agee had no trouble fielding this one. "The consensus opinion is that Martin Marietta—due to its recent heavy debt load to finance capital expenditures and poor showing in the stock market—will not be in a position to vigorously resist our offer." No one would easily forget Agee's words in the coming days. The board voted unanimously to approve the plan to acquire Georgia.

The next day, August 25, Bendix announced its offer for Martin Marietta. It planned to purchase 15.8 million shares of Martin—or 45 percent of the company—at $43 a share. Agee announced for the first time that Bendix had already acquired 4.5 percent of Martin. The bid totalled $1.5 billion. Eager that the offer be construed as friendly, Agee phoned Tom Pownall, the Martin president, and sent him a letter as well. But Agee had misread the Martin people. They would resist. If they could, they would prevent their company from being taken over. Pownall ignored the phone call and the letter. Agee instructed his investment banker, Jay Higgins, to call his counterpart at Martin Marietta, Marty Siegel. Higgins was to ask for a meeting between Pownall and Agee. Angrily, Marty told Jay that there would be a meeting only after Bendix withdrew its offer. Martin was not going to do any negotiating with a gun aimed at its head. Higgins reported back to Agee, who told him to get back on the phone with Siegel and inform him that Bendix was not withdrawing from the fray.

Tom Pownall was still wavering. He knew that if Bendix had made a truly attractive offer, he would have felt compelled to look at it seriously. That he owed to his stockholders. Fortunately for him, the offer—$43 a share—left a lot to be desired. That made it easier to resist. Instinctively, he preferred to fight Bendix. He felt strongly about his company. Besides, he had been Chief Executive Officer for only a few months: he didn't need the Bendix Gambit at this juncture. Still, how did one go about mounting a resistance? The people at Marietta, because of their work and their back-grounds, identified with the Pentagon and the defense establishment. The army was in their blood. So was taking a militant stand—for or against something. But Pownall knew he was not on firm ground in the Takeover Game; he had hardly met an investment banker before Marty Siegel.

And now Marty Siegel was giving him the options. They weren't pretty. Not at all. It was late in the game. So Martin had basically only two moves. It could search around for a white knight, a third company which would come in with a friendly offer higher than the Bendix one. That was problematic. It didn't preclude Bendix's topping the white knight's offer. Most important, it was not a real solution. It would still strip Martin of its cherished independence. Marty had another option up his investment banker's sleeve. It was a little-used one and so no one could map scenarios, no one could write an insurance policy for Martin that all would end well. Nevertheless, the option existed, and Marty thought it was worth a try. "What about hitting them hard?" he asked. Martin Marietta would make a counteroffer to buy Bendix!

Pownall didn't leap at the idea. It was not clear Martin could raise the hundreds of millions it would take to make the offer. Nor was it clear what shape Martin would be in after leveraging itself so heavily to get out of the Bendix mess. Then again, would the strategy succeed?

Precarious or not, the counteroffer looked like the best prospect for Martin. At least it held out the promise that the company would remain independent. So on August 30 the Martin board met and reached some dramatic decisions: it voted to reject the Bendix offer of $43 a share as inadequate. Martin, after all, in the past five years had invested $200 million more in capital expenditures than Bendix was offering. Next, the board agreed not to pursue a white knight. Finally, it opted to go after Bendix. It offered to buy up 11.9 million shares—or 50.3 percent—of Bendix stock at $75 a share. Bendix was then trading in the mid-50s per share. During Martin Marietta's crucial board meeting, Director Jack Byrne had handed Tom Pownall a lucky tie decorated with blue pennants and the words "Don't Give Up the Ship." It had worked for Byrne when his own company, Geico Corporation, the automobile insurance firm, was raided. So he advised Pownall to wear it throughout the takeover fight. Which Pownall did. As it turned out, he would need it.

The Marietta board saw the step as purely defensive. They dubbed it their ASSCAP, which stood for Assured Second Strike Capability. But someone gave it another name: the Pac-Man Defense, after the popular video game in which the forms gobble each other up. Marty Siegel had his own pet name for the ploy: the "dead man's trigger." When Jay Higgins, the Bendix investment banker, heard what Martin had decided, he quickly termed it the Jonestown Defense after the 800 cultists in Jonestown, Guyana, who had committed mass suicide in 1978 by poisoning their soft drinks. To dramatize the brutishness of what he thought Martin Marietta was doing, Higgins asked one of his aides to buy some packets of KoolAid, the drink the cultists used, which the investment banker then gave out as souvenirs. The plan at Martin, as at Jonestown, Higgins mused, was to leave dead bodies lying in the sun!

Pac-Man Defense, ASSCAP, dead man's trigger, or Jonestown Defense—it all came down to two multibillion-dollar companies engaging in an unprecedent game of corporate chicken. Could anyone really conjure what victory for Martin Marietta would be like? It would have to take on the staggering burden of paying off the money it had borrowed to purchase Bendix shares as well as the money Bendix had borrowed to buy Martin's shares. Beyond that, as *Fortune* magazine wrote in a retrospective piece on the Affair, a Marietta triumph would have converted "two perfectly normal companies with reasonable debt-to-equity ratios of one to three into a single corporate mutant with a $2.7 billion debt load on a $1.1 billion equity base."[7]

Bill Agee had no desire to let Bendix turn into a corporate mutant. And it seemed at first as if he would succeed. Government rules on takeovers gave Bendix an advantage over Martin Marietta. They required that a company must wait fifteen business days before buying any stock offered to them. This meant that Bendix's waiting period ended September 16. Because it made its bid five days after Bendix, Martin could not purchase the Bendix shares until September 22. By that time it would be too late for Martin Marietta. Bendix would already own it. But, as it turned out, the "waiting period" rule was offset by a legal quirk which played into Martin's hands. Martin Marietta was incorporated in Maryland, where the state law required ten days to pass before a stockholders' meeting could be called to dissolve a board—in this case, Martin Marietta's. Bendix, on the other hand, was incorporated in Delaware, where the law was more liberal: it permitted a majority stockholder—in this case, it would be Martin Marietta—to take control at once.

Confronting this presumed advantage for Martin, Bill Agee went into action, taking his own set of defensive measures against a takeover. He picked up some recommendations from his legal staff that had been lying around for a year—a couple of "shark repellent" amendments that, if adopted by Bendix, would have made it almost impossible for anyone to take it over and thereby would neutralize Martin's time advantage. On August 31 the Bendix board turned Martin Marietta's counteroffer down flat; it ordered up some golden parachute contracts—those large-sized severance packages which take effect upon a takeover—for Agee and some other senior executives. And it agreed to put the amendments to the stockholders. Agee began to feel good about Bendix's prospects. One unquestionable consolation was the large portion of Bendix stock—23 percent—which was held by the employee pension plan. Since there was no way Martin could get its hands on that stock—or so Agee thought—Bendix looked like a winner.

Marty Siegel was beginning to sense that the wind was blowing Bendix's way. Martin needed to talk to a third party—not a white knight, but someone who could help the counteroffer go through and hopefully relieve Martin of some of the debt that would pile up later. When Wall Street learned that Martin was interested in a third party, it was ready to bet heavily that Agee would come up the winner. Martin's original counteroffer now seemed to lack credibility; it appeared that Martin was not strong enough to undertake the takeover of Bendix by itself. In fact, the ploy to bring in a third party was most enticing to Marty Siegel and the crowd at Martin. At this point Siegel came up with the Harry Gray gambit. Harry Gray was the chairman of United Technologies, a $14 billion conglomerate which towered over both Bendix and Martin Marietta. The twentieth largest industrial firm in the United States, it had under its wing Sikorsky helicopters, Pratt and Whitney aircraft engines, Hamilton Standard aircraft controls and propellers, Otis Elevator, Ambac Industries, Carrier air conditioners, and Mostek. Siegel's idea was for Pownall to approach Gray with a proposal: Martin Marietta would, after purchasing Bendix, sell part of it to United Technologies. United would become Martin's "Gray Knight." It was not a bad idea on the face of it: Martin would be relived of major debts and United would acquire some valuable assets.

Harry Gray, however, had ideas of his own. Rather than accepting Marietta's leftovers from the Bendix deal, why not have United Technologies match the Marietta offer to take over Bendix? No matter who won—United or Martin—they would agree to divide the spoils. United would get Bendix's automotive and industrial divisions; Marietta would get a large portion of the aerospace and electronics operations. In effect, Harry Gray asked for all of Bendix save for the aerospace and electronics, where he thought Washington would raise an eye on antitrust grounds. Gray's counterproposal was accepted during a meeting on September 2 in the Park Avenue office of takeover lawyer Marty Lipton, acting as counsel to both the Kidder, Peabody firm of investment bankers (Marty Siegel's firm) and United Technologies. Representing Harry Gray was investment banker Felix Rohatyn of Lazard Freres. The agreement was announced five days later.

Until Harry Gray entered the battle, Bendix looked like a winner. But once the Martin Marietta-United Technologies scheme was sealed in Marty Lipton's office and announced to the world, Bill Agee would have been prudent to call the whole thing off. Moreover, Martin had scored another coup by enticing the trustees of the Bendix employee stock plan to tender those shares, 23 percent of the total outstanding—to Martin. Somehow the trustees, Citibank of New York, had been convinced by Martin Marietta's lawyers that they had a legal obligation to maximize the value of the stock plan's shares. Martin Marietta's counteroffer looked quite credible now. One way or the other, with Harry Gray on its side, Martin would have the clout to roll over Bendix. But there was that diehard faith in The Strategy which Bill shared with Mary, and with Bill's senior attorney Arthur Fleischer (of Fried, Frank, Harris, Shriver and Jacobson), and with the new investment banker just brought into the campaign, another whiz kid named Bruce Wasserstein. When the formidable figure of Harry Gray had joined the contest, Agee had sensed a need to expand his team of financial advisers. Higgins would handle the bid for Martin, and Wasserstein would defend against the United Technologies bid. This could not have made Jay Higgins happy, but Agee had other concerns on his mind. It was this move, some have speculated, that would cost Agee his company and his job.

Perella and Wasserstein's First Boston had been eagerly campaigning to get in on the action in the Bendix deal since late August, when Bendix first moved against Martin Marietta. The two men had made many phone calls, to Bendix, Martin Marietta, and others, to get a foot in the door. Perella had phoned Agee; then Wasserstein tried five days later. Then, as luck would have it, the September 6 edition of *Fortune* carried a highly flattering piece entitled "The High Rollers of First Boston," cataloguing its recent triumphs in arranging Megadeals for which it was paid Megafees: $14 million for helping Du Pont purchase Conoco; $17 million for aiding Marathon in its sellout for $6.2 billion to U.S. Steel. Bruce was described in the article as a "whiz kid, a brilliant architect of complex deals, although a little egotistical." He was making $1 million a year.

Bendix executives spent an entire day interviewing investment bankers to find a firm that would help them react to the United Technologies move. Finally, at 11 P.M. on September 8, Wasserstein was called into Agee's suite at the Helmsley Palace. The following morning Agee and First Boston concluded an arrangement: if Bendix succeeded in buying more than 50 percent of Martin Marietta, First Boston would receive a minimum fee of $2.75 million, and much more if a white knight entered to save Bendix. Ultimately, First Boston would receive between $5 and $6 million for helping to negotiate the rescue of Bendix by Allied. [We will have a lot more to say about First Boston's Wasserstein (see Chapter 6).]

The battle for credibility wore on. Agee had raised the Bendix offering price on September 7 to $48 a share for 18.5 million shares or 55 percent of Martin. Then, just three days before Bendix could begin purchasing Martin's shares, and with Bendix showing no signs of giving up, Tom Pownall realized that he would have to resort to a last-ditch ploy that was as creative as it was dangerous. He needed a way to show Bendix that Martin's counter offer was 100 percent credible. In making its counteroffer, Martin had erected a set of conditions which would keep it from going ahead with the move. It was now prepared to strip away most of those conditions so that it would become almost automatic that Martin would buy Bendix—regardless of what Bendix did. The only two conditions which Martin would keep would have Pownall withdraw his counteroffer if either (1) Bendix withdrew its offer or (2) the Bendix stockholders adopted the "shark repellent" measures (that would wipe out Martin's five-day advantage and effectively block its getting control of Bendix). In essence, when the Marietta board voted on September 13 to waive all but the two conditions, it was cocking Marty Siegel's dead man's trigger, sending a very clear message to Bill Agee.

It was probably no coincidence that Bruce Wasserstein spoke to Marty Siegel that very day for the first time about making a deal that would keep both sides from implementing the mutual self-destruction pact. Siegel walked away from the conversation feeling good. Agee was buckling—maybe. If Siegel could get all the contestants off the battlefield in one piece, it would be a remarkable achievement for Martin Marietta. Taking everyone back to Square One was an ideal solution.

In the final hours before midnight, September 16—Bendix's Moment of Truth, when it could begin to buy Martin Marietta—Agee continued to discount the possibility that Martin's Tom Pownall would actually pull the trigger. For a while on that day, it appeared that Martin had won a reprieve—when a federal judge, Joseph H. Young, ruled in Baltimore that all stock purchases were to be put off for ten days. Wasserstein and Siegel had been on the phones regularly at this stage to see whether the two sides could call their own truce. At 9 P.M. that evening, an appeals court judge in Baltimore reversed Young's ruling. And Bill Agee ordered Wasserstein to stop taking Marty Siegel's calls. Agee was determined to go through with the Martin purchase—which he did soon after midnight. By September 17 he had bought control of Martin, purchasing at first 52.7 percent, and eventually bringing the figure up to 70 percent, of the Martin stock. The one flaw in Agee's plan was its assumption that Tom Pownall would roll over and play dead, that he would take his finger off the dead man's trigger.

Buying 70 percent of Martin Marietta was not the same thing as winning the hearts and minds of Martin's senior executives. Given Pownall's resolve to buy Bendix no matter what, all that Bill Agee could try to do now was one of two things: (1) make it impossible for Martin to purchase Bendix six days hence on September 22, or (2) figure out a way to get Pownall to call off his dead man's trigger. Neither would be easy. On September 20 Bendix organized a "Unity Day" that was meant to show how much the employees wanted their firm to stay independent. In fact, one of its main purposes was to round up votes in favor of the "shark repellent" amendments; another was to make sure that employees involved in the stock option plan who had not yet withdrawn their shares from the Marietta tender pool, did so. It was a colorful day with "I Love Bendix" balloons, bumper stickers, pins, hats, and an airplane with a banner flying over Southfield headquarters, not to mention the short-skirted cheerleaders with pompons. But, even as "Unity Day" was occurring, Agee sensed that the exercise was futile.

He had already begun looking in other directions for a savior. If he could come up with a new bidder for Bendix, there would be a ten-day freeze on new stock purchases and Martin wouldn't be able to act by September 23. Agee turned to Edward L. Hennessy Jr., the 55-year-old chairman of Allied, the giant conglomerate, headquartered in Morristown, New Jersey. It was ranked number 55 in the country and had annual sales of $11 billion. Ironically, Hennessy for seven years had worked directly under Harry Gray at United Technologies; it was Hennessy who had set up the financial structure which provided Gray with the cash for his deals.

Meanwhile, by September 21, the day before Martin could begin buying Bendix, Agee realized that his best chance of reaching a favorable conclusion was to turn to Tom Pownall personally. Just before 10 A.M., he phoned Pownall and asked for a face-to-face chat. In fact, Agee wanted a chance to talk to the entire Marietta board; he was convinced that he could persuade them to listen to reason, to call off their plans, to give way to its new master, Bendix. Two hours later, Agee was winging his way with top aides and Mary Cunningham, who was no longer an employee of Bendix, from Detroit to Dulles International Airport. Pownall had promised to have company cars waiting to speed them to Marietta's headquarters twenty-six miles away in Bethesda. Marietta's welcoming committee was surprised to find Mary among Agee's entourage. They had heard all the stories about

Bill and Mary. For Agee, there was nothing unusual in bringing along his wife. She had been his closest adviser at Bendix, had worked with him on The Strategy; he had a hard time conceiving of negotiating without Mary around. Eager to meet the celebrity in person after reading all the stories, Marietta's executives found Mary's presence intriguing.

Agee kept hoping that he would get to see the Marietta board. First he had to sit and talk with Tom Pownall. When they finally huddled, Agee made him an offer that he hoped would bring the crisis to an end. Bendix would offer $55—or $7 more than Agee had paid for 70 percent of the Marietta stock—for the rest of Martin's shares. Marietta's board had grave concerns that if it pulled out of the plan to buy Bendix, it would risk a bunch of lawsuits from stockholders who would be disgruntled at losing out on such an attractive proposition. So Agee was prepared to indemnify Marietta's board in case there were legal actions. On top of that, he offered Martin four seats on the Bendix board.

But Pownall wouldn't budge. He was going to buy Bendix, and that was all there was to it. After three hours of rather fruitless talks, Agee pulled away from Marietta headquarters with nothing to show. During the ride to the airport Agee grew increasingly frustrated. At one point he ordered the two-car caravan to pull over to the roadside and alighted from his car. Suspicious that his car (provided by Marietta) might be bugged, he signalled his executives to walk with him up a nearby grassy knoll, where they conferred on yet another new strategy. The next step was to get to a pay phone and ask for more time with Pownall. The Marietta president had no great desire to go over the same ground with Agee, but keeping him pinned down did have one advantage as the deadline approached: he could not wind up a deal with someone else. Agee and his Bendix crew raced back to Bethesda. They talked for five more hours. Mary slipped in and out of the meetings. Sometimes Bill would take a break to chat with her away from the sessions. Pownall had the feeling that Agee didn't want to leave, that leaving would have been acknowledgement that his options had run out—which they almost had. Pownall was no less unyielding than before. Just after midnight the talks finally collapsed.

September 22—as the midnight deadline loomed—proved no easier for Agee. In Southfield Bendix stockholders were due to vote on the "shark repellent" amendments. Passage seemed quite doubtful. When a Bendix official who had convened the meeting realized that the amendments might not pass, he quickly ordered the meeting put off for a week. Suddenly from the audience appeared a group of Martin Marietta officials, rising from their seats, carrying cardboard cartons of stockholder proxies under their arms. Marching to the podium, they declared that the meeting was reopened. By some strange coincidence the lights then went out. Furious, but unwilling to yield, the Martin Marietta team simply moved over to a conference room at the nearby Michigan Inn and called a new stockholders meeting to order. The amendments were quickly voted down.

Agee placed some hope in the courts, but a federal district court judge in Baltimore refused to forbid Martin from purchasing Bendix. The Bendix attorneys tried to make the point that Bendix now owned 70 percent of Martin Marietta; were Martin to buy Bendix, that would run contrary to the wishes of the holder of 70 percent of the Martin stock, which was in fact Bendix. Martin's rejoinder to that won the day in court: Martin Marietta had a commitment to pay the Bendix stockholders who had already tendered their shares.

Amazingly enough, Agee still had a fallback position—Ed Hennessy. He had been secretly negotiating with the Allied Chairman for the past two days. Agee had read the handwriting on the wall. Unless he did something, Bendix and Martin Marietta would merge into one giant cripple, a company so weak that it would be in the throes of crisis from Day One. Agee didn't want to preside over such a "mutant." If he could do a deal with Allied, he might be able to keep Martin Marietta from acquiring Bendix. Under federal takeover rules any new bid would automatically put a ten-day freeze on share purchases; Marietta would be unable to purchase any tendered Bendix shares for at least ten business days. And Bendix, by then, would probably have succeeded in calling a special Martin Marietta stockholders meeting at which it would replace the Martin board and cancel Martin's offer to buy Bendix.

By late Wednesday, September 22, hours before Martin Marietta could begin to buy Bendix, Allied announced that it had made a $2.3 billion offer for both Bendix and Martin Marietta. The terms of the Allied-Bendix deal called for Allied to buy 13.1 million Bendix shares at $85 a share; Allied securities would be offered at $75 a share for the remaining 10.6 million Bendix shares. The $75-a-share price meant that Bendix stockholders could not assail Agee for selling out to Allied at less than United or Martin Marietta had offered. Bendix would become a subsidiary of Allied, as would Martin Marietta. Agee would be the new Bendix Chairman as well as President of Allied.

Incredibly, Agee had made a ghastly error. Waiting so long to finish off the agreement with Allied, he had not provided sufficient time for Allied's attorneys to file the necessary papers with the SEC in Washington before the 5:30 P.M. close of business. So Martin Marietta was still free to go for Bendix after midnight, which is precisely what it did. By Thursday, September 23, Martin Marietta had acquired 46 percent of Bendix's stock for some $900 million; the figure would rise eventually to 50.1 percent. The curtain had gone up on the Merger Theater of the Absurd. As it now stood, Bendix had purchased Martin Marietta, and Martin Marietta had purchased Bendix. And Allied had offered to buy them both!

Realizing that there was no way to stop Marietta from going through with buying Bendix, Allied's Ed Hennessy decided that he would make his own deal with Tom Pownall. Hennessy was aware that Agee wanted him to get both Bendix and Martin Marietta. But if Pownall went ahead and spent $900 million to purchase Bendix stock, Allied would be saddled with $3 billion of Martin Marietta and Bendix debts—not a very attractive thought to Hennessy. If only he could convince Pownall not to spend the money to buy the Bendix stock, he could see himself taking over both Bendix and Martin Marietta. Pownall agreed, seeing in the Hennessy offer a way out of the standoff with Bendix. Hennessy and Pownall cooked up a quick and, as it turned out, decisive deal: Marietta was to purchase 11.9 million shares of Bendix at $75; then trade those shares to Allied for some Marietta shares that Allied would be getting when it purchased Bendix. Allied was to retain $300 million of Marietta shares (39 percent of the outstanding Marietta stock), since Bendix had paid $1.2 billion to buy Marietta stock; and Marietta was to spend slightly less than $900 million to purchase the Bendix stock.

Hennessy and Agee met at 8 A.M. on Thursday, just two hours before the Bendix board was to meet, at which time Agee would bring the Allied deal up for the first time. Hennessy handed Agee a memo of intent to which he and Tom Pownall had agreed in Bethesda only ten hours earlier. Agee cringed. He had been led to understand that Allied would own Martin Marietta as well as Bendix, which would have permitted Agee, as the new President of Allied, to have control over Martin, providing a certain consolation for all the anguishing hours of the past few weeks. But here was the memo of intent making it dramatically clear that Martin Marietta would stay an independent company!

All that remained for Agee was to push the Allied deal by the Bendix board. But that, Agee knew, would be a monumental task. For days he had been suggesting to Bendix directors that it would be possible to survive the prospect of Bendix and Marietta buying each other's stock. The courts had been lending their support, and it seemed as if Bendix would prevail. Now he would have to come back to them with a proposal to be bought out by Allied.

As he almost always did, Agee had his way with the board, explaining that Bendix had very little choice; four directors resigned, but even that bold step could not prevent the board's approval. The board's support was of no consequence, since the Allied-Bendix deal made no difference: Marietta had already gone ahead and purchased the Bendix shares. Once Hennessy returned from Bethesda with his own deal with Marietta in the bag, he approached Agee again to revise their original deal; they came to terms on a $75/$85 offer from Allied. The original deal had Allied paying $1.11 billion in cash and $800 million in securities; the revised deal had Allied paying $900 million in cash and $1 billion in securities. Agee was to become President of Allied.

When the dealmaking ended, Marietta remained an independent company. And Allied owned Bendix.

Some were obvious winners, Martin Marietta for one. Its decision to resist looked wise, particularly since within a year Martin's shares were above the $48 a share offered by Bendix. Allied did not fare badly acquiring Bendix. Bendix employees and the remaining stockholders managed to get $85 per share for Bendix common stock, which was 70 percent more than their value when Bendix said it would move on Martin Marietta.

But the real loser, beyond all question, appeared to be Bill Agee. On the plus side, his own 47,055 Bendix shares were worth nearly $4 million. Trying to make the best of the situation, he left the impression that he was content to be the new Allied President, second man in an $11 billion corporation. But he had counted on being named Allied's Chief Operating Officer as well; and Hennessy decided against that. Precisely why wasn't clear. It may have had something to do with the kind of public exposure Agee continued to have. Named 1982's Most Intriguing Couple by *People* magazine, Bill and Mary were photographed in their bedroom; Mary had on a cable knit sweater; her eyes were closed, her head tilted away from Agee; she looked sweet and innocent, sitting on the edge of the bed. Bill was sitting on his knees in front of her, holding her hands. The business community once again was bemused by the Bill and Mary business. When Hennessy saw the photo, he was reported to have said, "I sure as hell wouldn't have done it."[8] Whether the photograph prevented Agee from becoming Allied's Chief Operating Officer, he stayed on board for only a short time.

Bill Agee would never quite get over what Hennessy had done to him, first by permitting Marietta to avoid being acquired, then by dumping him. About all that Agee could point to of a positive nature after the Bendix takeover was the increased value of Bendix's shares: around $50 before the takeover, $85 afterward. But then again, while that was supposed to be part of The Strategy—raising the value of Bendix shares—it was also part of The Strategy that Bill Agee would be there presiding over the triumph. And he was not.

The couple bought a home on Cape Cod and formed their own investment company named Semper (Latin for "Always"). Mary wrote a book about her own experiences at Bendix: she dwelt on the scandal, devoting much less space to the takeover battle.

Never again would anyone want to repeat the Bendix Affair. The tendencies displayed by the players, their frenetic insistence on going to the brink, their willingness to barter their companies as if they were just so many pawns on a chess board, seemed excessive, to say the least. When it was all over, the public had a much better idea of what the takeover game was all about; and what they observed proved a shock. Still, it did not totally turn them off to the new adventure in American business. The excesses needed curbing; that was unquestionable. But there was no reason to stop the game—now that Washington was in a supportive mood; now that the money suppliers were sympathetic; now that others had been shown how to play it. It was no coincidence that a shrewd businessman from Texas was joining the prowl in a big way.

Chapter 3

T. Boone Pickens: The Greatest Corporate Raider Of Them All!

T. Boone Pickens. Courtesy Photo Gittings.

The Bendix fiasco left the American business community reeling, plagued with embarrassment, frightened that a monstrous genie had been let out of the bottle. The specter of Bendix and Martin Marietta linking up into a mammoth financial cripple had heads shaking in dismay. Still, convinced that Bendix was an aberration of the American free enterprise system, and not an indication of a widespread malady, many American businessmen rallied behind the idea of mergers. For example, T. Boone Pickens, who was on his way to becoming the scourge of American business, thought Bendix was a mere tempest in a teapot: "Not everything is going to work the way you want it to. Those people knew what they were doing."[1] Nonetheless, a number of businessmen realized that the frantic bidding and counterbidding during the Bendix Takeover hurt their reputations. Golden parachutes, given prominence for the first time in Bendix, also hurt their image: the $4 million severance package given to Bill Agee raised new questions about this practice.

Seemingly characterized by suicide tactics and companies mortgaging themselves in order to buy each other, mergers certainly appeared ridiculous to the American people. Some constraint seemed in order. Naturally, Washington became the cauldron into which all these emotions were poured. The burning question was whether the politicians would feel strongly enough to curb mergers. Joe Flom, the takeover attorney, and others managed to keep the issue within the regulatory arena and away from Congress, where the damage to mergers might have been more severe. Marty Lipton, another takeover attorney, pushed for new legislation with stiff measures against hostile takeovers. The Securities and Exchange Commission, recommended 33 changes in all, but the M&A business was not slowed down.

So Washington did little in the wake of Bendix. The way was left open for the raiders. They had been active prior to Bendix, but no one quite knew when the bubble would burst—when the public would cast a wary eye toward their antics. If Bendix, with its patently reckless corporate behavior, did not bring in its wake significant reform of the takeover game, the raiders could feel free to pursue their quarry—and to go after even bigger quarry than before. That was the real meaning of Bendix. No one took it more to heart than T. Boone Pickens. Through the murkiness in the Bendix affair one light shone: the fact that, in the end, Bendix stockholders triumphed when the value of their stock rose dramatically. That outcome had more impact on Pickens' thinking than anything else in the scheming in Southfield.

His name itself assured that others would remember him. T. Boone Pickens. He would become the most intimidating of all the corporate raiders. And the most famous. Indeed, no one in American business in the 1980s, save Chrysler's Lee Iacocca, garnered so much public attention. The media began to latch onto the significance of modern takeover attempts, those billion-dollar deals which, because they were often "hostile," created the raw material for great drama. Naturally, the media began to focus on personalities—and on Pickens more than any other. *Fortune* magazine devoted six pages to Pickens in December 1983 at the time of the Gulf struggle, portraying him sympathetically as someone with an "uncommon desire to make money and a nose for good deals." A full-page photograph of Pickens showed him standing against the wide-open spaces north of his home in Amarillo, Texas, on his 40,000-acre ranch, boots barely visible, head bare, plaid shirt, leather vest. The Cowboy. But he was far more than cowboy. The ranch was his plaything. His true business address was Wall Street. "What sets Pickens apart," wrote *Fortune*, "is the passion he brings to the hunt."[2] When *Time* magazine decided to do a cover story on the corporate raiders of the 1980s in March 1985, it chose the Texan as its cover subject. Pickens was receptive: he invited the reporter aboard his corporate jet. "High Time for T. Boone Pickens; A wily raider shakes up corporate America" was *Time*'s complimentary headline. This time, Pickens was photographed aboard his corporate jet, white monogrammed shirt, tie open at the collar, looking very much the American businessman.

If Pickens had become the most famous of the corporate raiders, he was also the most controversial. Some wondered whether his raids against companies were an acceptable form of business behavior. He set Wall Street on its head with his intimidating air. What was he up to? Where would he strike next? Why was he so quiet? There were more questions than answers surrounding his enigmatic presence. The answers became crucial for Wall Street to discover.

He inspired fear, he inspired intense curiosity, and he inspired respect. Those who benefited from his moves against the corporate giants could not utter enough praise. The investment bankers and arbitragers loved him—for helping to line their pockets with gold. The stockholders loved him, too, their stocks often soaring as high as a Texas gusher. But the media couldn't quite adjust to a Texan maneuvering on Wall Street. TV interviewers introduced Pickens as "The Buccaneer of Wall Street" or "The maverick of the oil patch." It was inevitable that the media would make a connection, however tenuous, between Pickens and another famous Texan, the nefarious J.R. Ewing of the popular TV program, "Dallas." Both had made lots of money, both had wheeled and dealed. Pickens seemed amused. He had never even watched an entire episode, finding what he saw boring. But he did seem to know enough to note one important distinction between himself and the TV character: he didn't have J.R.'s problems with women!

When T. Boone Pickens played the Takeover Game, he acted like a general going to battle. The decision he would eventually make—whether to try to take over a certain company—was as carefully thought out as a declaration of war. Industrious, thorough, secretive, Pickens' staff acted as if it were about to launch an invasion. Planning and secrecy were critical, for the mere mention that Pickens was about to go after a company would send its stock up. He and his aides would study the prospective target down to the tiniest detail. Much of it was time-consuming detective work, sifting through annual reports and records of a firm's domestic oil and gas reserves, projected interest rates, and energy prices. The figures would be fed into a computer. By the time Pickens' staff had completed the preliminary research, he and his team would know more about the firm than most of its employees.

Once the decision was "go" on a corporate raid, the project became an ironclad secret known only to a few of Pickens' most trusted insiders. Nothing was taken for granted. A code name would be devised for the targeted firm—in the Gulf takeover fight, for example, it was "barrel cactus," named after a plant in Pickens' office. While a raid was in progress, Pickens would keep bank employees with potentially loose tongues in the dark by a cloak-and-dagger system reminiscent of the best spy tales. Funds that were earmarked as crucial for Pickens' deals would be kept in numbered accounts around the United States. When he wanted to transfer some money to fuel a takeover attempt, Pickens had an officer from his company, Mesa Petroleum, phone a bank and stealthily pass on a code word to a carefully selected bank employee. That employee called a second Mesa executive to confirm the transaction.

The Chief of Staff would then move into battle. Boarding his personal plane in Amarillo, where Mesa Petroleum is headquartered, T. Boone Pickens would fly off to the center of the financial world where deals are made or broken—New York City. And just like his military counterparts, Pickens the general would take up a forward command post; he would reside, not in a field tent, but in one of the city's deluxe hotels, either the Waldorf Astoria or the Helmsley Palace. He wanted to be close to the action, close to Wall Street, close to his investment bankers and attorneys—and the press.

Suddenly there was no longer any need for secrecy. Just the opposite. Once he was ready to make an offer for a company, he wanted to scream it from the rooftops. Publicity was what T. Boone Pickens needed. The object at this stage was for Pickens to make himself known to the stockholders of the firm he had targeted, to let them know that he had something of value to sell to them: a chance to get a higher price for their shares. No one would want to turn down such an offer. But for the game to work, Pickens would have to move to center stage. The stockholders would have to know that T. Boone Pickens existed and what he planned to do. So he turned to the newspapers, he called news conferences, he took out newspaper ads, and he gave interviews. He did whatever was necessary to place his bid—and the seriousness he attached to that bid—before the stockholders of his targeted firm.

Thus unfolded the Takeover Game as played by its master, T. Boone Pickens. Larger than life, frightening and maddening to those who would feel the brunt of his power, he appeared to emerge from nowhere. When he felt it was time, there he would be, nibbling away, investing a part of his millions in a company along with the millions of his partners. Did he really want to run one of the giants in which he invested? It was hard to believe otherwise. Why risk all those millions? Why go to all the trouble? Yet, T. Boone Pickens had only rarely taken over a company he was raiding. Usually he would come quite close and in the process frighten a lot of big-league executives. Like those who turned their backs on him when he walked into a room. Or scorned him in the press as a bandit, or a pirate. He had an answer for the scorn. Pirates didn't go around investing a billion dollars. What was more, three-quarters of a million small investors had earned more than $13 billion thanks to his efforts. Pirate indeed. Robin Hood, maybe.

Pickens pointed as well to his growing band of admirers. In the 1960s, when he spoke to college audiences, few would ask him how they could do what he had done. "They didn't give a damn what I did; they were probably turned off by it."[3] By 1984, when he spoke to nearly 30,000 students in eleven speeches, he found the response strikingly different. "Today they'll stand in line to come up and ask me a question. Generally, the question is, 'How can I get out and do what you did?'"

Given that kind of admiration, he bridled at being called a "raider." How could it be called raiding, he would ask rhetorically, when what he did was to buy a company's shares on the open market? Perhaps one day he would decide to take on the controls of a company, just to show them—just to show those fancy executives, with their monumental salaries matched by their egos, just how much better a job he could do. Pickens saw management as entrenched, so entrenched that it had forgotten what its main task was: raising stockholder values. CEOs especially bothered him. They made the difference in a company's leadership. He once told an audience of investors in Washington, "CEOs who themselves own few shares have no more feeling for the average stockholder than they do for baboons in Africa."[4]

Just how interested in taking over a company was T. Boone Pickens? Though he gave the impression that he merely wanted to buy a stake in the company so that he could threaten to take control of it, he apparently hoped from the outset to acquire a major corporation. David Batchelder, Chief Executive Officer of Mesa Petroleum, recalled that three weeks after he joined Mesa as an assistant to the treasurer in 1978 Pickens informed him that his goal was to acquire a major oil company. Batchelder thought Pickens was dreaming, but soon found out otherwise. For Pickens was playing a game which no one played better, a cunning game of watching, studying, probing, guessing when a company might be ripe for a takeover. As that was occurring, he would turn to the stockholders with a simple appeal: he would pay them more than the current market price for their shares. He insisted that he had no ulterior motive—such as making money for himself. To the average stockholder, it mattered not at all what Pickens' motives were—only that he would help boost the value of their shares. The four major raids Pickens made in the early 1980s left the stockholders laughing all the way to the bank. No wonder that he received letters from stockholders who wrote, "Dear Mr. Pickens, have you thought about our company?"

Corporate executives did not want Boone taking over their companies. And so they fought. They devised a variety of strategies. Even if the strategies cost the corporations dearly, getting rid of T. Boone Pickens was all that seemed to matter. Usually, when the company's officers became worried that he might in fact take over, they would enter into a deal. They would buy out the stock Pickens had accumulated, which by then was priced much higher than when he first began to invest; in return, Pickens would promise to abandon the takeover fight and to keep away from that company for many years, often 15 or 25. He walked away a happy, far richer man. The corporation was happy that he was taking a walk—but it had paid a heavy price for saying no to him.

Whatever his game, T. Boone Pickens has not done badly for himself. He has worked from a relatively small power base: Mesa Petroleum is a dwarf in the oil industry, with sales of $413 million in 1984. Yet, in three years between 1982 and 1985, Pickens made over $800 million for Mesa and its partners. His most spectacular success came in 1983 when he maneuvered Gulf, then the fifth largest American oil firm—with 1984 sales of $28.4 billion—into selling out to the fourth largest oil firm, Chevron—with 1984 sales of $29.2 billion. The pricetag was an astounding $13.2 billion; the merger was the largest in business history. Personally for Pickens, it was a bonanza, earning for him and his partners a hefty $760 million. This and other successes have shaken up the oil industry, forcing American business men to reexamine the old rules by which corporations lived and worked. His arrival has made the earth tremble under the feet of the corporate warlords, and many have wondered: Just where did T. Boone Pickens come from?

His background is that of an oilman, not a financier. He was born within sight of working wells on May 22, 1928, in Holdenville, Oklahoma, the only son of Thomas Boone Pickens and Grace Marcian (Molonson) Pickens. Young "T Bone," as his father liked to call him, was raised on a street of white clapboard houses and green lawns. Holdenville (population, 6,300) was a cow town surrounded by pastures: cattle grazed alongside active oil pumps. Young T. Boone's father, an attorney for the

Phillips Petroleum Company's land acquisition department, was an inveterate gambler who, rather harmlessly, liked to bet on college football games. But, more perilously, he had no qualms about risking the family's capital on oil-lease speculations, building and destroying fortunes. Pickens could never forgive his father for losing those large amounts of money. Though it was the height of the Depression, the elder Mr. Pickens liked to drive around town in a fancy Pierce-Arrow, earning him a reputation as well-to-do. Young T. Boone found the car an embarrassment: whenever Father drove him to school, "T Bone" would insist on being dropped two blocks away. In contrast with his father, T. Boone's mother was a practical woman who rarely made hasty decisions and had a gift for analysis. Her son deeply admired his mother's caution. One can imagine some of the "discussions" he and Mother may have had about Father's love of gambling. So practical was she that Holdenville's officials sought her out to run the city's gasoline-rationing program during World War Two. A gambler for a father, a cool, analytical figure for a mother—T. Boone Pickens would always say that he'd had great luck with his genes. The family traced its ancestry back to the same part of England that produced a distant kinsman by the name of Daniel Boone.

Boone's first "merger" may have come at age 14 when he joined various newspaper routes on neighboring streets with his original route of 28 customers; he wound up with 150 clients. During high school, young T. Boone moved with his family to Amarillo (population then 170,000), at the time the unofficial capital of the Texas Panhandle. That city has remained Pickens' home. He received good grades in high school without much effort. He did have a geography teacher (his aunt) who would not give the youngster an A even though he apparently deserved one. She criticized Boone for not working up to his potential. He would not forget the criticism for some time—until he had proved himself later in life. Though he was not tall at five feet, eight inches, Boone was a star guard on the Amarillo High School basketball team, which in his senior year made it to the state playoffs. So it was no surprise that Boone entered Texas A&M on a basketball scholarship in 1947. When he broke his elbow, he was forced to give up the scholarship; he transferred to Oklahoma State for his sophomore year. While in college he had the reputation of being good at any game, enjoying youthful pranks, and therefore lacking seriousness. At one point, he thought of becoming a veterinarian or a basketball coach. He married his high school sweetheart, Lynn O'Brien, one of the prettiest blondes in the city; she was 17 years old; he was 20. A geology professor had a positive influence on him; after two years on the Dean's List, Pickens graduated in 1951 with a Bachelor's degree in geology.

He went to work for Phillips Petroleum. The place had no time for his ideas, making him unhappy from the start. He remained for four years in growing frustration until one day in 1955 his wife asked him why, if he disliked the work so much, did he stay on. The question encouraged him to do something he had long wanted to do. Returning to the office immediately, he gave notice, packed up his things, and drove off. Pickens wanted to do his own exploring for oil, to prove how good he could be as an "oil finder." Taking the $1,300 in severance pay from Phillips' profit-sharing plan, he had just enough to purchase a 1955 Ford station wagon that was large enough to hold his exploration gear.

One searched for oil by chasing down rumors over dusty back roads in Texas and Oklahoma. Nights were spent bent over maps studying geological strata. It was work that Pickens had been trained for; it was work he loved. He made sure to know everything possible about oil drilling. That first year he had no financial backing. But in 1956 he took $2,500 in cash and a $100,000 line of credit from his wife's uncle and another local investor and launched his first firm, the Petroleum Exploration Company, based in Amarillo.

In this as in his later business adventures, Pickens would be applauded for doing his homework. He liked to say that he managed to succeed where others failed because he rose earlier in the morning and worked harder. That, plus an uncanny understanding of the business, made Petroleum Exploration thrive. To keep drilling, one needed backers; with his easy, persuasive manner, Pickens managed to win the ear of local dentists, doctors, attorneys who liked to invest in small-time drilling. He came off sounding like a good geologist—and a good businessman. It was a hectic time for Pickens. He had found some one hundred investors in the first few years, but always more money was needed. His mind raced in many directions at once. Watching one well in the dry air under a boiling Texas sun, he would rush to a telephone booth to try to convince an investor to give him cash to seek samples from another well. In 1959, he ventured beyond Texas and Oklahoma, setting up a company called Altair in Canada with $35,000 in backing. His luck would be—not bad. From the oil and gas fields he would work there, Pickens eventually earned some $600 million when he sold out to Dome Petroleum in 1979.

By 1964 Pickens' operations had grown to over three hundred drilling groups working on 4,000 properties. He wanted to take the company public, but investors balked, not eager to risk their cash flow from the producing wells for stock with an uncertain yield. Pickens won the day. He took no founders' stock, an oversight he would later regret; for a number of years he received only his salary. Pickens chose the name Mesa for the new company after the familiar formations of the high plains near Amarillo. Other oil companies had owned service stations, refineries, tankers, and pipelines. Not Mesa. Pickens decided that he would stick to what he knew: drilling, exploration, and production. There would be no potentially money-losing sidelines. Pickens' only attempt at diversification failed in 1974 when he was forced to sell the firm's cattle business at a $19 million loss. Mesa realized an impressive profit almost from the start. In 1969, Pickens took a giant step toward making it a major exploration company: he bought the Hugoton Production Company with its huge gas field north of Amarillo. After acquiring 17 percent of Hugoton's stock, he convinced its managers to agree to a merger; this was an early Pickens takeover bid— a friendly one and thus different from his later efforts.

His ability to find oil was impressive—never more so than in 1970, when Mesa became the first independent oil exploration firm to get involved in offshore drilling, which had always been monopolized by the oil giants. In time, Mesa would become America's most successful independent oil company. Then in 1975 Mesa, as part of a consortium, discovered a big oil field in the North Sea; Pickens named the field after his second wife, Beatrice, whom he had married in 1972 after divorcing Lynn, mother of his four children. He had known Beatrice at Oklahoma State; she had married a fraternity brother. By all accounts, she has shown an interest in Pickens' work that Lynn did not, and that seems to have accounted for the break-up of the first marriage and the success of the second.

Pickens made a shrewd move in 1979: the high costs of exploration in Alaska were beyond Mesa's means, and oil fields abroad were, as Pickens put it, "at the mercy of radicals and unreliable foreigners,"[5] so he searched for a new approach. The result was the Mesa Royalty Trust. On November 1 every Mesa stockholder received a unit of the Royalty Trust for each Mesa share he owned; Mesa kept 10 percent of the trust units. Three months later the price of Mesa's stock, which had been $40 a share the previous July, zoomed up to nearly $60; a unit of the oil trust sold at $35. Mesa's stockholders and T. Boone Pickens earned a healthy profit. What Pickens had done was indeed enterprising: he had divested himself of a full half of his company and at the same time, kept it!

Pickens succeeded in the '70s because he almost always seemed to be one step ahead of bad news: he knew when to get out of a situation just before it would cause him enormous damage. When in 1979 the Canadian government decided to impose new energy regulations that made it unwise for American firms to invest in Canadian oil, he sold Mesa's Canadian operation for $600 million. The tale was repeated the same year just before the British government levied a heavy tax on North Sea oil production: Pickens realized a $65 million profit by divesting Mesa of its operation there—just in time.

He began to play the takeover game in earnest in the early 1980s. By that time oil companies looked like fertile ground for him. After all, in 1979 the Organization of Petroleum Exporting Countries (OPEC) had nearly tripled the cost of oil, and so shares of the major oil producers rose sharply. Only three years later—in 1982—prices started to drop as a world glut of oil occurred. Meanwhile, American energy reserves were diminishing. Pickens saw a chance to make a move: oil company stocks, he concluded, were undervalued.

He waged his first campaign against Cities Service, the Tulsa, Oklahoma-based oil company which ranked as the nation's 20th biggest. It was a daring move, considering that Cities Service was at least three times Mesa's size in assets; and over eighteen times larger in total sales (in 1981 its assets were $8.5 billion and its total sales $408 million). Trying to make a "friendly" offer, Pickens on May 31, 1982, phoned Cities Service Chairman Charles J. Waidelich and offered $50 a share for 51 percent of the company—a deal worth $1.6 to $1.8 billion. Pickens had already acquired 5 percent of Cities Service a year earlier. Its stock was trading just below $30 a share, as oil prices had been on the decline. A day after Pickens' phone call, Waidelich refused the offer and decided that the best defense was to go on the offensive. In a move much like what Martin Marietta would seek to do just three months later against Bendix, Cities Service offered to buy 51 percent of Mesa's stock at $17 a share. But herein lies the difference between Waidelich's offer and Martin Marietta's. Waidelich offered only one dollar more than the trading price of Mesa's stock. It is hard to understand why anyone at Mesa should have been intimidated—yet Pickens and Mesa were. The shoe was on the other foot. What could Pickens do? Still confident, he departed Amarillo for New York to press the fight and seek support for his bid.

Fortunately for Pickens, in August, Occidental Petroleum emerged as a corporate white knight, buying Cities Service for $65 a share. Cities Service did not have the aggressive instincts of Martin Marietta; it was not prepared to fight to the bitter end. Thus, Pickens was helped out of a situation, and he reaped a fat dividend for his endeavors. He managed to wind up with a $31.5 million profit—an impressive sum for a seeming novice in the takeover game. Pickens sensed that this formula might be tried on even bigger fish. Cities Service was not the only undervalued corporation around. To get involved in a larger way, however, meant getting more backing; Pickens still had inadequate financial clout to take on the big boys.

General American Oil Company was Pickens' next target. In December 1982 he announced a $520 million cash tender offer for a majority of the company's stocks. "Looking for oil and gas isn't going to do you any good now," Pickens told the *New York Times* on December 21, "with prices stabilized or dropped back to some degree. Consequently you've got to do something different. We're not going to commit big dollars to exploration. We're going to commit big dollars to acquisition." But acquisition was not what General American had in mind. The company went on the offensive, employing a series of tactical maneuvers to keep Pickens at bay. He didn't like what he saw. Therefore, in January 1983, Pickens filed suit in federal court, charging General American with "kamikaze tactics" that were keeping his firm from making a fair bid. He withdrew the suit that same month when Phillips Petroleum negotiated an accord in which it purchased General American for $1.2 billion. Once again, a white knight had come to the rescue of a company targeted by Pickens. Phillips agreed to pay Mesa $15 million to cover the costs of Mesa's bid; in return Pickens pledged to give up his quest of General American. In the stock run-up Pickens managed to earn another $43.6 million profit.

Now it was time for Pickens to go after even bigger fish.

What was T. Boone Pickens like? It's hard to find out, if only because few are totally objective about this larger-than-life figure. His admirers are awestruck at his success; his detractors have suffered in one way or another by being excluded from his beneficence. So neither the fans nor the critics are objective. One of the shrewdest assessments, I thought, came from someone who had recently spent a week with him. "To understand Pickens," he said, "or a lot of these raiders, for that matter, you have to realize that some like Pickens are nonestablishment types. It is best to see Pickens as someone who is simply trying to win the respect of the establishment." I also sought out people who had spent a lot of time with Pickens. I talked with someone who had worked closely with Pickens during the 1980s. "You know," he began, "they all do what they do to make a lot of money. Boone had an ideological dimension and there is an enormous amount of appeal associated with the fact that this guy has been willing to take on . . . so-called establishment companies . . . to challenge them."

The Pickens acquaintance found the Texan "very gracious, very charming, very sensitive, and a very caring man"—adjectives that one normally doesn't associate with aggressive businessmen. But, he said, "I have been with him when the battles were the hottest and heaviest and I have never seen him lose his temper, lose his poise. I have never seen him blame somebody, fly off the handle." By way of example, he recalled being summoned one evening in 1985 during Pickens' Unocal fight to a meeting of the Texan's main advisers. "I walked into the room and instead of the principal advisers, all the people who worked with them, maybe fifty to seventy-five people, were there. They were being treated to a beautiful steak dinner with wine, a little roast hosted by Boone. It was his way, when things looked the darkest and everybody was really tired and exhausted from the fight, of saying thank you, don't despair, and keep your spirits up." After a few hours the main advisers were quietly taken to another room.

Disagreement exists over whether Pickens' expressions of concern for the stockholders are genuine. According to one former Pickens aide, who is skeptical, "It helped the notion that he was a friend of stockholders and disarmed people who thought he was a Texas desperado. It made the public think that he was a kind of Robin Hood." Another Pickens-watcher noted, however, that Boone has a populist strain in him: "He really does believe he's fighting for the shareholder."

Pickens averages twelve-hour workdays, sleeps no more than five hours a night. He gets his best ideas during his 20-minute morning showers. He is on the phone constantly; he has twelve in his home alone. At his ranch he has a radio beam that can reach him anywhere on its 14,000 acres. For those who have trouble keeping up with him Pickens has little patience: he has fired people for coming to work late or leaving early for the weekend. He points to his low blood pressure (110 over 70) to explain how he can handle so much work. Acquaintances of Boone make a big point of how he never loses his composure, even though he has risked more than $1.3 billion in big purchases in major oil firms.

Even-tempered as he is, Pickens is also driven by a keen sense of competition that goes back to his basketball playing days; he recalled once how excited he was when he first could jump up and touch the net. In tandem with that competitive instinct is Pickens' love of gambling: he and his friends would bet as youths who would pay the check at the next table. He also took bets on how the Cities Service board would react to his offers and on long putts during his golf game.

Pickens eschews rich foods, likes the simple things of life such as "Granny Apples," nuts, and, above all else, raw carrots. At 10 A.M. when he's in his Amarillo office he has a trolley come around to bring him a bowl of raw carrots. Sports are important to him. From basketball as a youth he went on to golf and tennis; he is also a crack bird shot with a double-barrel Browning. He encourages his employees to be athletic. In the company racquetball competitions, he is often at the top of the ladder. His employees know that athletics are close to his heart, so in 1979 they gave Pickens a life-sized bronze statue of himself crouching and ready to let go with a backhand. It dominates the T. Boone Pickens Fitness Center at Mesa's headquarters. Consistent with his love of athletics is Pickens' campaign against smoking, which is forbidden at his meetings and on his corporate plane ("If you must smoke, please step outside," warns an inscription on a needlepoint cushion inside the plane).

One of Pickens' big joys is making a lot of money, and that is precisely what he has done. In 1984 he was called the highest-paid corporation executive in America with more than $20 million in salary, cash bonuses, and deferred compensation. Pickens held 1.5 million shares of Mesa Petroleum and had options for almost 5 million more. His stocks and options were valued in March 1985 at about $100 million. He has a small golden parachute in case Mesa is ever taken over: two years' salary or just under $1 million. He could also exercise those stock options.

Pickens has some large holdings as well, including his 2B Ranch, where he and his wife stable eleven horses and hunt together. He has a 6,500-acre Oklahoma cattle ranch and a vacation retreat in California's Palm Springs. His year-round home is in Amarillo, a $1.5 million house with a sunken tennis court, a 20-foot-high glass-enclosed gallery, and a library with over 1000 volumes, including a collection of rare illustrated books on American Indians.

In the late summer of 1983, Pickens chose to go after one of the giants of the oil patch—Gulf Oil. There was no seemingly sound reason to imagine that his tiny Mesa Petroleum, with its 7,000 employees and 1983 sales of $422 million, could go up against such might: Gulf was the fifth-largest oil firm in the United States and had 40,000 employees. But, as it turned out, Gulf was ripe for takeover—at least in Pickens' determined view. Gulf's management had made some costly errors in judgment and so its financial reserves had been dwindling. Wall Street had turned sour on the company; its stock was selling at only $38 a share. Some thought it should have been at $114 a share. Pickens spotted an undervalued company that just might be conquered.

He began buying up Gulf stock: by October he already controlled 8.75 percent of the firm and was prepared to nearly double that amount. He spoke openly about what he was trying to do: "Very simply we're buying the stock for investment purposes. Gulf stock is selling at a huge discount when compared to appraised value." Gulf, however, didn't scare easily. To stave off Pickens it leaned on his bankers, and four of them agreed to withdraw their support for his financing. This was unusual. A Wall Street investment banker told me about a conversation with a friend on the credit committee of a major financing institution; he asked about the analysis his friend had made to deal with the problem of risk in giving credit to Pickens. "We never lost money with Boone," the friend said. My investment banker acquaintance shot back, "I understand that. But what kind of analysis did you do?" The credit committee man said, "I'm telling you, we never lost money with Boone. It's better than lending to Argentina. It's better to lend to Boone."

In November 1983 Pickens organized a meeting in New York with two hundred financial analysts and money managers to assure them that he would not cut any separate deals with Gulf. He would not sell his shares to Gulf at a premium but would continue his effort to take over the company. Most thought he would make a serious bid to take over Gulf, or at least seek a white knight with the idea of earning a goodly profit in the process—but they were glad for the reassurance. It was pouring rain outside, but the crowd couldn't stay away and miss the unusual chance to see what this man was like—this man with the strange name, with the great derring-do, this man who had sent chills running down the backs of the Wall Street community. Pickens took fifteen minutes to work the audience. Like a politician, he shook hands, answered questions, moved easily while his face was bathed in the strobe lights. Once on stage, he introduced his wife to the audience. "Bea's here to catch any soft fruit that comes my way." None came. He made his pledge—there would be no separate deals with Gulf. He only wanted to increase the value of the stockholders' shares. What was management worried about?

All this was music to the audience's ears. They wanted to believe him. Someone asked him what he would do if Gulf tendered for Mesa stock. "If they offer a premium, they've got it," came Pickens' reply. The audience gave a nervous laugh, as if they knew Boone was not going to let Gulf indulge in any Pac-Man games with his own company.

Despite Pickens' public assurances, Gulf was worried. Perhaps Pickens' next move might be to snare a seat on its board of directors. That seemed fairly easy to do. But, if Gulf (which was incorporated in Pennsylvania) could reincorporate in Delaware where the law was stricter, Pickens might be stopped. In December 1983 Gulf called a special meeting of the stockholders to reincorporate the Pennsylvania firm in Delaware. This would help keep Pickens not only from electing board members, but also from calling special stockholder meetings and from submitting charter amendments to stockholders. Pickens disclaimed any interest in getting on the Gulf board, saying he was already on too many boards. He denounced Gulf Chairman James Lee's reincorporation plan, and both men traveled around the country like candidates for political office, whipping up support for their respective sides of the argument among the institutional investors who controlled one-third of Gulf's stock: Pickens sought to kill the reincorporation plan, Lee sought to win backers for it. Investors often hosted Pickens one day, Lee the next. Full-page newspaper ads appealed to the investors. One read, "Your choice, your voice, your vote." When the stockholders voted on December 2 to reincorporate in Delaware, the result was a defeat for Pickens.

For the moment, T. Boone Pickens had been constrained. He would now have more trouble electing directors to the Gulf board. He insisted, however, that he had bought his 13.2 percent stake in Gulf simply to persuade Lee to create a large royalty trust that would spin off about $750 million a year in cash flow to stockholders. His idea was to put Gulf's oil-producing properties, which gave off continuing income, in trust; this would avoid a corporate tax on earnings. The earnings of the trust would go to unit holders as royalty payments. Just as shares were traded on the stock exchange, so too would units in the trust. This proposal was submitted to Gulf's stockholders and in January 1984 they turned it down, believing that it would serve only to dissipate the company's exploration cash.

Nothing seemed to daunt Pickens. In interviews he turned philosophical: he was glad that stockholders seemed to be catching on; starting to understand that their assets were being depleted; showing some desire to act. All this shuffling around, as he called his own role in the Takeover Game, would help to restructure the oil industry.

He turned to Drexel, Burnham and Lambert as well as Lehman Brothers, two major investment banking houses in New York, to help him raise more cash to buy additional Gulf shares. Meanwhile, ways were open to Gulf to fight Pickens. Gulf could acquire a smaller company to increase its debt. Or, Pac-Man-style, it could try to take over Mesa Petroleum (though, after the Bendix-Martin Marietta affair, few corporate executives would have wanted to try that except as a last resort). Gulf could seek to buy back Pickens' stock at a premium at once, rather than wait, as it did, until February 1984. Or it could adopt some "shark repellent" techniques: staggering the terms of board members or enacting rules that required a sizable majority of stockholders to approve a takeover. But Gulf's management, fearing that taking such steps would lower the value of its stock, didn't act quickly enough.

By the early part of 1984 the circle was closing in on Gulf. With Washington giving its approval to the Texaco-Getty deal, it now appeared that big oil companies were vulnerable to takeovers, that even big and powerful Gulf could fall. Things were looking up for Pickens. He had been in touch with Cincinnati financier Carl H. Lindner, Chairman of the Penn Central Corporation. Lindner agreed to invest $300 million in Mesa, and so Pickens was able to put in a bid of $65 a share for 13.5 million Gulf shares. That would have raised Pickens' holdings of Gulf stock from 13.2 to 21.4 percent. A proxy fight was in the offing.

"Unfair and inadequate" was Gulf's response to Pickens' offer. Gulf insisted that it was not for sale, but it understood that this statement had little practical meaning: the only question was whether Gulf could find a buyer of its own choice. By February, the company was becoming desperate: it tried to reduce its attractiveness by declaring that it would buy its outstanding shares if Pickens managed to gain 51 percent of the stock. At times, Gulf feared that it was fighting for the very life of the company: Pickens didn't deny reports that he was giving consideration to selling off Gulf's assets—and earning perhaps as much as $12 billion—once he obtained control.

It was time for Gulf to prevent a bad situation from getting worse. Pickens and his backers were about to raise their stake to over 21 percent. A hostile takeover seemed imminent. Gulf executives sought the best deal. Into Pittsburgh came three prospective buyers, each bankrolled by $6 billion or more. The rules of the game, as laid down by Gulf, were that by 9 A.M. on a Monday morning each had to make his bid—without seeing those of the two other competitors. The jackpot was Gulf Oil. Seven hours after the bids were in, Chevron—Standard Oil of California (Socal)—was chosen the winner. Best known for its Chevron gas stations, Socal had come in with a cash bid of $80 a share, or $13.2 billion—the highest price one American corporation had ever paid for another. The name of the new oil company, now the nation's third largest after Exxon and Mobil, would be Chevron—after Socal's trademark.

Pickens' incredible feat had been in gauging that Gulf would not take him seriously and would not be equipped to do battle with him with all of its energy and will. Had Gulf taken him seriously early on, it might have erected adequate defenses. But it did not. And so Pickens stayed in the game, built up his stake in Gulf, and kept the management on its toes, fearing a takeover. Using the conventional tactics of the corporate raider, Pickens led Gulf into believing that it had no alternative but to seek another buyer. And when that buyer appeared, Pickens would realize a profit, a whopping $760 million! For, in buying Gulf's shares, Chevron was buying Pickens' as well—at $80 a share. He and his group had paid an average of $45 a share for their 22 million shares.

Pickens was a hero to Wall Street. The arbitragers held him in great respect. They should have: he had earned a mind-boggling $300 million for them. But it was the stockholders who truly took him into their hearts. Not surprisingly: he had made millions for them. "We really did work on behalf of all the stockholders," Pickens said afterwards. "Gulf's stockholders are participating in a run-up of $5.8 billion. We just happen to have 13.2 percent."[6] Some believed Pickens was a frustrated man: the speculators had profited by his adventures far more than the little stockholders he always talked about. It was said that if he could have spun off a royalty trust in the Gulf episode, he would have been far more pleased.

The Gulf-Chevron merger, spurred by T. Boone Pickens, had major reverberations for the takeover game. Until the Gulf deal, oil companies had not wanted to go after one another. But in the first half of 1984 alone, apart from the Gulf takeover, Texaco had purchased Getty for $10.2 billion, and Mobil had absorbed Superior Oil for $5.7 billion. The real significance of Gulf was in demonstrating that the giant firms could be knocked over. By generating $63 million in fees for the investment bankers (Merrill Lynch, Morgan Stanley, and Salomon Brothers), Gulf supplied a good reason for other Wall Street financial advisers to take a serious look at the takeover game and decide to go for a piece of the action.

Washington's reaction to Gulf was a whimper. Whatever bitterness was felt toward Pickens, it did not produce a surge of congressional sentiment against takeovers. One senator sought some limitations, but he did not get very far. Senator J. Bennett Johnston, a Louisiana Democrat, looking at Gulf, wanted to stop oil companies from diverting what he contended were billions of dollars away from the exploration for new oil into the purchase of undervalued companies like Gulf (and Getty as well). After Texaco bought Getty, Johnston looked around and saw other takeover candidates in Sun, Phillips Petroleum, Union Oil, Superior and Atlantic Richfield. He introduced a bill that would have effectively barred mergers for six months among the top 150 oil firms; it was defeated by a 52–42 vote.

No battle was more bruising for Pickens than his campaign in 1984 to take over Phillips Petroleum, a company best known for producing Phillips 66 gasoline. At first he acquired a 5.7 percent interest in the Oklahoma-based corporation at an average of $43 a share. Then, on December 4, 1984, he proposed a tender offer for 20.6 percent of Phillips outstanding shares at $60 a share, or $900 million, a move that prompted the firm's executives the next day to obtain a temporary restraining order to prevent him from acquiring control. Phillips would not simply let Pickens walk all over the firm. Phillips, like Cities Service, Superior, and General American, was represented by Marty Lipton, who by now had perfected the "poison pill" defense. Deciding to swallow a "poison pill," Phillips instituted a recapitalization plan that doubled the company's long-term debt, making a takeover gambit prohibitively expensive. Or so one would have thought.

Public pressure was applied to Pickens as well. It came from the townspeople of Bartlesville, Oklahoma, home of Phillips Petroleum. The entire town came to the firm's support: a local church sponsored 24-hour prayer vigils to stop Pickens. Local residents began wearing BOONE BUSTERS T-shirts. An anti-Pickens song was written and sung at a public meeting attended by almost 4000 people. The words went like this:

> There's gonna be a meeting at the old town hall tonight.
> And if they try to stop us, there's gonna be a fight.
> We're gonna get our company out of this awful fix.
> 'Cause we don't want to change our names to Pickens 66.

All of this hurt Pickens very much. "After all," he said later, "I'm a native Oklahoman, born and bred. Did they think I would shut down the whole town? Those people had things on backwards. They thought the town owned the company. The town didn't own the company, the stockholders owned the company, and the shareholder is the forgotten man."[7]

To quell Pickens, just before Christmas, Phillips bought back his stock purchased before the tender offer at $53 per share. Phillips, for its part, had to agree to a financial restructuring that would make the value of all stockowners' holdings the same as what Pickens received. The arbitragers were irritated at not reaping the benefits of a takeover at $60 a share, Pickens' original offer. They had gotten used to Pickens bringing them millions of dollars. Instead, they lost $100 million and adopted a slightly less respectful attitude toward the man from Texas.

Phillips stockholders soon confronted another takeover bid by Carl Icahn, but they eventually managed to avoid an Icahn takeover by making a deal with him. (See Chapter 4.) Pickens, who with his partners earned an $89 million pretax profit, had to promise as part of his stock buy-back deal with Phillips not to launch a Phillips takeover attempt for at least fifteen years. This seemed all beside the point: raising its corporate debt to $7.3 billion to stave off Pickens and later Icahn, Phillips wasn't a very attractive takeover target after the battle was over.

Even though Pickens embittered the management and the employees of Phillips and disappointed the arbitragers, he was still highly thought of on Wall Street. The *New York Times* on March 5, 1985, reported "unqualified admiration" on Wall Street for Pickens' "ability to come out ahead—and improve the lot of Phillips' stockholders in the process."

While moving against Phillips, Pickens had his eye on Unocal, then the twelfth-largest American oil producer with 1984 sales of $11.4 billion. It was the same story: Pickens spotted a company with hidden value and supposedly poor management, a combination which put it at the top of his "hit" list. "Unocal," said Pickens, "is obviously strong but its executives haven't done very much for the stockholders."[8] He began acquiring stock quietly in October 1984 and by the following February owned 13.8 million shares, for which he had paid nearly $600 million. The stock rose correspondingly from $36 to $48 a share. By February 14 Pickens was the largest single Unocal stockholder. By this time, however, Pickens was a known quantity; his tactics were too familiar, too often-used for him to march in, buy up his shares, and wait for management to buckle. For many reasons, some of them directly related to T. Boone Pickens, American management had grown determined to make life tough for the corporate raiders. Phillips had been an important watershed. Unocal would provide one more experience when corporate management would simply not cower to T. Boone Pickens.

This would become his toughest fight.

Fred L. Hartley, Chairman of Unocal, and a company employee since 1939 when he started as an engineer, decided to wage war against Pickens. The Unocal Chairman could have sought a white knight. But he would have none of that. He saw Pickens as part of a larger problem. Hartley would save Unocal from "financial barbarism, terrorism or gangsterism, call it what you want."[9] In March, the firm sued its principal lender, Security Pacific National Bank, for dealing with Pickens, for allegedly lending money to him to finance his purchase of Unocal stock. Pickens, undeterred, sought alternative financing. Three weeks later he had purchased another 6.7 million Unocal shares—his holdings now were up to 13.5 percent.

In April he announced an $8.1 billion offer for the firm. "Grossly inadequate," cried Fred Hartley, countering with his own bid to buy back Unocal's outstanding shares at $72 a share. There was nothing unusual in Hartley's buy-back plan—except for one incredible wrinkle. All stockholders could participate in the offer—except Pickens. Was this legal? Would Pickens stand for it?

On May 13, while Pickens was losing a proxy fight to unseat Hartley, a Delaware Court ruled that Pickens' Mesa Petroleum could not be excluded from Unocal's exchange offer—and the $180 million profit. But in a shocking surprise four days later, the Delaware Supreme Court reversed the lower court, upholding Unocal's unorthodox plan. That reversal would stand in the Takeover Game as a great milestone, a key moment in the slowing down of the corporate raiders. For what the high court's decision of May 17 appeared to do was to permit firms incorporated in Delaware to use almost any defense against unfriendly tender offers. It was one of the worst blows to corporate raiders in general, and specifically to T. Boone Pickens. It was "the biggest surprise I've had in thirty-five years of business," Pickens said of the court decision. "That call was like Doug Flutie (at the time a star quarterback in pro football) throwing a Hail Mary pass and making a touchdown. They (Unocal) were extremely lucky."[10]

The Supreme Court said that corporate directors have leeway under the "business judgment rule" to discriminate against minority stockholders if they think it's in the best interests of the majority. Unocal faced, in the court's view, a "grossly inadequate, coercive, two-tier, front-end-loaded tender offer" from a raider who apparently was simply after a premium for his own shares. Therefore Unocal was justified in preventing Mesa from a partial buy-back of its shares for debt securities valued at $72 each. The raiders had always dreaded this day, when the courts would turn aggressive, when judges would move away from their old attitude that it was better to let the marketplace and businessmen work out their own problems. The Delaware Supreme Court was saying: things have gone too far, the behavior of Mr. Pickens and his fellow corporate raiders, having caused American corporations such grief, must be contained; Congress was not willing to enter the fray; so the courts must. The point of the ruling was simple: if you are T. Boone Pickens, a board of directors of a target company can keep you at bay—and the courts will support them.

One big question: would the new court ruling encourage action against raiders in other arenas? At first blush the answer appeared to be no. Washington's attitude was: fine, the courts have stepped in, now we don't have to. Just three days after the Delaware court ruling, the SEC said it had decided against pressing Congress for legislation to limit hostile takeover practices; it would permit state courts and the marketplace to deal with such activities. Thus, the Delaware decision would serve as a new stumbling block for the raiders, but not a fatal one.

Pickens at first figured his losses in the Unocal exercise at $300 million; and so he felt he had no choice but to make a deal: Unocal agreed to pay Pickens the $72-a-share price it had offered in its own buy-back scheme, but only for some one-third of the Texan's 23.7 million shares. More important, Hartley won from Pickens a pledge to sell off his remaining shares slowly, and to refrain from further takeover attempts against Unocal for the next 25 years.

Confronting a $305 million loss, cut down to size by the Delaware Supreme Court decision, forced to get his cash out of Unocal more slowly than presumably he would have liked, T. Boone Pickens appeared to be down. But was he out? Pickens thought it interesting how quickly one could go from being a hero to a nobody in the public's eye. He acknowledged that the court decision had temporarily stopped his momentum. But he vowed that he hadn't lost it forever.

It became obvious, after some time, that he was very much alive financially and flourishing. Mesa announced it would report an $83 million after-tax gain from its Unocal dealings! How could this be? In the terms of its peace agreement with Unocal, Mesa realized a $189 million gain from the sale of one-third of its holdings to Unocal; but Mesa lost $305 million on the depreciated value of the other two-thirds of the shares (which it had to hold for at least one year). That came to a $116 million pretax loss. Under standard accounting practices, that would result in a $63 million after-tax loss. But Mesa used an obscure provision of tax law that allowed it to treat the $590 million proceeds of the sale as a dividend, only 15% of which was taxable. It posted a paper loss of $639 million on the depreciated value of its total investment of $1 billion. That produced $198 million in tax benefits, which, minus the $116 million pretax loss on the deal, turned into an $83 million after-tax gain. Had Pickens taken a loss, it was believed that this could have stopped him from further raids. But, landing on his feet, as he did, few believed that he would be kept from trying again.

The Pickens defeat raised the question of whether the golden era for raiders, as the *Wall Street Journal* called it, was over. Had the court setback curbed takeover fever? The courts seemed upset about greenmailing but not about takeovers as such.

By August 1985 Pickens was apparently making plans for yet more raiding. At least that was the conclusion drawn from his plan to reshape Mesa. In announcing a major reorganization of his company, he told everyone that he was temporarily out of the takeover business—but no one quite believed him. Mesa's board approved a plan to transfer the bulk of its assets into a limited partnership. Pickens was to become general partner of the new firm. Rather than signaling that Pickens' takeover days were over, the step appeared to suggest just the opposite, for it gave him more leeway if he wanted to acquire firms outside the oil business.

One new development did suggest that Pickens might be out of the game for a while. In the fall of 1985 he signed a contract containing a $1.5 million advance for writing his memoirs, one of the largest ever. The publisher was Houghton Mifflin, which won over six others. Presumably Pickens' book would draw back the cover on some of his secretive, mysterious

Pickens didn't quit the takeover game. In February 1986, in his first move since he failed to take over Unocal, his Mesa Limited Partnership offered $200 million in cash, or $22 per share, for KN Energy, Inc., a natural gas company. Though Pickens did not acquire the company, KN's stock went from $17 a share to 22½ when he made public his offer, proving once again the power of T. Boone Pickens, corporate raider.

corporate raiding. Reporters asked Pickens the predictable questions about whether he might consider a takeover of one of the mighty publishing firms. He didn't say yes, but he didn't say no either. The book, said Pickens, "would be about a routine American boy who grew up to be a businessman."

In March of 1986 Pickens found himself in the unaccustomed, but appealing, role of white knight. This time the raider was Irwin L. Jacobs, the Minneapolis investor who had offered $23 a share—or $763 million—for Pioneer Corp., a gas-rich independent energy firm around the corner from Mesa Petroleum in Amarillo. Jacobs had built up a 14 percent stake in the company. Chairman David Culver of Pioneer rejected that offer and then worked out a friendly deal with Pickens, who spent $860 million worth of his limited partnership units in the reorganized Mesa firm for the company. Pickens paid $24 a share, only $1 more than Jacobs had been offering. The deal was a first for Pickens: unlike Cities Service, Gulf, Phillips Petroleum, and Unocal, Pioneer was now his company. This time he had not been swept aside. This time he would become boss. The new Mesa unit gave Pioneer stockholders equity in the merged Mesa-Pioneer company plus the right to a $1.50-per-unit annual distribution for five years.

The Pioneer purchase put Pickens in a strengthened position to engage in even more takeovers. Having acquired Pioneer, which had almost no debt, Mesa would be able to increase its borrowing power to some $800 million. Then, using margin financing, Mesa could purchase as much as $1.6 billion in the stock of a target firm. For that reason, it was rumored that Pickens might go after Mobil Corp or Atlantic Richfield Co. in 1986 or 1987. So, T. Boone Pickens was expected to continue as corporate raider par excellence, getting the detectives working again, and employing the secret codes, and putting in place those secret bank accounts. In the winter of 1986 one of the burning questions on Wall Street was still: what was T. Boone Pickens up to next?

At first even oil executives, some of whom were victims of T. Boone Pickens' aggressive actions, thought he was doing a service to the oil industry by shaking it up. There was no question that Pickens had radically altered the industry's shape: two large companies, Cities Service and Gulf, had disappeared, recast into new companies as the result of battles traceable directly to Pickens. Other oil firms had avoided hostile takeovers by virtue of restructuring efforts such as getting rid of assets, laying off thousands of employees, and adding billions of dollars of debt to their balance sheets.

In time, those oil executives would grow wary of T. Boone Pickens. Some argued that his effort had proven costly: had he refrained from his hostile forays, the oil companies might have taken the cash that had gone to pay off that debt and put it into oil exploration. When oil prices collapsed in the winter of 1985–1986, the oil companies no longer could consider drilling. What they were left with were large debts.

So there was growing hostility toward Mr. Pickens. But he simply shrugged his shoulders as if to say, "So what." Oil executives could debate all they wanted whether his raids helped the oil industry. The question was quite meaningless to him. All that mattered, as far as he was concerned, was whether the owners of the company—the shareholders—had benefited: he knew the answer was positive.

In the spring of 1986, Pickens announced a new project—not a takeover bid this time, but more of a crusade to help the 47 million stockholders in the United States. "I believe there are two constitutencies in America that are not represented in Washington," he said in April of 1986. "The first is the taxpayer, the second is stockholders. I'm gonna do something about the stockholders . . we're going to get them represented." He planned to organize a nonprofit group which would lobby on their behalf. A monthly newsletter would be distributed as well: it would warn stockholders about any pending legislation against their interests and about new defensive techniques used by management. He hoped to have the new organization functioning by the end of 1986. The new endeavor appeared to be a thinly disguised vehicle for the launching of Pickens' political career. He did not discourage such speculation, hinting that he might try for the governorship of Texas in 1990. Pickens noted that politicians and managements were not that different: "Once you find a politician lying to you, he won't be around very long. Once stockholders realize management has been lying to them, they won't be around either." As the third-highest-paid executive in the United States in 1985—with total compensation of $8.4 million—Pickens could afford to devote his efforts to whatever he wished.

Chapter 4

Carl Icahn: The Raider Who Got Himself
An Airline

Carl Icahn. © Joyce Ravid.

Al Kingsley, a round-faced, solidly built man whose office around the corner from Carl Icahn's looks like a tornado struck, tells a lovely little yarn that suggests how his mysterious, incredibly successful boss works. It happened in 1982, when Icahn owned less than 5 percent of a certain firm. Kingsley won't divulge the firm's name. Icahn was hoping, as he often does, to increase his investment to 20 or 25 percent of the company. He was prepared to sign a "standstill agreement": we promise that once you meet our conditions, we won't press our case further, buy more stock, or try to win control of the company. Icahn wanted to reach 25 percent, and then he would stand still. A meeting was called, the chairman of the board and his investment banker on one side of the table, Carl and Al on the other.

"Come on outside, Carl," the investment banker suggested.

Once outside, the banker began, "Look, you've got a terrific plan. But they don't like you. We know you've been in litigation before. If you start buying more stock we're going to take you to court, and we're going to dilute the hell out of you. Or we'll sell off our crown jewels. On the other hand, you just bought the stock a couple of weeks ago, you can walk away with a $10 million profit. You can think it over. Talk to me tomorrow morning. You want to think about it?"

"No," said Carl unhesitatingly, "I'll take the $10 million."

Al Kingsley told me that story one cold February morning in the customary manner of a "Wall Street watcher." One hand pecked at the keyboard of a computer terminal to call up different stock quotations. One ear listened to his secretary outside answering his phone calls to decide whether he wanted to be interrupted. He took a couple of phone calls from the boss, calling in from his Westchester estate, inquiring about a certain board of directors meeting, checking on a few points in his TWA struggles. Kingsley apologized for each interruption. But he never let go of the thread of that story. For him, the story was crucial in order to understand what makes Carl Icahn tick. "According to the definition of greenmail," Al said excitedly, "that was greenmail." But, he went on, in case I hadn't quite gotten the point, the investment banker had initiated the buy-back proposal himself. Icahn had not given the chairman of the board an ultimatum: give me the 25 percent stake or else. Not at all.

In this way Carl Icahn made his millions. Of the small club of take-over artists operating in the 1980s, few could match Carl Icahn for the shrewdness of his investments, for his uncanny ability to take advantage of business opportunities. Nearly every name in the book has been thrown at him: bounty hunter, predator, piranha. Yet, he has also been awarded the highest form of flattery: some who once were Icahn's adversaries have asked later to join him as partners in some new deal. In some ways he is the classic corporate raider. While he did not invent them all, it was Icahn in the late 1970s and early 1980s who raised the tactics of the takeover game to a new height. Like Pickens, he managed to alienate a multitude of corporation executives who feared for their company and their jobs, but at the same time he endeared himself to stockholders who saw the value of their stocks soar.

In one important way, Icahn stood in marked contrast to the other takeover raiders of his day. Though he had engaged in his share of raids, and walked off with millions in profits, in some instances he actually took over the target company. That happened in his pursuit of Baird & Warner, ACF, and TWA. The question had been raised often: how would one of the raiders perform, a Pickens or an Icahn, if he actually got his hands on a company? Both men had assailed corporate management assiduously. As the media watched Icahn, the TWA Chairman, perform on a day-to-day basis, there was a chance to find out.

Icahn's record on the road to TWA was impressive. And the more successful he was at the takeover game, the greater his appetite appeared to be. In one of the better descriptions of his maneuverings, *Time* magazine wrote on May 20, 1985: "For Takeover Artist Carl Icahn, the raiding game is like eating Chinese food. As soon as he finished munching on one company, he craves another." Indeed that seemed to be the case. Since the late 1970s Icahn had averaged one raid every six months. It was in large measure Icahn's success, coupled with the activities of T. Boone Pickens, which in the early 1980s awakened the American public to the arcane phenomenon of corporate takeovers. By the time the public realized what was going on, Icahn and the others had a firm grip on the game, knew how to play superbly, and seemed almost unbeatable. Icahn, in the telling words of the *Institutional Investor* in October 1982, had elevated the practice of takeovers "to something of an art." And there seemed little that could be done to deflate his balloon. The *Wall Street Journal*'s Paul Blustein bemoaned Icahn's dominance in the takeover field, asserting in late 1982 that "it was time to come to grips with the fact that Mr. Icahn is on the verge of becoming an epidemic. His corporate raids have proven pretty much invulnerable to legal counterattack."[1]

All this proved was that Carl Icahn had been right and his Uncle Elliot—just a bit too cautious. Back in the 1960s, Icahn was lucky to have a rich uncle—Elliot Schnall. Of course, Elliot was fortunate to have Carl Icahn as a nephew as well. Back in the 1960s, Carl made a fortune for his uncle; that was when Carl was involved in options and arbitrage. Elliot didn't even know what Carl was doing, but it worked like a charm. They had been a great team. Elliot bankrolled Carl so that the latter could acquire a seat on the New York Stock Exchange; and the two of them were drinking buddies during after-work hours—and sounding boards for each other. So it was perfectly natural that Carl would turn to Elliot in 1979 when this new idea hit him. Carl explained to his uncle that he planned to go after undervalued firms. Convinced that he was crazy, Elliot tried to talk some sense into his nephew.

"What do you know about undervalued companies?"

"Look, I'm going to do it."

"Carl, forget it. I think that you're taking too many risks."

"In risk there is reward and I'm going to do it." Carl wasn't too bothered by Elliot's misgivings.[2]

By the spring of 1979, Icahn introduced what was essentially a new wrinkle in risk arbitrage. This was his game: he would go beyond the standard arbitrager's gambit of buying probable takeover stocks in anticipation of stock price increases and holding them against a formal tender offer. Rather than just invest in a company and then wait for someone else to take it over, why not try to take it over himself? Icahn liked the idea. Al Kingsley, now Senior Vice President at Icahn & Co, recalled those days: "We thought if we became activists in the company we could make something happen. We thought if we said the company was undervalued people would realize that it was, and things would start to happen."[3]

Indeed they did. Icahn began with the Chicago-based real estate investment trust, Baird & Warner. The stock was selling for $8 a share when he took control in a proxy fight. He renamed the company Bayswater, after his boyhood neighborhood in Queens.

Icahn's first real contest was Tappan. Remember Tappan stoves? Same company. Based in Mansfield, Ohio, Tappan was a major American manufacturer of stoves and ovens. It had been around since 1881, and Richard Tappan, grandson of the founder, was now the chairman. With its stock selling at only $8, but its book value at $22, Tappan was ripe for Carl Icahn's ploy. It was a game which required great patience, hard work, and a good eye for opportunity. Carl Icahn thought he had a winner in Tappan. He began buying up the stock, and when he had passed the 5 percent mark, he filed the required 13D disclosure statement with the SEC. That alerted Richard Tappan, who phoned the New York investor. Just what was Icahn planning to do? Icahn said he wanted a seat on the board. He contended that once on the board he would hire an investment banker to search for a buyer for Tappan. But Tappan's management thought differently. It feared that Icahn would use the board seat as a launching pad for taking over the company; then Icahn would sell off some of Tappan's less profitable assets. "I wasn't going to let Icahn walk in and sell piecemeal an enterprise my family had spent their lives building," Richard Tappan said later.[4] Nothing of the sort happened. Instead, Icahn was successful in winning the crucial vote to force Tappan Co. to seek an acquirer. When the airlines went on strike, jeopardizing the delivery of pro-Icahn proxies for the vote, Al Kingsley was nominated by Icahn to rent a car and drive from New York to Mansfield, Ohio, with a shopping bag full of proxies—so that he would arrive on time. He did. Soon afterward AB Electrolux, a Swedish-owned home-appliance producer, offered Tappan $18 a share for its stock and the company had its white knight. Where did that leave Carl Icahn? Much richer. Having invested $1.4 million, Icahn made a $2.7 million profit on the 330,000 Tappan shares he had bought at around $10. "You can't beat that kind of return," Icahn said delightedly.

There is a marvelous footnote to the Icahn-Tappan story, and it concerns Richard Tappan. Most of the corporation leaders we meet on these pages have only contempt for the raider. Not so the Tappan chairman. He admired Carl Icahn and what he had managed to do for himself. Tappan understood that Icahn's foray had had the effect of pushing up Tappan stock. Never mind the takeover. The stockholders had benefited, and that, after all, was what management was supposed to be interested in, wasn't it? Upon hearing of the nice words Richard Tappan was saying about him, Icahn called him up to say thanks. During that phone conversation the hunted said to the hunter how about letting me join the hunt? Icahn must have been a little stunned. He had just done battle with this man, defeated him soundly, forced him to accept a white knight while Icahn was sitting back earning a couple of million of dollars. Here was the hunted asking to be part of his next deal. Icahn liked the idea. It was certainly good public relations to have one of the hunted aboard. And so Tappan came in. He never regretted it. Since 1979, his investment in Icahn's deals has increased sevenfold.

Things worked even faster for Icahn at Saxon Industries. A paper products distributor and manufacturer, Saxon, like Tappan, was also undervalued by more than half. Its average price in 1979 had been $6 to $7 (Icahn paid $7 a share) but its book value was put at $16.50. Between July 1979 and February 1980 Icahn and eleven partners (one of whom was Richard Tappan!) purchased 766,700 shares, or 10 percent of Saxon's stock. Matching his strategy at Tappan, Icahn sought representation on the Saxon board. He asserted that he wanted to find a buyer for the firm. Preferring to avoid a proxy fight and a chase after a white knight, Saxon paid Icahn and his partner $10.50 a share for their stock, far higher than what they originally paid. So for their $4.6 million investment, Icahn's partnership earned a six-month return of $2.2 million! Again, nice work.

There was a footnote as well to Saxon, but this one must have sent chills down Icahn's spine. While Icahn had been clever in getting Saxon to offer a buy-back of his stock, he would not know until quite some time later just how clever he had been. For, as it turned out, most of the assets which had attracted him to Saxon in the first place had been fictional! By 1981, Saxon was the 381st-largest industrial firm in America. But then it all fell apart. Its president, Stanley Lurie, pleaded guilty to six counts of conspiracy, mail fraud, securities fraud, and bank fraud involving Saxon. He was given a five-year sentence for what one magazine called his "accounting magic." Saxon filed for bankruptcy three months before Lurie was ousted as chairman in June 1982. How fortunate Mr. Icahn had been to take his money and run when he did.

By now, after Tappan and Saxon, Carl Icahn had what could be called—for lack of a better word—a system. He and Al Kingsley would first dig deeply into their research files, looking for companies with poor performance records. If a company's book value (the net worth of its assets) was higher than its stock value, there was a chance it was worth pursuing. But, beyond that, Icahn would look for companies in which the managers owned little stock in the firms. Then the research began in earnest. Now Icahn had to make 100 percent sure that this was a company in which he wanted to invest millions of dollars. He compared the work to a chess game: each effort has its own problems, its own solutions, but each was in a sense a game.

Icahn doesn't like to think of himself as a gambler; that suggests a certain recklessness. He likes to call himself a risk-taker. Someone who makes all the necessary calculations and then plunges into the game, knowing that more than likely he has found himself a good thing. He likes to think that whatever risks exist are acceptably low.

The media kept calling Icahn a raider, but he didn't like that term. Why not state the obvious? He was merely taking part in corporate democracy in its highest form. Whenever he bought his first stake of 5 percent in a company, he would call up the chief executive officer and invite him out for a lunch, which Icahn hoped would be cordial. It usually was. Then the CEO would go back to the office, call up his lawyers, and bring suit against Icahn. If he was bothered by the lawsuits, Icahn didn't show it. He liked to think of those suits as part of the negotiations. Icahn's next step was to force the company's board of directors to solicit acquisition offers. If the company pressed ahead with that option, fine. As the Tappan experience showed, Icahn could hardly lose. If the company proved stubborn, he was happy to let the issue go to a proxy fight. What group of stockholders would turn down the kind of offers he was making? There was nothing illegal in what he was doing. If the company wanted him out of the way, as Saxon clearly did, he would go away—after cashing in his stock and earning millions of dollars. What makes takeovers possible, in Carl Icahn's view, is inefficient management:

> You have a lot of undervalued companies out there, undervalued assets. And there's a lot of capital around. One of the major reasons so many of these companies are undervalued is simply management, the bureaucracy that has built up in management over the last couple of decades. It's sort of a corporate culture.
>
> You almost take it as a given. You have to pay a premium for control. You wonder why. What you're really saying is that a company with management is worth a lot less than a company without management. . . . What does this say about management? That's what the whole takeover thing is about.

> As a result of what is going on, even where companies don't get taken over
> but are in a fight, they usually do a lot better afterwards. . . . What I do is to make
> money, no question . . . but I think it's salutary. . . . Shaking these companies up
> makes them a lot more productive.[5]

Icahn's next target was Marshall Field, the Chicago retailer. He had purchased over 20 percent of Marshall Field's shares for about $15 a share. He indicated that he wanted control of the company. That led Angelo R. Arena, Marshall Field's President, to call Icahn "a notorious corporate opportunist."[6] To escape Icahn's clutches, Marshall Field turned to a white knight, Batus Inc., the American arm of Britain's BAT Industries tobacco and retail group. Icahn had no complaints. He wound up drawing a $17 million profit in six months for his original $13 million investment when Batus bought his shares at $30 a share. Executives would complain, as Arena had, that Icahn was just out to make a buck, that he was merely a short-term profiteer. "What's wrong with making a profit?" Icahn shot back. "They're making it sound like, 'If Icahn makes a profit, that's bad. Put him in jail.'"[7]

The man knew how to make a profit. Not always did he seek a hostile takeover. One of his most profitable ventures came in 1982 when he took home $3 million in just one month after investing in Anchor Hocking, the glassware maker. That represented an annualized return of 816 percent on an investment of $4.4 million. Another occurred in 1983 when he paid $27 for one million American Can Co. shares; six weeks later the company paid him $35 a share to buy back the shares. But his greatest coup was the $19 million profit he made on a $35 million investment in Gulf & Western. He had purchased 3 million shares in the early summer of 1983 at about $19 a share: he sold them back three months later at $29 a share.

His most notorious corporate raid came against the Virginia textile firm of Dan River. Icahn had put up $14 million to try to take over the firm, purchasing Dan River stock at $12 a share. The townspeople of Danville, Virginia, site of company headquarters, thought he was playing with their lives and their livelihoods, and they tried to get him to stop trying to acquire Dan River. Some one hundred townspeople purchased stock for the first time, hoping that this could save the mill. They invested their retirement funds or vacation savings. Dan River sued Icahn for buying Dan River stock in alleged violation of security rules, but the suit was dismissed. Then Dan River cooked up some defensive measures, issuing new stock to try to dilute Icahn's investment. He contended that they were using "abusive defensive maneuvers." Icahn charged that the stock issue was not legal. He kept on buying Dan River stock. Icahn grew increasingly less popular. In a cartoon, the *Greenville News* in South Carolina portrayed him as a thug waylaying a startled Dan River and demanding: "Wanna sell me some stock?" (That cartoon now hangs on a wall in Icahn's office in midtown Manhattan.) Others were accusing Icahn of being less than honest. Dan River tried to stop him with a lawsuit based on the RICO federal law—for Racketeer Influenced and Corrupt Organization Act. The statute's civil side permitted companies and individuals to bring RICO lawsuits because it defined racketeering—its intended target—very broadly; legitimate businesses and businessmen were using the law against one another in court, as in Dan River and Carl Icahn. A federal appeals court refused to permit the use of the RICO statute against Icahn. After a six-month struggle, Dan River's managers took the company private in a leveraged buyout, purchasing all outstanding shares at $22.50 each. Once again, Carl Icahn fared spectacularly. Though he had won few friends, he gained $8.5 million.

The company was "saved" from Carl Icahn, but questions were asked whether the surgery had made the patient better or worse. His move forced Dan River into selling off several unprofitable operations, closing eight of its twenty-eight plants, and cutting the payroll from 14,500 to 9,300. When he was asked if Icahn's prowling had improved the company, Dan River CEO David W. Johnston Jr. candidly observed that this was like asking a man recuperating from a serious heart attack, who had given up smoking and drinking, whether he was happy to have had the heart attack.

Carl Icahn was born and raised in Bayswater, Queens. His father was an attorney, but he practically retired because of poor health when Carl was a youngster. His mother was a schoolteacher. His father was a frustrated opera singer who had hoped for a career with the Metropolitan opera but wound up as a cantor in the local synagogue. From that experience Carl acquired a certain distaste for organized religion in general, and Judaism in particular, views which Carl's father successfully passed on to his son. If the father could not be an opera singer, he could at least provide his only child Carl with some appreciation of music. So the youngster took piano lessons and learned to love classical music as his father had. While he talks little of the way his parents may have influenced him, Icahn did say once that his father had taught him to find out what he wanted to do, and then go for it. The youngster had also acquired an urge to achieve perfection. If perfection meant making more money than he could have dreamed of as a child, he has achieved that.

While at Far Rockaway High School, Carl had excellent grades. He became something of a chess whiz as well. His top grades got him into Princeton, the first Far Rockaway graduate to be accepted to that Ivy League school. He worked his way through college as a cabana boy and a construction worker. That may have explained why his college chums saw him as a poor kid from New York. Not the hard-core poverty type, but certainly someone with limited means. With his mother pressing him to be a doctor ("She kept saying go get security, be a doctor"), Carl rebelled a bit, passing over a pre-med program for a major in philosophy.[8] Watching Icahn maneuver in the business environment so craftily in the 1980s, one has a hard time imagining him pondering Plato, Kant, or Bertrand Russell. Yet, he won the prize for the best senior thesis for "An Explication of the Empiricist Criterion of Meaning." Much later in life, Carl would confess to an interviewer that looking back on that thesis, he scarcely understands what he was writing about. Nonetheless, he apparently remembered enough to tell another interviewer that empiricism—the use of observation and experience, not theory—appealed to him particularly "because it recognizes as knowledge that which we can arrive at through the senses."[9] He sold ads for the *Daily Princetonian* and considered heading for Wall Street after graduation. But his mother—at least temporarily—won out.

He entered the New York University School of Medicine. "What the hell else was there to do?" he asked rhetorically in our interview. But during his two years there he found little to excite him. "I hated it," he told me. Besides, he was becoming something of a hypochondriac. He actually quit medical school twice but returned for one more try. Finally he threw in the towel, knowing that he would disappoint Mom, but determined to seek another career. The year was 1960. "I just decided I'm going to do what I want to do," he recalled. His mother's reaction: "You're making the greatest mistake of your life. You needn't come home anymore."[10] But there is no evidence that mother and son parted ways.

Icahn spent six months in the army. While a private at Fort Sam Houston in San Antonio, Texas, he won several thousand dollars playing poker in the barracks. He then headed for Wall Street, where he had wanted to go all along. He joined Dreyfus Corp. as a trainee in 1961. In his first year with the firm, after investing his poker winnings, he made $50,000 for himself, exploiting the bull market. That looked easy. Carl sensed that he had a knack for reading the tea leaves of the stock market. True, there was Jack Dreyfus, telling him to be careful or otherwise he would lose his shirt. What did he know? If only Carl had listened. The market collapsed in 1962, and in the process young Icahn was wiped out. He was forced to sell some of his dearest personal possessions, among them his proudest: a new white Ford convertible Galaxie. He had to sell the car to pay for food and rent. Meanwhile, as he tried to figure out how to recover, he might have taken comfort from the fact that this would be the only time in his life he would be in serious financial difficulty. But he couldn't know the future.

Indeed, that was the chief lesson he learned from the whole experience: there was no way to predict the future, no way to predict which stocks would rise or fall. In short, there was no System on the stock market, no matter what others said, no matter how easy it had seemed just before it all crashed on top of him. The experience would stay with him for the rest of his days: never, never would he play the stock market; never would he put his money in something so fraught with risk. He needed something far less chancy. He needed something that others hadn't gotten into quite yet, so he could make his mark. He found it in options—contractual rights to buy or sell a security at a certain price for a specified time. He entered the options game just as it was getting popular.

Icahn became manager of the options department at Tessel, Patrick & Co. in 1963; he continued in that work for Gruntal & Co. from 1964 to 1968. By the late 1960s, he decided to begin his own business. But he needed backing. So he turned to his uncle, Elliot M. Schnall, who owned a firm that made loose-leaf binders. During the 1960s, Carl had made a lot of money for Elliot through shrewd investments. The two were close; after work, Carl, still a bachelor, and Elliot, recently divorced, would head for "21" and drinks. Sometimes they would double date. At some point Carl, who was going to invest $100,000 of his own, asked Elliot to loan him $400,000 so he could buy a seat on the New York Stock Exchange. Having made so much money thanks to nephew Carl, it was time for Elliot to return the favor. The loan was granted. In 1968, Carl opened Icahn & Co., his own firm, which engaged in options and arbitrage.

His specialty was takeover arbitrage, and the business took off. Because Icahn & Co. is a privately held firm, it does not publish its earnings. So there is no way of knowing how much Carl Icahn is worth. Still, in December 1983, news reports put the net worth of his company at over $100 million. "Our firm has been very successful," Icahn told me in understated fashion. "We built up a lot of capital over the years."[11]

It is just as difficult to penetrate into Carl Icahn's inner world of plots and deals and maneuvering. Icahn's right-hand man Al Kingsley noted in our interview: "We have to go through a whole network that has to be carefully orchestrated. To be secret. . . . Everyone wants to know what Carl is doing." His stock purchases are made through a maze of corporations and partnerships, some of which carry ornithological names, such as Crane, Pelican, or Condor, to conceal for a while that a man named Icahn is involved. Icahn's basic strategy is to purchase 5 percent of the firm's stock; he then submits formal disclosures of his holdings to the SEC. But he has ten days to do so. During that brief time he quickly purchases even more stock, so that by the time executives turn around he has as much as 20 percent or more of a firm. By then the target company is truly on the defensive. Much of Icahn's strategy depends on complete secrecy. The minute anyone knows what he is thinking or doing, speculation begins, and that will inflate the stock price; the bidding becomes that much more costly. So Icahn remains furtive for as long as possible.

Perhaps that is why he has in large part worked as a loner. For years, only he and Kingsley tossed around ideas in what must have been one of the most productive "financial think tank" operations ever. The two men complement each other, their opposite talents merging to more than the sum of two parts. Kingsley has been the legman, rifling through corporation reports, looking for that hidden ingredient that will get Carl Icahn sitting up and taking notice. Icahn gets ideas from other sources as well, but, according to Kingsley, it was just the two of them working together for twenty years; only in the mid-1980s did Icahn flesh out the staff to include a corporate lawyer, junior analyst, banker, and a trader. Icahn and Kingsley both liked keeping the operation small. "You depend on yourself to see that things are done," noted Kingsley.[12]

> Icahn suggests that a takeover is more difficult than it seems: There's a lot of pitfalls. It looks simple, but . . . you put a group together and say, 'Let's go take over xyz. We'll just buy the stock. We'll take over them.' But it's very tough because when you're in it, there are so many pitfalls, so many headaches. First of all you put together a group of partners. Then every partner has a lawyer, and every lawyer wants something to say. So I would never do that. I learned that you only do it with limited partners. Nobody has anything to say where I'm concerned. They put in money with me and that's it. But of course I put up most of the money so that's a big plus. But that's the problem of this game. Your own partners can hurt you.[13]

Even Icahn's closest colleagues acknowledge that he has his demanding side. But then again, why shouldn't he? Once he had found a formula that was worth millions to him, was there any reason to behave differently? To act as if he needed the advice of others? Still, by the evidence of those who have seen him up close, he was not the easiest person to have as a boss. Gail Golden went to work for him in the late 1970s as an executive secretary. She found the job through an employment agency, which warned her that the position had little stability; the previous record for holding the job was only two years, and there had been lots of turnover. The advice they gave her was that Icahn was excitable. Gail found that to be true. "He can change from a hearty laugh to a bubbling rage in seconds," she observed. "He wants everybody's total commitment. The only thing that impresses him is hard work." Then she quickly added that he was "very funny, very warm, approachable. He's on the level. Anyone who comes in with an idea, he'll listen to."[14] It didn't take me long to notice that the boss was indeed demanding. In the hour or so in which I spoke with Al Kingsley, Icahn was on the phone from his Westchester estate twice, asking questions, spewing out ideas, keeping everyone in the office on their toes.

Icahn is a tall, athletic-looking man. He has a long, oval-shaped face. His accent is heavily New-Yorkish. He speaks in short, quick bursts, but his choppy sentences seem always well thought out.

Amazingly, the man is well liked even by his adversaries. That perhaps is Carl Icahn's greatest accomplishment. Making millions is one thing. Others have done that. But few have won the esteem of business rivals as has Icahn. He is noted for his fairness, his honesty, his ability to make his word his bond. "It sounds funny but I was always ethical," he told me in our interview. "I have always lived by my word, so to speak. I think that's the way to be. . . . The funny, ironic part is if you do that over the years, it really pays off tremendous dividends." He offered one example: when he started his firm he came under pressure to do underwriting. There was fast money to be made, half-million-dollar commissions and the like. But he thought it improper on his part to ask his customers to spend $3 million for 30 percent of a company which was not worth anything near that.

The attorneys and the investment bankers who sat across from him in the TWA deal appear to be among his warmest fans. Indeed, James Freund, the attorney from Skadden, Arps, Slate, Meagher & Flom, who helped TWA to defend against Icahn, was quoted in *The American Lawyers* in December 1985 as saying:

> On the chess computer I have, you see all the moves the computer is contemplating. It's like that with Carl. He thinks out loud, and he's trying a lot of things out to see how you react, to see how he feels. Things may seem widely disparate. It's not all random, either—he's thinking out loud, but also with a purpose. And the most important thing he says in any meeting, I've learned, is the last thing he says. It's like the computer—at the end it goes click, click, click, and it makes its move.

Michael Zimmerman, the investment banker who advised TWA, when interviewed on the MacNeil-Lehrer news program in November 1985 called Icahn "the most worthy adversary I think I've ever faced. The man's business is taking over companies. He works very, very hard at it, and he's very, very good at it."

Even Icahn would acknowledge that, though he is a loner, he could not do what he does on his own. He needs partners. After he became successful, and a Carl Icahn investment was considered gold, he had no trouble attracting people into his deals. Indeed, he once joked that a couple of his friends did so well from joining him in some deals that they went ahead and changed their lifestyle, they quit working! Not Carl Icahn, of course. By October 1985 he could turn to a pool of some two hundred to three hundred investors who were glad to get in on one of his deals. New backers could come in sometimes, but at a minimum $5 million investment. His old friends had first choice, and thus it was not easy for a newcomer to break into the club. The old-timers would have to put in only half to three-quarters of a million dollars. Icahn had a soft spot for them: they had been with him through lots of deals.

Though he doesn't go looking for partners, if he meets someone on the tennis court or at a cocktail party, and he takes to the person, he might invite him to participate in a deal. He met Dave Mahoney at a cocktail party. They then had dinner, talked, and Mahoney invested $1 million in the Aero Limited Partnership through which Icahn gained control of TWA.

Carl Icahn is very good at it, I would suggest, because he loves what he's doing so much. "The game for me is—just a game," says Icahn. "It's like a game and you're collecting money . . . and you see how well you can do at it. I always did arbitrage and I always did well. It developed into creating a business and this is just creating something. It's just building up capital. But it's also doing something salutary."[15] Icahn has melded a feel for the numbers with a sharp intuitive sense for what endeavor is going to make money. He has always been looking to buck the crowd, to get involved with projects that others were not aware of, or weren't prepared to join. First it was the options game, then it was hostile takeovers. It didn't bother him or surprise him that he was in a distinct minority when he began going after undervalued companies. Uncle Elliot thought he was crazy. And Wall Street couldn't quite understand why anyone would want to pursue such seeming nonstarters. His explanation made some sense. "I look at companies as businesses," Icahn said late in 1983, "while Wall Street analysts look for quarterly earnings performance. I buy assets and potential productivity. Wall Street buys earnings, so they miss a lot of things that I see in certain situations."[16]

That mild understatement explains how Carl Icahn got into the takeover business. But it doesn't explain why he remained in it and pursued it as aggressively as he has. One reason may be that he was so superb. As Icahn says: "I think I'm good at what I do. I think in the takeover business I would say I'm as good as anybody in this area. . . . I have a good mind for this type of thinking. It's like a chess game. I was always a good chess player."[17]

> He had other qualities too. And he enjoys talking about them: I'm a pretty one-track kind of personality, sort of obsessive. I think that's one of the hallmarks of success. It's a very competitive world and if you're not going to be an obsessive type of individual, very involved in what you do, competition is going to get you sooner or later. You have to be very involved. . . . Ideas come to you . . . not necessarily working and sitting at a desk. . . . I have a certain ability to take advantage of the breaks, of the lucky breaks. People let their egos get in the way and don't take advantage of certain breaks, of certain great opportunities.[18]

But having done so well, having made his fortune, it might have seemed reasonable, even logical, for him to cash in his chips and go home.

Home to "Foxfield," his 38-acre estate in Westchester, north of New York City, with its twenty rooms, tennis court, and swimming pool, with its peace and quiet, assured because Icahn bought up the two adjacent lots on either side. But that was not something he longed for, that was not some long-range goal that lurked behind his 15-hour days, his 2 A.M. meetings, his intense phoning, his demands placed on his office staff. His wife Liba, a former ballerina from Czechoslovakia, knows that only too well. She would like him to slow down and even thinks at times it would be nice if he didn't work. From the standpoint of their finances, he certainly doesn't need to work. "But then," as she noted, "where is he going to go from here? You know, regular family, the husband works, and there's always something, at least financially, to look forward. . . . The point is that he doesn't need any more money, but it's the game, as he says."[19]

Yes, for Carl Icahn, it's the game. You can tell it's the game when you hear that he's named his German shepherd attack dog "Shiloh" after the Civil War battle. That was to mark his triumph in the Dan River campaign: it was at Shiloh that the south began to lose to the north; Dan River was the south, and Carl Icahn was the north. And then he named his Westchester estate Foxfield; that had been the secret code word he had employed in the takeover attempt of Marshall Field. Yes, it's the game. "What turns me on," he told *Fortune* in March 1985, "is the excitement of it all. I really believe in what I'm doing. Don't get me wrong. I like to win. But I love to rock boats that should be rocked. Sometimes I wonder why I keep doing it. I've got enough goddamn money."[20] The money, as he put it, simply was a way of measuring success or failure at any given moment. "The money is like the chips or the points or something," he said in that McNeil-Lehrer interview. Rocking the boat, that's what he liked. "You sort of really are in a sense fighting a very strong establishment, and it's become exhilarating to see if you can outmaneuver them."

He's turned his office, on the 27th floor of a Manhattan skyscraper, into a kind of Carl Icahn museum. On the walls are neatly framed covers of annual reports of over a dozen companies he has pursued, the trophies from the hunt. He also has a framed copy of an article he wrote in 1983 for the *New York Times* ("Stop the Oppression of Stockholders") as well as the uncashed $100 check the *Times* sent him. Then there's a photo with Icahn's face superimposed on the face of a golfer. Some nongolfer executive gave it to him after hearing Icahn say once too often that the only time business executives get off the golf course is when he files a 13D (indicating he's obtained 5 percent of their firm).

The office looks more like a living room. Beautiful wood chairs. Carpeted floor. On the day that I saw Icahn, he had worked his fatigued, athletic-looking six-foot three-inch body into his desk chair; he was holding some gold object in his hand and, like a juggler, tossed it here and there. His hair was combed to the side but fell slightly down over his forehead.

The desk was neat with a *Barron's* and some other material neatly in place. A computer terminal was off to the left. A lamp in the shape of a cannon and a bottle with a ship inside it sat on the desk. Not surprisingly, there was a TWA plane model on the windowsill to his left; and another on a table at the other end of the office.

By the end of 1983 Icahn had decided to shift his strategy. In the past he had been successful at goading a firm into buying him out at a premium. That had left him with lots of money. Millions in fact. But he had not really acquired a big company. He wanted to become more activist. "There are certain situations," he said toward the end of 1983, "where my group will be more effective by taking full control of companies, which should be more beneficial to everyone."[21] He made a start with ACF Industries, the ailing railcar maker. By September 1983 he had purchased 27.3 percent of the company. In June 1984 he acquired it, his first big acquisition, for $468.7 million. As was expected, he started to sell off its parts; Icahn earned $360 million for three divisions, leaving only the railcar division intact. He closed the New York headquarters, dismissing most of the 180-person staff.

"Is Icahn For Real?" Phillips asked in a full-page newspaper ad; could he really raise $4.2 billion to pay for the deal? Icahn retorted with his own ad, which he wrote himself: "Is Phillips For Real?" He pointed out that his investment banker, Drexel Burnham Lambert, had needed only two days to round up $1.5 billion. Icahn seemed to be in a perfect situation: either he would take over the $13.7 billion company; or he would still reap millions of dollars in a buy-back.

The showdown came when Phillips stockholders had to vote on the restructuring plan which their management had struck with T. Boone Pickens. If they rejected the plan, as Icahn hoped, he would be free to pursue his own takeover. In late February, as the big vote approached, Phillips distributed white proxy cards to stockholders which had "Phillips Petroleum Co." on the heading. Icahn sent around his own blue cards which had an incredibly similar design. Their heading was "Phillips Petroleum Co. Stockholders Protection Committee." The ploy sent Phillips executives into a rage: Icahn was trying to dupe stockholders.

Three days before the scheduled vote, the same townspeople of Bartlesville, Oklahoma, who had held prayer vigils to keep Pickens from taking over Phillips, poured Trop-Arctic motor oil, a Phillips product, on a batch of Icahn's blue proxy cards which he was using to solicit shares. That set off a bonfire. Suddenly it rained, but even that wasn't enough to douse the fire. Or the Bartlesville crowd's dismay with Carl Icahn. The drenched Bartlesville crowd yelled, "Burn, burn, burn." Women baked heart-shaped cookies with the Phillips 66 logo and sent off a batch to Icahn with the

Icahn came close—or so it appeared—to taking over Phillips Petroleum as well, his first multibillion-dollar takeover target. His move came soon after after T. Boone Pickens had agreed just before Christmas of 1984 to sell back his 5.7 percent of Phillips stock for $53 a share. Phillips management had struck a deal with Pickens in which stockholders would get a package of debt securities and equity worth $53 a share. On February 12, 1985, Icahn countered with his own takeover bid of $4.2 billion: he would buy 45 percent of the company at $60 per share. That plus the 5 percent he already owned would have given him majority control. Phillips proceeded to create a poison pill—stockholders would have the right to exchange each share for a one-year 15 percent senior note worth $62. The rights could be exercised only if a raider had acquired 30 percent of Phillips' shares. Icahn's offer was made conditional upon the board's rejection of the capital-restructuring proposal and the dissolution of its poison pill.

message stuck to it, "Have a Heart." A photo studio posted a sign: I CAHN/YOU CAHN/WE ALL CAHN/LICK ICAHN.

Nevertheless, Icahn's newspaper ad barrage convinced Phillips stockholders that they were being shortchanged. A truce was called a few days later. Icahn was ready to make a deal. On March 3, with its back to a corner, the Phillips board made a better offer that finally satisfied Icahn. It would swap IOUs with a face value of $62 each for half of Phillips' outstanding shares, adding $4.5 billion in corporate debt. Icahn dropped his tender offer and promised that he wouldn't try another raid for at least eight years. He declared victory and withdrew, gaining at least $50 million for a month-long foray. "I'm happy the stockholders benefited," he said at the time. "But I'm no Robin Hood. I enjoy making the money."[22] Icahn's holdings were then worth more than $75 million under this proposed buyback. In my interview with Icahn he pointed to the Phillips episode as one of the highlights of his career. "I felt good when I won the Phillips thing, because it seemed like we weren't going to win. We were David fighting Goliath."

Interestingly, Phillips appeared to come out of the Pickens and Icahn raids stronger. Within the next year it had sold $1.6 billion worth of its assets representing 10 percent of the total. It had paid back $2 billion in debt and reduced costs by $300 million a year. Even though it had taken $400 million in asset writedowns, which had diminished net income by half, Phillips had a cash flow of $2.1 billion that was about the same as in 1984. Its revenues were up somewhat to $15.8 billion. It still had $6.8 billion of debt by March, 1985, a very high 78 percent of total capital. But it was shedding its assets, however reluctantly. One was the Pier 66 Hotel & Marina in Fort Lauderdale, Florida. Some had called that the Boone Docks, a reference to the apparent likelihood that Pickens would get control of the place. Phillips sold it for $50 million.

To return to Icahn, there followed a brief skirmish with Uniroyal, the

Connecticut-based tire maker. In April 1985, soon after Phillips, Icahn had built up his stake in Uniroyal, making a hostile bid of $18 a share. When Uniroyal was taken private with the help of a friendly merger with a Wall Street investment firm, Clayton & Dubilier, which had offered $22 a share, Icahn withdrew his offer, promising not to increase his holdings for six months. He made over $16 million in his foiled attempt to take over Uniroyal.

Only three days after Uniroyal ended, he was announcing that his next target would be Trans World Airlines. If he could pull off the takeover, it would be his greatest coup. It would help him change his image from being just a speculator in companies to someone who actually bought them. Though it had experienced financial difficulty, TWA was indeed a prize: it was the largest international airline serving the North Atlantic. In January 1985 *Fortune* had described it as the third least-admired major corporation in America. Icahn smelled a ripe deal. On April 29 he crossed the 5 percent mark. Only 10 days later, he had acquired 20 percent of the stock, having spent, along with some other partners, $95 million. TWA's executives were shellshocked and depressed. They'd had no idea that Icahn was making inroads into the company so quickly. He not only had one-fifth of the company, but he had developed a major psychological edge if he wanted to take on more.

Once TWA's bosses realized that Icahn had pretentions of taking over the company, they turned red with anger. "Mr. Icahn's presence is uninvited and undesirable," fumed TWA President C.E. Meyer. Rather than give in, he filed suit and asked the Department of Transportation to check whether Icahn was "fit" to run an airline. Then came the May 20 full-page ad from TWA, an open letter to Carl Icahn, saying that, "If you thought we'd just stand by and do nothing while you try to take over our company, think again!" A guessing game began: did Icahn genuinely want to take over TWA? Howard Hughes was his boyhood hero, it was said: of course Icahn wanted the airline. Eight days later, a federal judge refused the airline's request to restrain Icahn from buying more shares. Weakened, with no defenses available (thanks to a $1.3 billion debt), TWA was, in the colorful words of one of its takeover advisers, fighting with an unloaded gun. With Icahn holding so much TWA stock, greenmail was ruled out. Grudgingly, TWA's management said it would submit Icahn's proposal to stockholders in sixty days—but only if it could not come up with a white knight. Salomon Brothers was given the task of conducting the search. It polled one hundred airlines, but only Texas Air's Frank Lorenzo wanted TWA.

For a while it appeared that TWA and Frank Lorenzo would indeed do a deal, creating the second largest American airline after United. Houston-based Texas Air was offering $925 million for TWA. If Icahn would go along with the deal, which appeared likely, he stood to gain $50 million by cashing in his 35 percent stake. He might well have, had it not been for the intervention of TWA's unions, led by the Air Line Pilots Association (ALPA). They wanted no part of Frank Lorenzo, fearing that he would void union contracts and cut employee salaries, as he had done elsewhere. ALPA Executive Council Chairman Harry Hoglander quietly approached Icahn with an unprecedented proposal. What thus transpired was described by the *New York Times* on August 31 as "one of the most unusual alliances in the history of the high-stakes, frenetic, takeover game." The unions proposed that Icahn should purchase TWA; in return the 3,500 TWA pilots would accept a 26 percent pay cut (calculated to save $145 million a year); they would receive a block of the airline's stock as compensation. Icahn agreed, promising not to dismantle TWA or dispose of any job-related assets. With the new deal in his pocket, Icahn raised his bid in early August to $24 a share, or over $500 million for the remaining two-thirds of the stock. This was $1 higher than Lorenzo's offer. Icahn went ahead and raised his share of TWA to 45 percent. But Lorenzo countered with a $26-a-share offer. It was one of Icahn's most severe tests. His critics insisted that he was interested only in greenmailing TWA into making him a big profit. Icahn denied such claims vehemently. He was clearly on the spot. To sell out now to Lorenzo would mean that he could reap the incredible sum of $124 million! But he vowed that he wanted to buy TWA.

Icahn asked himself precisely what was he, corporate raider or the potential head of a major corporation? It was around this time that he offered some rather pessimistic views about the fate of the raiders. It seemed self-evident that he was turning away from raiding—at least for a while. In a talk with a reporter he noted, "It's a tough game. There are a lot of times when they're writing bad things about you and all, so the guy with the big money says, 'Hey, who needs it?'" He noted that takeover raiders were suffering somewhat, Pickens had just had a rough time with Unocal. Only a handful were still actively engaged in the game. The four he mentioned were himself, Irwin Jacobs, Jimmy Goldsmith, and T. Boone Pickens. "That's about it. And I don't know how many times Pickens is coming out any more. If they come up with more legislation, there will be nobody. And that's really bad for our society."[23]

In the end, Lorenzo agreed to end the merger pact he had concluded with TWA, walking away with $43 million when the agreement was canceled. Victory came to Carl Icahn on August 20. That was the day he learned by phone that the TWA board had rebuffed Lorenzo's bid, which was higher than his own. Icahn put on the jacket and cap of a TWA pilot and marched around his office, proudly announcing, "We got ourselves an airline."

By early October, Icahn and his partners had bought over 52 percent of the airline for $350 million and were offering to buy the rest for some

$520 million. He was named Chairman of TWA on January 3, 1986, in a bitter-sweet ascendancy. At the time he had paper losses of $87 million on the 52 percent stake in TWA. He had also agreed not to withdraw the $320 million he had invested in the airline, thus losing the chance to invest these funds in other takeover targets. So it was that *Newsweek* led off its January 20, 1986, story, "That well-known greenmail specialist may soon be forced to sign his name Carl Icahn't." The play on Icahn's name must have brought a grimace to his face. With TWA still in the doldrums, reports persisted that Icahn would in time look for a buyer. But he assured employees in a letter that "I have never sold or liquidated a company after gaining control." That was true, but then again he had acquired only a few companies. In early March TWA acquired the St. Louis-based Ozark Air Lines for $250 million. Ozark had been TWA's main competitor at Trans World's St. Louis hub. The purchase was a shrewd move on Icahn's part, for it would increase TWA's annual traffic by 30 percent to some 27 million passengers and tighten its hold as the fourth-largest American airline. It was a coup for Icahn, who had come to realize that only by growing could the major airlines survive competition. Meanwhile, the business community was eager to know if he could hack TWA—or was this, as a *Fortune* cover story in March suggested, "The Comeuppance of Carl Icahn." Time would tell. By acquiring TWA Icahn had gone far to erase the image of the corporate raider who slips in and slips out, carting his huge profits off with him. He had said all along that he was in the TWA game to buy himself an airline. He had done just that. Now everyone was wondering: what would he do with it, now that he had himself an airline? Would he be content? Or would his eye be poring through business reports again?

During the spring of 1986 it appeared that Icahn might not keep TWA very long. At least he was threatening to sell all or part of it to ease his burden. And it was indeed a burden. In March, a strike by 6,000 flight attendants grounded almost half of TWA's flights. In the last quarter of 1985 TWA posted a $123 million deficit. Its losses for 1985 were $217.1 million. "I was looking for a challenge," Icahn said at the time "I got it." If Icahn couldn't solve his problems with TWAs unions, he was planning to call it quits. "I am not going to stand by and watch this company bleed to death," he said. "If we can't make money, I will cash in my chips." Were he to do that, he would be taking a large loss: he had paid $310 million for his 16 million TWA shares; but in late March they were worth less than $250 million. Icahn held out hope that TWA would bring $1 billion if it were liquidated; that would mean a $200 million profit for him. But he wasn't rushing into anything. It seemed likely that Carl Icahn, now the owner of an airline and no longer a raider on the prowl, would need all the patience he could muster.

When we met during the winter of 1986, Icahn gave the impression that he might not participate in the takeover game in the near future. It was getting too difficult:

> Now, with all the rules, there are a lot of moments of truth that look easy but are not. You have to make a lot of tough decisions fast. . . . Some of the things they do now, some of the court cases have not been too good for the guys who do takeovers. They upheld some of these poison pills. . . . They weren't obstacles before. But now with some of these court cases upholding poison pills you have to worry about them. Before you'd just fight them. You'd work around them. You could sort of play your chess game with them. But now it's made the chess game a little bit more difficult. I think some of them will be reversed.

Yes, the chess game was a little more difficult. "That's why," said Icahn finally, "there aren't too many in the game. It's a tough game. If it were easy. . . . . ." His voice trailed off.

In May, Icahn was back in the takeover game, this time eyeing Viacom, the large broadcast and cable-television firm which had been viewed as a suitable takeover target for some time. Its stock had been trading at around $67 a share, but was thought to be valued more truly at $100 a share.

At first Icahn had acquired 9.9 percent of the stock, but by May his holdings had jumped to 19.9 percent. He revealed at the same time that he had made an offer of $75 a share for the company but had been rebuffed. The final curtain on the Icahn-Viacom deal was drawn on May 22 when Viacom repurchased almost 17 percent of Icahn's stock. That eliminated the prospect of his taking over Viacom and gave him a profit estimated at between $17 and $35 million. Viacom said it would give Icahn $62 a share in cash, plus warrants to purchase 2.5 million Viacom common shares, and $10 million worth of free commercial air time on the company's television and radio stations.

The newspapers debated whether Icahn had once again engaged in greenmail. Icahn would only say that his arrangement with Viacom was preferable to a hostile takeover fight. What was certainly true was this: Icahn's burdens stemming from his takeover of TWA had not kept him from dabbling in the takeover game. If he had gone after Viacom, there was no reason to assume he wouldn't be going after others in the near future.

Chapter 5

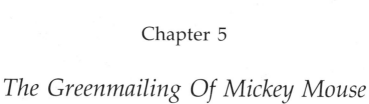

*The Greenmailing Of Mickey Mouse
And Donald Duck*

Saul P. Steinberg. Courtesy Hugh Brown/Reliance Group Holdings, Inc.

Corporate raiders were at the apex of their powers. They seemed virtually unstoppable. Investing in companies, building up a stake, they sent fear and loathing through corporate America. The defenses which managements erected in the early 1980s were ineffective. It was possible to ward off a raider using one of a variety of tactics—but at an almost unthinkable price. Recruiting a white knight kept the raider away but still brought the company under new ownership. Adding large debt to a company's balance sheet saved the firm from new owners but saddled the present ones with new, undesirable burdens. Selling the crown jewels reduced a company's appeal but at a heavy cost.

One tactic promised to be far easier to implement than these measures. It also appeared to be a way of ridding oneself of a corporate raider with the least pain and disruption to a firm. Furthermore, usually the stockholders did not have to be consulted in advance. The tactic had been used increasingly in early 1984—and had come to symbolize some of the less pleasant sides of the takeover game, it had a name.

Greenmail.

A play on the word "blackmail," greenmail referred to the buying off of an investor who accumulates shares and then makes a tender offer or threatens a proxy fight. The management, sensing that the investor—or more accurately, the corporate raider—may succeed in putting together the financing to take over the company, decides to make him an offer he literally can't refuse. It offers to buy back his shares at a premium, in return for which the raider will agree to drop all plans for a takeover bid for a period of, say, ten to fifteen years.

Greenmail had been practiced in the past but only rarely. In the 1980s it seemed to be happening at an alarming rate: in March 1984 alone, greenmail was paid four times by managements eager to avoid takeover struggles:

- Texaco bought back 9.8 percent of its shares for $1.28 billion from the Bass family.
- Warner Communications paid Rupert Murdoch $180.6 million for his 7 percent interest in the firm.
- St. Regis bought the 8.6 percent of its firm held by Sir James Goldsmith for $160 million.
- Quaker State Oil Refining gave Saul Steinberg $47.1 million for his 8.9 percent share of the firm, handing him a $12 million profit.

In one month, $1.6 billion in greenmail had been paid to keep corporate raiders at bay.

As greenmailing increased that spring, it gained an increasingly worse reputation. Managements despised the practice. The very name, greenmail, conjured up something sinister, less than ethical. Stockholders in companies offering greenmail to a raider felt they were being ignored; and perhaps worse, they felt they deserved to profit as much as the raider had from the management's largesse. Articles appeared in the press, spotlighting the practice for the first time and asking questions about what it all meant for American business.

The SEC's advisory committee met in late March 1984 to discuss the issue. Among the participants were Marty Lipton, Joe Flom, and Bruce Wasserstein. The committee proposed a new law requiring that "targeted buy-backs" of a company's shares (otherwise known as greenmail) at a market premium first be agreed upon by a majority vote of all stockholders. Purchases of shares that were held for more than two years would be exempt from the votes. In May legislation was introduced by Representative Timothy E. Wirth, a Democrat from Colorado, that would prohibit corporations from paying a buyout premium to stockholders of more than 3 percent unless the majority of stockholders approved. In the end it was not adopted.

No wonder then that so much fuss was raised when Saul Steinberg began his foray against Disneyland Productions that spring.

Certainly there was nothing new in what Steinberg was doing. He had done it himself in the past. He has boasted that no one has greenmailed as much as he has. Most of his greenmailing had occurred in the 1970s; some dozen firms bought back his stock for a premium. If there had not been a corporate raid against Disney, the notoriety would have undoubtedly settled on another similar incident. But, when Saul Steinberg chose to go after one of America's most enduring and well-loved icons, it was understandable why the battle would command such a widespread audience and arouse such controversy.

Walt Disney Productions. The name conjured up Mickey Mouse and Donald Duck. Disneyland. Fantasyland and Tomorrowland. Mickey Mouse watches. Animated cartoons. The Mickey Mouse Club. And, of course, the founder of all this, Walt Disney. He was a man who had made more children happy than perhaps anyone in the history of entertainment. So firm did he stand on his pedestal in the eyes of children—and parents as well—that he and the Disney family who had taken over the empire seemed virtually irremovable.

Saul Steinberg, however, was going to give it a try.

The Steinberg move against Disney Productions has been characterized as one of the wildest and most controversial of business struggles, entering along with the Bendix Affair of 1982 into the major leagues of messy dealmaking. Disney Productions had made no acquisitions in the past and ordinarily carried only a small debt; but in less than four weeks in 1984 the company engaged in a rage of dealing designed to keep Saul Steinberg at bay that had Wall Street shaking its collective head: it purchased one firm for $200 million in stock, suggested buying a second firm for $337.5 million, and cut a deal with Saul Steinberg priced at $325 million.

The tale began as corporate raids generally do, in the depressing balance sheets cropping up at Disney Productions. The company which Walt Disney founded in 1923 with brother Roy was clearly on the skids. For decades children's movies and Disney Productions had been almost synonymous. Then along came *E.T.* and *Star Wars*—and the youngsters switched their allegiance to other studios. Once *The Wonderful World of Disney* was all the rage on network television. But in the early 1980s Disney had no major hit show on the air. Those two grand theme parks, Disneyland and Walt Disney World in Orlando, Florida, remained the crown jewels of the Disney Empire, but attendance had been level for nearly the entire decade. One sign of how far Disney Productions had drifted: in March of 1984, its Touchstone Division offered *Splash*, an adult movie with Daryl Hannah playing a mermaid. One wit observed that Snow White might have blushed had she taken in *Splash*. After 1980—when it had earned $135 million—annual profits of Disney Productions had dropped 30 percent. All of this less-than-exciting news sent the Disney stock dropping—and led many to speculate that the company, solid enough with $1.3 billion in revenues in 1983, seemed ripe for a corporate raider. Disney's real estate had an estimated value of $2.2 billion; its film and program library as well as its cable television channel were worth $420 million. That had led to the view that Disney stock was undervalued.

One event during the spring pushed Disney Productions into the category of takeover target. On March 12 Roy E. Disney, son of the cofounder, and a near carbon-copy of his famous uncle, resigned as a company director. He had spent twenty-three years working at the Disney studio—as film editor, cameraman, and writer. In 1977 he quit, bothered that Ronald W. Miller, the company president and husband of founder Walt's daughter Diane, had allowed him little decision-making power. Roy thought animated features, which had been Disney's enduring anchor, deserved more attention. He called the place a real estate company which happened to make movies. He wanted Disney to concentrate on the creative side—motion pictures—that had won it not only financial success but also most of its fame. The business, in short, was being poorly managed.

Saul Steinberg, then 44, watched the market tape bring forth the news that Roy Disney had resigned. He was the chairman of Reliance Group Holdings with annual revenues of $2.5 billion. The main element of that company is Reliance Insurance. Steinberg had acquired the insurance firm in 1968 and then took it private in 1981. By 1985 it had $4.2 billion in assets, most of which were held in government and corporate bonds. Like everyone else, Steinberg knew there had been problems in the Magic Kingdom. Now the most visible evidence of inner turmoil appeared. Blood was in the water. The shark decided to move in closer. Saul Steinberg began buying Disney stock that day at $50 a share. Within the next week, word was out. Someone was going after Disney Productions. The stock began to rise.

Saul Steinberg was born in Brooklyn on August 13, 1939. His interest in financial matters was evident at an early age. His father was the proprietor of a small rubber-manufacturing plant. By the time Saul was in Lawrence High School (in Lawrence, Long Island) he was reading the *Wall Street Journal.* He entered the University of Pennsylvania's Wharton School of Business at the age of 16. Only an average student—he received Cs— Steinberg apparently preferred to engage in finance rather than study it. While a senior, he bought 3 percent of the O'Sullivan Rubber Company; he then threatened a proxy fight if the management did not agree to diversify into automotive parts. This was 1959, twenty years before people started to use the word greenmail. But here was O'Sullivan buying Steinberg's shares back from him at three times the cost.

A professor suggested that same year that Saul do a senior thesis on "The Decline and Fall of IBM," the giant computer firm. Saul agreed; but once he got into the research he found IBM to be, not a firm in trouble but, in his words, "an incredible, fantastic, brilliantly conceived company with a very rosy future."[1] When he reported these findings back to his professor, the professor refused to believe them. Clinging to the idea that IBM was not worth much, the professor wouldn't even look at the research. So Steinberg wound up having to write on another topic. That did not dampen his belief in the value of computer leasing, a business in which he thought there was good money to be made. He was right. In 1961, two years after graduating, Saul began a computer-leasing firm in a Brooklyn loft, using $25,000 borrowed from his father. During the first year he earned $56,000; $100,000 the second. Shortly, it was IBM's largest customer. Steinberg and his co-workers never even saw the computers they rented. Four years later when he took the company—Leasco—public, it had assets of $5.4 million. Wall Street was attracted to its stock during the 1960s, as it sold at over fifty times its earnings. By the time he was 29 years old, Steinberg was a multimillionaire. Taking advantage of Leasco's success, he purchased ten small companies, using Leasco's stock and cash to pay for them. In 1968 he paid $300 million to purchase his largest company, Reliance Insurance Co., then a conservative fire, life, and casualty firm that was 150 years old and almost ten times the size of Leasco.

His raid of the nation's sixth-largest bank, Chemical, in 1969, brought him a certain amount of notoriety. He was only 29 years old. Steinberg had been looking for alternatives to the insurance business: he had not been making profits from it. He thought of buying a bank so that he could sell insurance products through the bank's branches. He was talking about creating an integrated financial services company. The Chemical Bank executives thought little of his idea—and of him. The bank received support from a variety of sources: investment banks, U.S. senators, and Nelson Rockefeller, the Governor of New York. Steinberg could read the handwriting on the wall. He withdrew, selling his Chemical stock for a $36 million profit. The bank and its supporters came to think of Steinberg as an outsider, a bête noire—a view that took Steinberg by surprise. He said afterward that he had always known there was an Establishment; he had simply assumed that he was part of it!

He concentrated on his insurance firm, hiring new managers, reinvesting the portfolio, moving into title and life insurance. After losing $45 million in 1974, the company steadily moved into the profit column, so that by 1984 it was earning $118 million after taxes, a remarkable accomplishment, considering the recession and increasing insurance claims. But his record was marred by a series of incidents which hurt his reputation. Woodmere Academy, a private Long Island school, sued him in 1972 for allegedly failing to pay part of the $375,000 he had pledged to build the Barbara Steinberg Library and Computer Center—named for his first wife. Though he called it a misunderstanding, the state supreme court ordered that he pay. Then in 1976 he lost a lawsuit which he brought against Barron's for printing an article which assailed Steinberg's "questionable accounting practices in the computer-leasing business." Finally, in 1978, he ran afoul of the SEC, which charged him with encouraging friends to purchase stock in Pulte Home Co., a Michigan construction firm. Steinberg, a director of that firm, had allegedly sold his own shares for a profit when the stock price rose dramatically. He was forced to sign a consent decree: he did not have to admit the charges but did have to promise to avoid such behavior in the future.

The New York Times case did not help Steinberg's image. He disclosed in 1980 that he had bought 5 percent of the newspaper. Though he claimed that he never intended to threaten a takeover, Steinberg acquired the reputation of being a most unfriendly suitor at the time. At a luncheon with the Times executives, Steinberg reportedly left in a huff when a Times lawyer accidentally called him "Mr. Silverman." Why Steinberg was insulted has not been explained. But, in his anger, he retaliated by purchasing more Times shares. Though Times executives reportedly feared he might try for a seat on the board, he never owned more than 7 percent of the company; and one Times executive insisted that Steinberg's investment was friendly.

The charges of corporate malfeasance got to Steinberg. He decided to take Reliance private in 1981; then he would not have to worry about stockholders or a board of directors—and he could invest in whatever he wished. Because he would be investing his own money, Steinberg believed that he would make better investment choices. And so he undertook a leveraged buyout of Reliance for $550 million, one of the largest ever undertaken.

An acquaintance of Steinberg's summed him up this way: "He's a kind of Peck's bad boy. He's financially brilliant. During the Disney take-over he bought his office staff Mickey Mouse shirts. I think he likes to excite people. He gets a thrill out of that. Underneath, though, he wants to be liked or respected. But, you never know when he's going to take a piece of your leg with all that winsome impishness." By the early 1980s, though, Steinberg was putting some of that winsome impishness on the shelf. The Disney deal was one of the few aggressive deals he would undertake in that period. For 17 years prior to 1984 he had not engaged in a corporate raid.

Stories appeared telling of a new Saul Steinberg, the Master Raider who had mellowed, who no longer sought corporate violence at every turn. He was said to be worth $400 million and was therefore one of the richest men in America. He gave 5 percent of his annual net income to charity. The Metropolitan Museum of Art was his special project: he was its largest donor. Steinberg had developed a relaxed daily routine that seemed to suggest a content, uncompetitive sort. He rose each day at 6 A.M., exercising in a private gym in his apartment. He walked his two young boys to school each morning and would sometimes get to work late in order to stay home and play with his baby. He walked the twenty blocks to his Reliance Group office at Park Avenue Plaza on 52nd Street in New York City. He had a sign on one wall that said in Hebrew, "Thou shalt not speak to the press on the phone." (Steinberg noted often that the phrase "on the phone" should have been left out.) Some $500 million of Reliance's cash assets were invested in the stock market. Steinberg was said to be buying large stakes in as many as twenty firms, hoping that the stock would jump and he could make a large profit. He was a busy reader of all the financial publications, scrutinizing them with great care for the tiniest detail that might be of value.

Disney Productions needed a line of defense. One week after Roy Disney resigned from the board, an important meeting occurred in New York between senior Disney executives, en route to France to explore the idea of a European Disneyland with the French, and the firm's advisers from Morgan Stanley, the investment bank, and from Skadden, Arps, Slate, Meagher & Flom, the law firm. Bob Greenhill of Morgan Stanley suggested that Disney extend its line of credit at once. To delay any further, he said persuasively, would be to invite trouble, because once Disney became a takeover target, the bank would not agree to the extension. So on March 27 the Disney executives proposed and won board approval for the tripling of its line of credit from $400 million to $1.3 billion. Playing down the threat from Saul Steinberg, Disney announced that the extra credit was merely for "general corporate purposes." Privately, the Disney executives knew that it would come in handy to buy up a company or two as a defense. Buying companies was a good way to fend off a raider. Disney could purchase the new firm with fresh Disney stock, thus reducing the proportion of stock the raider owned. Of course, one didn't just go out and buy a company. It had to be the right company. It had to be one that Disney wanted. Then again, perhaps, even at this early stage, sensing the way raiders were working these days, Disney may have realized that a war chest might be needed to pay off a greenmailer.

Meanwhile, Steinberg labored quietly, buying up share after share. On March 29, he announced that his firm had purchased 6.3 percent of the 34.6 million shares in Walt Disney Productions. It was simply an investment, Steinberg said. Such a pronouncement from a corporate raider was about as calming to management as a hijacker's telling them he was about to take them on a plane trip to Libya. Share after share went into Steinberg's company. By April 3 his stake had risen to 7.3 percent, a week later to 8.3 percent. It was common knowledge by now that Disney Productions might be taken over. The only question was who would do it. Roy Disney seemed a possibility. It was thought when he left the board that he planned to sell his shares. But by April 11 Roy's Shamrock Holdings Inc. had built up a 4 percent stake in Disney; he apparently wanted to get his hands on even more. Other giants of the corporate world appeared interested as well, such firms as RCA and Coca-Cola. Rupert Murdoch, the press magnate, also apparently had his eye on Disney.

Toward the end of April Steinberg's true colors became clear. He notified both the Federal Trade Commission and the Justice Department's Antitrust Division that he planned to acquire 25 percent of the Disney shares. That elicited the first public comment from Disney Productions on the Steinberg gambit, and it was not friendly. His forays, the company said on April 25, "are not in the best interest of Disney shareholders." That, of course, was open to question. If Steinberg eventually made a bid to buy out Disney, stockholders might gain handsomely. The management in fact meant that a potential Steinberg bid for Disney was not in the best interests of management. Few would dispute that.

It was time for Disney Productions to put up the barriers. The board met on April 30 at Disney's headquarters in Burbank, California. Ron Miller, the Disney president and a former tight end for the Los Angeles Rams, proposed that Disney Productions think about buying new properties. He called the secret acquisition plan Project Fantasy. At that same meeting Miller was given a golden parachute worth $500,000 annually through April 1988. Finally, Joe Flom of Skadden, Arps convinced the board to rewrite parts of its corporate bylaws to make it more difficult for a raider like Saul Steinberg to move against the firm.

On May 17 Disney agreed to pay $200 million in 3.3 million shares of new Disney stock to acquire Arvida Corporation (the Project Fantasy team

had code-named it "Resort Company"). Arvida was a real estate development company in Florida that was controlled by the Bass Brothers of Texas.
From start to finish the Arvida acquisition had taken Disney under two
weeks. Was Arvida a good buy for Disney? Some thought not. The Disney
management was assailed for paying too large a price. But management
contended that the acquisition would help expedite the development of
15,000 acres of undeveloped land near Epcot Center and Disney World
near Orlando.

The company's strategy seemed clear: the price Disney was paying
represented between 8 to 10 percent of the company's shares. Disney
management controlled an additional 10 to 15 percent. So anywhere from
18 to 25 percent of Disney's shares were now inaccessible to a raider. Since
Disney bylaws required that holders of 80 percent of the shares had to
approve any merger, the Arvida purchase appeared a shrewd move to
keep Saul Steinberg at a safe distance. But was it enough? Disney's management wasn't certain.

Steinberg kept up the attack. On May 25 he received the green light
from the FTC and the Justice Department to build up his share in Disney to
25 percent. Three days later he informed Disney Productions that he might
seek full control of the company. By the first few days of June Steinberg
revealed that he would try to remove directors on the Disney board. More
trouble appeared on the Disney horizon: both Steinberg and Roy Disney
were annoyed at the Arvida purchase, insisting that it was a waste of
Disney's corporate assets. Roy hinted that he might team up with Saul
Steinberg to take over the company. Perhaps for that reason, Disney Productions erected one more barrier to defend itself. On June 6, it announced
that it was acquiring Gibson Greeting, a Cincinnati-based maker of cards
and wrapping paper. Disney planned to pay $307 million—roughly the
market value of the 6.2 million shares Disney planned to issue in exchange
for Gibson's 10 million outstanding shares—a further dilution of Saul
Steinberg's growing stake in the company. Disney executives insisted that
Saul Steinberg was not part of their consideration in going after Gibson,
that Gibson was a good business and that was all there was to it. Yet,
Disney finalized the deal just a bit over two weeks after learning that
Gibson could be bought. The effect, no matter what Disney officials said,
was to raise another barrier in front of Saul Steinberg.

Indeed, the Gibson tack was a clever move on Disney's part. Steinberg's share was now only about 11 percent. Now he would never be able
to take over the company. He would never be able to come up with the
needed cash. Disney Productions lulled itself into a sense of security about
the raider. In the meantime, Steinberg was planning his next move. He
formed a new holding company and called it MM Acquisitions. MM stood
for—guess what? Mickey Mouse! Was this some bad joke being played on
Disney? Was it Steinberg's way of announcing that one day Mickey Mouse
and all the other parts of the Magic Kingdom would be his? He never said.

To acquire part of the financing for the Disney takeover, Steinberg turned to Kirk Kerkorian and to the elderly Fisher brothers who ran the Fisher Financial and Development Company. Kerkorian was owner of 50.1 percent of the MGM/UA Entertainment Company. Fisher was a major commercial real estate firm in Manhattan. Steinberg struck his own mini-deals with both. He got Kerkorian to agree to invest $75 million that would give him a 20 percent stake in the Disney takeover. In return he had a 60-day option to purchase the Disney studio and film library for $448 million. Fisher put in an equal amount and thereby gained the exclusive rights to acquire undeveloped land near Walt Disney World and Epcot Center in Florida as well as near Disneyland in California. Steinberg raised $1 billion in all by creating a group of partners who would agree to split up the company.

On June 8 he was ready to make his move. On that day MM Acquisitions offered to purchase 37.9 percent of Disney for $67.50 a share. This would have raised his stake to 49 percent. Since a few months earlier the Disney stock had been selling for a third less than $67.50, the Steinberg offer appeared to have every chance of success. Steinberg also made an alternative offer: he would purchase all 37.9 million shares of Disney at $72.50 a share—or $2.75 billion. But the directors would have to agree in advance to withdraw their own offer to purchase Gibson Greetings.

Later, during a deposition he gave as part of a lawsuit, Steinberg noted that late in the evening of June 8 Laurence Tisch, Chairman of Loews Corp., and a friend of his, phoned him, urging him to sell out, to agree to greenmail. "I listened," Steinberg said in that deposition,

> and he told me the reasons, which were basically that if we did not sell out, that Skadden, Arps and Morgan Stanley did really not have control over this client, and this client might do dangerous and stupid things.
>
> And the dangerous and stupid things that they were threatening, and they had also expressed this to Mr. Hodes (Steinberg's lawyer), was that if we completed our tender offer, they would during the tender offer make a tender offer for the remaining shares subject to our tender offer. . . . Assuming our tender offer was successful and theirs was successful, we would have owned 100 percent of a company with well over $2 billion in debt, and it would have been a very serious problem for us. . . . I believe that they indicated that they were prepared—I didn't hear this directly, this came to me secondhand—to pay $80 a share.

What Steinberg was saying was this: if he actually bought 49 percent of Disney Productions, the managers of that company would then make a tender offer of $80 a share for the other 51 percent of the company's stock. Upon buying the stock, they would then retire it. Steinberg would be left with control of all of the outstanding shares of the company. What a prize! The new company Steinberg would inherit would have more than a $2 billion debt because of the purchase of the stocks by the management. In effect, Steinberg was saying: he had been blackmailed into taking greenmail. Erwin Okun, the chief spokesman for Disney, had a "no comment" to those Steinberg accusations.

David Kay, the head of mergers and acquisitions at Drexel Burnham Lambert, the investment banking house which had arranged financing for Saul Steinberg's tender offer, had some harsh things to say about Disney Productions afterward.

> Management conducted an utter scorched earth policy. They were going to make sure that if they weren't running Disney, it was going to be a company that no one wanted to run. They were a client out of control who did not do what their advisers suggested, and who did things that in the final analysis led to their doom.[2]

It took the board very little time after being informed of Steinberg's latest offer to decide on a buy-back of his shares. Steinberg at first insisted that Disney pay him $80 a share for its stock. Disney proposed $73 a share. On Monday, June 11, Steinberg and Disney agreed on a figure of $77.50— or $325.5 million—for its 4.2 million shares. Steinberg had paid $265.6 million for his stake. As part of the package, Disney agreed to reimburse Steinberg for $28 million in expenses that arose from his stock purchases. In all, he walked away with $60 million. For his part, Steinberg agreed not to acquire any Walt Disney shares for the next ten years. Disney, in turn, promised to protect Steinberg from lawsuits arising out of the buy-back.

The greenmailing of Mickey and Donald seriously hurt the Disney balance sheets. With less than $10 million in cash at the end of March, Disney had to borrow the full $325.5 million—using its recently arranged $1.3 billion line of credit. Beyond that, Disney had added $190 million in debt from the purchase of Arvida. The Steinberg buy-back and the Arvida acquisition raised Disney's debt to $866 million, 76 percent of its equity. Before Disney had ever heard of Saul Steinberg, its debt was merely one-fourth of its equity. In response to all this Disney's stock fell $10 as soon as the Steinberg buy-back was announced. Others were displeased about the Disney deal with Steinberg. Stockholders wondered why they could not reap some of the benefits that accrued to Steinberg. The stock would plummet $20 soon after the buy-back. It eventually recovered and rose to nearly $130 by February 1986.

Roy Disney thought the Steinberg buyout a bad move, largely because the stockholders would be left out in the cold. He had favored a leveraged buyout of the company. So strong were his feelings that he planned to bring suit to have the greenmail payment to Steinberg rescinded. In addition, he planned to win an injunction that would block the Gibson Greeting deal on grounds that it was a waste of Disney's corporate assets. The day before he was to file his plans with the SEC—on June 20— the Disney board learned of his intentions from a leak to the press; this led them to search for a quick compromise. Agreeing to drop his proxy fight,

Roy won the right to return to the Disney board and the appointment of two of his allies. He also became Vice Chairman and Director of Animation.

Like blackmail, greenmail appeared—in the case of Disney Productions—to be something of an epidemic. No sooner did Saul Steinberg depart from the scene, having taken his money and run, than another group of investors appeared, headed by corporate raider Irwin Jacobs of Minneapolis. He had watched the Disney stock drop sharply and began accumulating it, becoming in mid-July the company's largest stockholder. Jacobs announced during that troubled summer of 1984 that he had purchased 5.8 percent of Disney and was hoping to get his hands on more stock. Jacobs' opposition to the Gibson Greeting deal gnawed at the Disney board. When it refused to reconsider the Gibson acquisition, Jacobs responded by buying even more Disney shares and threatening a proxy fight. By mid-August Jacobs had his way: the board decided to call off the Gibson purchase. Jacobs offered the Bass Brothers $65 a share for their stake in the company; but they turned him down. So he sold his shares to them in October for $61 each. This left the Basses in effective control with 24.8 percent of the Disney stock.

A year after the Steinberg fight with Disney Productions, the company appeared headed for recovery. Roy Disney had succeeded in getting it to concentrate on movies; plans called for Disney to increase production to fifteen films a year.

As for Saul Steinberg, he was not through with Disney, not by a long shot. In February 1986 he asked a California court to let the group he represented reclaim the 4.2 million Disney shares he had sold in the summer of 1984. Steinberg's Reliance and Disney's directors became codefendents in over twenty lawsuits filed in California and New York courts by disgruntled Disney shareholders who had challenged the buy-back of 1984. Arguing that Disney Productions had not kept its commitment to protect Steinberg's group from legal actions, Steinberg said he was prepared to give up the $32 million in profits from the 1984 arrangement in order to get the shares back. Were Disney to acquiesce, it would mean that Steinberg would double his money, since his original stake was valued at $542 million by February of 1986; the stock had closed on February 19 at $129.12. Steinberg had sold his shares to Disney for $77.50—for a total of $325 million. As of the spring of 1986, the issue was still unresolved.

Just how problematic is greenmail? Many found it, in Marty Lipton's phrase, "a disgrace."[3] Agreeing was Greg Kieselmann, comanager of institutional research at Morgan, Olmstead, Kennedy & Gardner, a Los Angeles brokerage firm. As he put it in *Time* in June 1984: "It's like watching your mother getting ravaged by New York thugs."[4] Well, if it wasn't quite as melodramatic as that, greenmail still had few fans. Nonetheless, some academics pointed to studies that show stock prices actually rising after a company had been greenmailed. The very name, though, suggested something that needs curbing. However problematic greenmail was, there was widespread outrage and dismay after the Disney Productions buyout of Saul Steinberg. Predictions abounded that greenmail would be curbed— that the Disney case would be the last greenmail case.

With the hue and cry which arose over the Steinberg greenmail of Disney Productions, raiders became more careful to avoid the impression that they were intent on such a practice. That is not to say that greenmailing abated over the next few years, only that, as one participant in takeovers noted, "The transactions are done now in the dead of the night so that they won't get noticed as much." Press releases are written about the deals, but those parts which might be potentially unattractive are played down by publicists in the hope that newsmen will not pick up the scent.

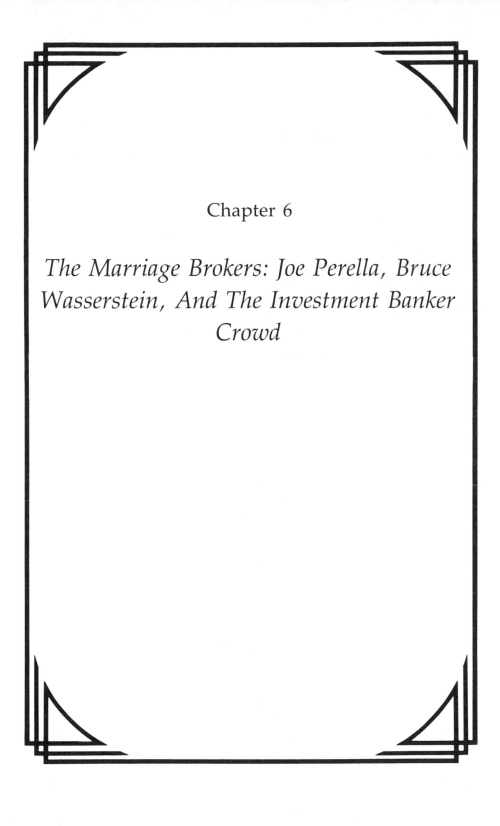

Chapter 6

The Marriage Brokers: Joe Perella, Bruce Wasserstein, And The Investment Banker Crowd

Joseph R. Perella. Courtesy The First
Boston Corporation.

Bruce Wasserstein. Courtesy The First
Boston Corporation.

Jay F. Higgins. Courtesy Salomon
Brothers, Inc.

They were too old to be members of a college fraternity, yet the atmosphere in the private dinner room was reminiscent of that kind of group. The man in charge was clearly Jay Higgins, the 40-year-old whiz kid who at the time (he has since become co-head of corporate finance) ran the Mergers and Acquisitions Department at Salomon Brothers, a top investment banking house. I had met Jay that afternoon for an interview at Salomon Brothers' headquarters on the 46th floor of 1 New York Plaza. I guess the meeting went well, because he invited me to join him that evening for "an M and A dinner." It turned out to be the winter get-together for Higgins' teammates, a stag affair designed to serve as both an expression of gratitude for hard work done and a chance for a pep talk about the future. The guest of honor was Marty Lipton, the takeover attorney par excellence. A young member of the Salomon M&A department quickly explained that Higgins and the team at Salomon had a special place in their hearts for Marty.

The dinner conversation was light and breezy. Drexel's snaring of investment banking whiz Marty Siegel from Kidder, Peabody had tongues wagging. Lipton was asked what he thought of the move. He thought for a moment, then said, "He came to me for advice." "Well," someone at the table asked, trying not to sound too curious, but obviously dying to know, "what did you say?" Marty said, "I told him to take the job."

If Marty seemed an outsider, I was no less an obtruding figure. Or so I thought. Jay introduced me to everyone as someone writing a book on corporate takeovers, and no one seemed at all surprised by my presence. However, I was surprised. When I commented to a dinner partner that ten years ago I doubted I would have been invited to such an event, he quickly agreed. The point was this: the once-crusty, once-sacrosanct community of investment bankers was now coming out of the closet. Mergers and acquisitions—a decade earlier the phrase would have meant little to the average man on the street—was suddenly dramatic headline-making stuff. The art was practiced by men: this was nearly an all-male club, and these men had been a very private group. Rarely if ever would they have talked to reporters in the past; they would have been aghast if their names had appeared in the newspapers, and crestfallen if a photograph appeared.

But now the public's hunger was rapidly growing: it was eager to know as much as possible about this arcane game Wall Street was playing. With billions of dollars at risk, and fees paid in the millions, high drama was certainly unfolding. Stars were being born. Media stars. Men who only a few years before could never have imagined that their faces would appear on the covers of national magazines. Men who would find that making millions of dollars in private was a luxury which they and their investment banking colleagues would no longer be allowed. As the appetite for news about the stars like Jay Higgins and the others increased, the stars themselves came to realize the best way to handle the public's mounting interest was to be as open as possible. Not an easy adjustment for a group used to the kind of secrecy prevailing in the KGB or the CIA. Sitting down to dinner in that Italian restaurant on the east side of Manhattan that winter evening, I sensed that my presence there was part of the new openness.

The more the public learned about mergers and acquisitions, the more it became apparent that the main practitioners numbered no more than twenty, an incredibly tiny and chummy fraternity to which there seemed to be no entrance requirement. The rewards of membership were astounding—fees ranging in the millions of dollars, not to mention the psychological kick that came with belonging to America's newest and most mysterious elite. The watershed date for all of this was 1974. That was the year when the first of the modern hostile takeovers occurred. The corporation which launched the takeover was International Nickel Company (INCO) and its investment banker was Morgan Stanley, the Cadillac of the investment banking firms. Until INCO moved against the Philadelphia battery maker, ESB, Inc., hostile takeovers bore for investment bankers and law firms the moral stigma of spitting on the floor, in the colorful phrase of takeover attorney Marty Lipton. Even if somehow you could overcome that stigma, there was no way you could afford anything as adventurous as trying to knock over a big-league corporation: the banking establishment frowned upon providing loans for such high-risk, nervy gambits.

Gradually that would change. A new merger boom would hit the business community in the late 1970s. But this time the stakes would be much greater. As it became easier to organize large-sized mergers, as the profits to be made in them became apparent, an intense competition began among the investment banking community for a piece of the action. A parade of investment banker stars would emerge, at first Felix Rohatyn at Lazard Freres, Ira Harris at Salomon Brothers, and Bob Greenhill at Morgan Stanley; then others, Michael Milken at Drexel Burnham Lambert, Joe Fogg and Eric Gleacher at Morgan Stanley, Jay Higgins at Salomon Brothers, Geoffrey Boisi of Goldman Sachs, and Marty Siegel at Kidder, Peabody. Some would represent the new breed of corporate raiders, T. Boone Pickens, Carl Icahn, Saul Steinberg, Sir James Goldsmith. Others would line up in defense of corporations under attack. The investment banking stars would become, if not household names, then at least media personalities with reputations that would add luster and respect to the firms for whom they worked.

One might have thought that the images of Morgan Stanley or Goldman Sachs needed no burnishing. But, suddenly, as the rules began to change, as hostile takeovers became fashionable, as the means to accomplish those takeovers became available, and as more and more outsiders staked claims for participation in the takeover game, competition intensified. As it did so, the old established investment banking houses began to sense that they too would have to adjust, to modify their style and their techniques if they were going to survive. No company altered its personality more than did First Boston, located in the heart of Manhattan—and no company reaped as much success for itself by adjusting so magnificently. Many explanations for the triumph of First Boston would be proferred. Nonetheless, the real credit belongs to two men, Joe Perella and Bruce Wasserstein—a brilliant, unconventional team whose passage through the thicket of the takeover game would come to symbolize the emergence of a new breed of investment banker. After First Boston's dynamic duo hit town, no one would ever conjure up an image of an investment banker as the passive, staid, respectable stereotype described in the pages of Stephen Birmingham's *Our Crowd*. While investment bankers had once advised executives over a golf game, that casual approach was no longer part of their bag of tricks, owing in no small part to Messrs. Perella and Wasserstein.

For the first time on staid, gentlemanly Wall Street, the tactics of the street were employed. The First Boston duo are not likely to be found on a golf course; but you might well find them phoning the clubhouse to grab that CEO as soon as he finishes his round of 18. Known for their aggressive, unconventional methods, the First Boston team would go after a client even after another investment banker had been hired by that client. That was the case in the Bendix-Martin Marietta Affair, when Wasserstein kept on the phones and was finally hired by Bendix's Bill Agee—despite the fact that Bendix had already employed Salomon Brothers. In fighting for a client, Perella and Wasserstein have acquired a reputation for avoiding the obvious and coming up with new, ingenious tactics. Looking back to First Boston's situation in the mid-1970s, it is no wonder that Perella and Wasserstein felt they needed to adopt aggressive, activist techniques. For starters, it would help their firm stay alive.

First Boston, by the early 1970s, had reached a low point. Its competitors started to pass the word that First Boston might be closing soon. Other investment banking houses, like Morgan Stanley and Goldman Sachs, were beginning to expand their merger and acquisition departments, sensing that the merger business might soon pick up. But First Boston was forced to hold back for reasons that were perfectly understandable. In 1969, it had represented the Bangor Punta Corporation when the company made a successful bid to acquire the Piper Aircraft Corporation. Chris-Craft Industries, a rival suitor, brought a suit against Bangor Punta, members of the Piper family, and First Boston for allegedly violating federal securities laws. A court awarded Chris-Craft $38 million in damages, most of which First Boston was expected to pay, inasmuch as its pockets were deeper than those of the other defendants. The $38 million represented about half of First Boston's total capital. Throughout the early

1970s the suit cast a pall over the investment banking house, even though in time (1977) the decision was reversed by the Supreme Court. Throwing salt in the wound was the fact that First Boston had received a fee of under $100,000, a peanut-sized amount considering the other, heavy costs. No wonder that mergers and acquisitions were dirty words around First Boston when Joe Perella joined the house in 1972.

The son of Italian immigrants, Joe Perella was born in Newark, New Jersey, in September 1942 and spent his first ten years there before moving to nearby Union, where he went to Union High School. He graduated from Lehigh University in 1964 with a degree in accounting. His first job was as a Certified Public Accountant with Haskins & Sells; he worked there six years but in time became dissatisfied with accounting. There just wasn't enough action: "When you're in there doing an audit, making a royal pain in the ass out of yourself, the business people are worrying about 1986 and you're in here auditing 1985. The numbers are historical numbers."[1] He had no interest in being a CPA all his life. While at Haskins & Sells Perella had the opportunity to put together registration statements for a few clients involved in mergers and acquisitions. Tasting the excitement of the field, he frustratingly went through the motions, all the while curious to know more. "I would go to the printers to work on these statements, and these bankers would come in, smoke a couple of cigars and leave. I said, 'Who are these guys, anyway?'"[2] Perella paid little attention to the bankers then, but during his fourth year with the firm he applied to the Harvard Business School. It took him another two years before he actually enrolled as an MBA student. The year was 1970 and he was 28 years old.

During his summer break at Harvard in 1971, he worked for the World Bank, attracted to that institution because it was then led by Robert McNamara. But once on board he found the experience worse than being an accountant. He would try to tell himself, as did his colleagues, that they were there to bring succor to the developing countries of the world, but something was missing. As Perella recalled in our interview: "I could not measure my reward based on my contribution to the development of a country like Colombia, and then have somebody give me a report saying before the World Bank got involved, there were two pigs per hectare and twenty years later, there were five pigs per hectare." He wanted to work for an organization that made a profit, that was "bottom-line" oriented. As someone who acknowledges that he thrives in an intense atmosphere, Perella found the relaxed pace at the Bank somnolent. What he missed was simple: "There was no pressure to make a buck."

He would try to remedy that, but first there was Harvard. Since his parents could not pay for his tuition, Perella sought scholarship help. He was awarded one by the prestigious investment banking firm of Goldman

Sachs. Though the firm paid half the cost of his MBA, it did not offer him a job afterward. He tried to take courses with those professors who had the best reputations; by the second year he began focusing on investment banking as his favored career choice. That field would not waste his accounting background. No one, including Joe Perella, thought about becoming a mergers and acquisitions specialist at Harvard Business School in the early 1970s. Receiving his MBA in 1972, he joined First Boston at a salary of $18,000 a year. He spent his first six months there in a training program in the corporate finance department. He worked on a few merger assignments, which he enjoyed, in part perhaps because he handled them well. During February 1973 the head of the corporate finance department approached Perella, who was winding up his six-month trainee assignment, with an offer he felt he could not refuse—although to others at First Boston the proposal might have seemed a banishment from the centers of power.

"You worked on a couple of these merger assignments," Perella's boss began, "and you seemed to know what you were doing. You liked it, and we don't have anyone specializing in that subject in this department. You think you'd like to try your hand at starting something like that up for us? You want to think about it?"

"No."

"Why not?"

"You've been here twenty-four years," intoned Joe, choosing his words carefully. "I've been here twenty-four weeks. I'll do it. Don't worry about it."[3]

No one gave Perella's appointment a second thought. He was known around First Boston as the guy who had just gone through the Harvard Business School, just finished a training program. He decided to go slowly, to establish his credibility with the senior folks. No one thought enough of Perella's mergers and acquisitions "department"—that first year he *was* the department—to offer him any manpower. By the second year he took it upon himself to grab some talent from the undergraduate schools. It was too early for him to recruit a few Harvard MBA's. Perella soon decided that the corporate finance department's personnel were not ideal material for the M&A team he wanted to build. He noted: "If the client wanted to go to the bathroom, they went to the bathroom. If he wanted to build a wall, they built a wall. They were jacks of all trades. I wouldn't add the second phrase, master of none."[4]

As the mergers and acquisitions business grew under Perella, his need for more staff—more horsepower, in his oft-used phrase—became acute. The man who would give him the staff was George Shinn, who took over as chairman of First Boston in 1975. Shinn knew that First Boston was in trouble; it needed to improve its staff and to develop expertise in the new fields of investment banking. Perella sensed that the merger field was about to explode, but he had to impart that message to George Shinn. Fortunately for both of them, and for First Boston, Perella was persuasive. A year after Shinn became chairman, Perella received the mandate to increase his staff. Eventually he recruited his single most significant addition, Bruce Wasserstein.

Perella decided that little was to be gained from relying only on one law firm, as First Boston had in the past. In his own mergers and acquisitions work, Perella sought a variety of attorneys, including those two renowned takeover specialists, Marty Lipton and Joe Flom (see Chapter 8). Retained by Combustion Engineering, Perella had been asked to advise the company in its white knight purchase of Gray Tool Co. of Houston; Gray Tool faced the threat of a corporate takeover from another firm. Perella sought out attorney Sam Butler of Cravath, Swaine, and Moore, the prestigious New York law firm, who agreed to serve as legal adviser. Butler showed up at the initial meeting with a junior associate named Bruce Wasserstein. He looked scruffy, he was chubby, but none of that mattered to Perella. Twenty minutes into the session Perella thought to himself: "I don't know who this guy is but he's some smart son of a gun." Combustion Engineering acquired Gray Tool for $66 million, and Perella was impressed with the way the Cravath firm worked, and especially the way Wasserstein had performed. He informed Butler that he would offer Cravath most of First Boston's M&A work but only on the condition that Bruce Wasserstein be the chief Cravath contact. At Cravath, however, an associate worked in one specialty and was then rotated to another. Wasserstein was due to leave mergers and begin an 18-month stint in municipal bonds. Grimacing at Perella's proposal, Butler acknowledged meekly that Wasserstein was set to move over to another partner and wouldn't be available.

"This is crazy, Sam." Perella couldn't believe Cravath's casual attitude toward his potentially profitable offer.

All Butler could say in response was: "That's the way our system works."[5]

Perella wouldn't accept Butler's no. The following year, 1977, he called Wasserstein directly and said to him: "Hey, I'm getting tired of this Byzantine system you guys have over at Cravath. I wanna work with you on this—let's you and me figure it out." Perella asked whether he could hire an associate directly, or if Cravath insisted on his hiring only a partner. Confessing that he had never been asked such a question, Wasserstein checked and then phoned Perella back to say, "It's OK. You can call an associate."

"OK, I'm calling you and I want to hire you on this Babcock & Wilcox fight." United Technologies had raided Babcock & Wilcox Co., the electrical power plant manufacturer. Perella had a client, Cities Service, of Tulsa, Oklahoma, which had expressed interest in becoming a white knight; counsel was required. Wasserstein heard about Perella's frustrating talks with Sam Butler. And he heard of Perella's strong desire to work together. At one stage, Perella had a bright thought. "Why don't we cut through all this b.s.? Why don't you just come work directly for us?"

"Gee," replied an astounded Wasserstein, "I never thought of that."

And so on July 1, 1977, First Boston acquired Bruce Wasserstein. He was hired as a vice president at almost double the $50,000 he had been making as an associate at Cravath. No one then could have sensed how shrewd a move Joe Perella had made. No one could have known that the investment banking field—and the American business community in general—was about to be taken by storm. A storm which Joe Perella had started and which Bruce Wasserstein was going to put in motion.

Born in New York City, Bruce Wasserstein is the son of Jewish Eastern European immigrants who had prospered in real estate and textiles. Even as a youngster his mind was working overtime, looking for ways to work out new strategies in the children's games he played. He especially liked the games in which he could play leader and order others around. The stock market also interested him early on, to the point where in eighth grade he wrote a term paper on the subject. While he was in high school the family moved from Brooklyn to Manhattan. There he attended the McBurney School while taking courses at Columbia University. Bruce entered the University of Michigan at the age of 16. He became Executive Editor of the *Michigan Daily*. That interest in the written word is reflected in his great delight in coining apt and cute phrases for his investment banking antics. He graduated with honors in 1967, having majored in political science.

At age 19 Bruce entered the Harvard Law School with plans to study for a joint degree in law and city planning. However, when the university started a dual-degree program in law and business, Bruce took that on. The law particularly attracted him. He worked on the *Civil Liberties Law Journal* and spent a summer engaged in a Ralph Nader study on the administration of antitrust rules. Another summer he walked through seven of New York's poorest areas to help take inventory of social services under the aegis of the War on Poverty. Considering the praise he would win later for his astuteness in law, it is ironic that Bruce failed to make the law review. He was in the top 2 percent of his class at Harvard Law School. In 1971 he graduated with high distinction from the business school as a Baker Scholar and earned his J.D. cum laude from the Harvard Law School.

In 1972, the year Joe Perella came to First Boston, Bruce was a Knox Traveling Fellow at Cambridge University. There he wrote a paper on British merger policy, and, he earned a graduate diploma in comparative legal studies in economic regulation. He coauthored two books with Mark

Green, an activist-attorney: *With Justice for Some* was published in 1971; *The Closed Enterprise System*, appearing in 1972, attacked the Federal Trade Commission for its confused antitrust policies. He joined Cravath at the age of 24. His colleagues thought him a quiet, scholarly figure with good chances of eventually becoming a partner.

By the summer of 1977 First Boston had virtually stopped making money. The mergers and acquisitions group was only four people, Joe Perella and three others. They had put together a few deals, but there were not that many opportunities—yet. During the summer and early fall of 1977 the M&A group at First Boston was not involved in even one deal. A major turning point for the Perella-Wasserstein team came in September when First Boston gathered one hundred of its investment bankers for a day of self-examination in Tarrytown, New York. Charts were trotted out to show how the company was doing in a variety of fields.

Mergers and acquisitions was the laughingstock of the meeting. So poor was its record that it did not even have a place on the charts. Soon after Tarrytown, Perella pressed for more resources. In addition to Wasserstein, he hired three others, bringing the group up to eight, still too small to have much impact. Perella did not want to acquire a reputation as an empire builder, so he commissioned a study by two Harvard Business School students on prospects in the M&A field. His plan was to use the study to legitimize his request for more staff. Meanwhile, a pair of deals came along that would set the First Boston team on the correct path. One was Combustion Engineering's acquisition of Vetco. The other was Kennecott Corp.'s rescue of Carborundum Co. from a hostile takeover attempt by Eaton Corp. First Boston earned its first two big fees—$1 million for the Combustion/Vetco deal and $2 million for the Kennecott/Carborundum one—in a single month, November 1977. The management at First Boston began to sniff the profits that could be made from the new merger wave. By 1978 Perella was able to increase the M&A group from four to eighteen. The small, energetic crew handling M&A under Perella was called, half-affectionately, the "Manson Gang." It may have been due to the black beards sported by Bill Lambert, who would become the number 3 man in the operation, and Gangleader Perella. Or it may have been due to the rough-and-tumble tactics they were employing.

In 1979, Perella became worried that he might lose Wasserstein to another firm. He wasn't about to let that happen. "I knew exactly what they would do," Perella recalled. "They'd come to Wasserstein and ask how much are you making. We'll double it and that's it. I felt Bruce was competent enough to have his own group somewhere else on the Street. So I wanted him to have the psychological equivalent of having his own group and therefore not have to leave First Boston."[6] Raising the subject with his boss, Jack Hennessy, Perella insisted that Wasserstein be invited in at once and informed that Joe wanted him as codirector of the M&A group. Hennessy asked Perella if he was certain he wanted to take such a step.

"Yes, I am," he replied with great self-assurance. "Do it right now. I can never bitch to you about this. You didn't impose it on me. I'm imposing it on myself." Wasserstein was called and on the spot given coequal status with Perella. Together, they have run the M&A group ever since.

Their personalities offered some stark contrasts, but that seemed to make them more effective as a team. The most obvious contrast is in their physical appearance: Perella is tall, thin, balding, always well dressed, and has a beard. Wasserstein is short, chubby, and has tousled red hair. Perella was known as charming and reassuring, the one who found the clients, nurtured them, made them feel comfortable doing business at First Boston. Yet, he brought an aggressiveness to his pursuits which resulted in bringing in the most business of anyone in the firm's fifty-year history. Part of Perella's charm is his extroverted, easygoing personality. Once, a visitor to his office pointed to a painting of a shark, with teeth flashing menacingly, and asked Perella if it was meant to signify anything. No, said Perella, but then he gave that cute smile and winked, as if to say indeed it did. He seems full of life all the time, full of opinions, he just about smothers you with his personality. He seems constantly in motion, probably because most of the time he is. My interviews with him were spread over three different days, largely because it appeared impossible for him to isolate himself from the flow of business swirling around him. In the middle of the first session he begged time out to take a phone call, he read a two-page memo which the caller had asked him to look at immediately, and then he called the person back. That done, he returned to the interview, as if the interruption had never occurred.

Wasserstein is the more cerebral of the two, more deliberate. One colleague likes to point out that he is always thinking and expressing himself in outline form. More reserved than Perella, Wasserstein chooses his words much more carefully, taking his time to answer questions, cringing when his codirector talks too openly. Wasserstein is known as the better strategist of the two, the better at figuring out what a client should do. (Perella, as one would expect from his softer personality, is considered the better at getting the client to do it.) Wasserstein's acquaintances speak of his giant ego, his inability to suffer fools easily, his dislike of small talk, the fear he strikes in some executives who have a hard time figuring out his machinations. His attitude toward the public attention showered on him seems a bit contradictory: he has a reputation of enjoying every flattering word written about him; yet when interviewers try to learn more about him, he recoils. Once a reporter asked him about his outside interests. He replied sharply, "The thing is, I'm just not that fast or clever to come up with the right answer."[7]

But he has been fast and clever in coming up with a number of strategic wrinkles that make Bruce Wasserstein one of the preeminent players of the takeover game. His mind is working all the time; given a set of facts, he does not try to impose the past on them but looks for a new way of achieving what he wants. Hence, he is known as someone who more often than not will pull a rabbit out of the hat. There is no debate that many of the strategic wrinkles associated with the modern takeover game originated in the fertile mind of Bruce Wasserstein. One is the "lock-up" tactic. It is worth describing, for it shows not only how imaginative Wasserstein is but also how Joe Perella guides his forces through a deal.

The tale began in the spring of 1980 when the chairman of Pullman, Silas Keehn, turned to First Boston for help in finding a white knight to save Pullman from a hostile takeover bid from J. Ray McDermott & Co., the New Orleans builder of offshore oil rigs. "A situation like that," *Forbes* wrote at the time, "is to people like Joe Perella exactly what a nice, bloody piece of meat is to a shark."[8]

Eyeing the bloody piece of meat eagerly, Perella and four young associates ran through a list of hundreds of companies, vetoing antitrust risks, cash-poor firms, and companies known for making decisions too slowly. Perella wanted only "real players." The list was whittled down to sixty-five, and First Boston then turned over the annual reports of the top fifteen prospects to Silas Keehn. Two weeks passed. Perella and his team, now numbering twenty-five, called around to the sixty-five firms to ask if they would be interested in merging with Pullman. A sign of interest from a firm elicited a rush of material, some public, some confidential, from First Boston—pertaining to Pullman. In addition, First Boston and Pullman staff became available for questioning.

By early May a hostile takeover attempt appeared imminent: Pullman's stock was suddenly trading at a much higher volume. The bid came on June 30 when J. Ray McDermott sought 2 million Pullman shares at the $28 market price; that would have given McDermott 23 percent of Pullman; it already owned 5 percent of the company before the June 30 bid. Gambling that Pullman could not come up with a white knight, McDermott kept the offer low, hoping to get the company on the cheap. It was then that Bruce Wasserstein weighed in with his "lock-up" concept. He proposed that Pullman offer prospective white knight Wheelabrator-Frye, the New Hampshire engineering firm which was only one-third Pullman's size, the exclusive option to purchase Pullman's engineering and construction divisions—its "crown jewels"—for $200 million. That would mean that no matter who bought Pullman, Wheelabrator or McDermott, Pullman's "crown jewels" would go to Wheelabrator. McDermott would be deterred from going ahead with the deal. The "lock-up" worked, and First Boston won a $6 million fee. The tactic was highly effective, but when Wasserstein tried to use it in the U.S. Steel/Marathon Oil deal, the Sixth Circuit Court of Appeals ruled against it, calling it manipulative. Other courts, however, have allowed it.

A second Wasserstein "wrinkle" was designed as a way for raiders or white knights to induce stockholders to tender shares speedily. Wasserstein called it the "front-end-loaded two-tier offer," a mouthful of a phrase that essentially worked like this: someone would make an offer for a large portion of the target's outstanding shares at one price; he would at the same time offer to buy the rest of the shares at a second, lower price. Stockholders were thus greatly encouraged to rush to get the good price at the beginning (the front end) so that they would not be caught with a lower price later on. Accordingly, the takeover was made much more likely. Wasserstein employed this tactic in Du Pont's takeover of Conoco and in the U.S. Steel/Marathon deal. As any number of observers have pointed out, it was not Bruce Wasserstein who actually invented the "two-tier" takeover strategy. That had been around for some time. What he did was to make the key refinement: making the first cash tender offer worth more to a target company's stockholders than the second-step merger. Indeed, the "front-end-loaded two-tier" offer was employed for the first time, so say the takeover historians, by J. Ray McDermott against Wasserstein himself in the 1980 Pullman affair. Wasserstein has said diplomatically that he doubted his rivals really understood its full potential.

For such legerdemain Wasserstein has earned fans as well as critics. The fans find in him the qualities of a magician. Of course, doing M&A work is just not that easy, and no one knows it better than Wasserstein. "It's like playing a football game in a bathtub," he has said.[9] Perella certainly agrees: "Every new deal is like walking through a minefield."[10] Nevertheless, the admirers all have their favorite Bruce-is-the-greatest stories. They love to point to the time he taped up six large sheets of manila paper and, off the top of his head, drew the entire deal's flow. "This is why it won't go this way," he would say. Or, "here's what we'll do if it does that." They also love to recall the occasion when he stepped into a situation after lengthy, messy negotiations had led nowhere. Showing up in old sneakers, no socks, and faded jeans with a hole in the seat of his pants, he reclined into a chair, peered at the documents, and figured out immediately what was key to the deal and what was not. Within forty-five minutes he had finalized the outlines of the package; all that remained was for the attorneys to put it down on paper.

Perhaps because of such wizardry critics say Wasserstein is too gimmicky, too pushy, not a nice person. And a hundred other things. Of course, one's being on top of the heap, as Perella and Wasserstein are, encourages such naysaying. One of the strongest charges against Wasserstein came in August of 1985 when executives of Beatrice Co., the large food company, became convinced that he had threatened to turn the company into a takeover target if Beatrice did not hire First Boston to defend it against a takeover. According to the *Wall Street Journal,* Wasserstein denied making such a threat. What he did was simply to predict that Beatrice would be taken over.[11] That is what happened: Beatrice was in the spring of 1986 taken over in a $6.2 billion leveraged buyout by Kohlberg, Kravis, Roberts & Co.

Fighting for clients is what the game is all about. Perella and Wasserstein will go after clients even after another investment banker has been chosen. They don't give up. They're constantly trying to work out their own end of a deal. No doubt that is one reason they have done so well. That has given them an image of being slightly pushy. They just don't give up. As Perella observed, First Boston used to be criticized for being sleepy. Now that it was making money, it was called too aggressive.

First Boston's earnings in 1978 had been only $1.8 million. But the following year its mergers and acquisitions effort improved impressively. By 1980, M&A fees were double those of 1979, as First Boston was involved in $5.7 billion worth of deals. The real turning point for Perella and Wasserstein came in 1981, the year of their multi-billion dollar Du Pont-Conoco deal. First Boston would handle $32 billion worth of mergers and acquisitions that year. The two men had met with success in the recent past, but their successful handling of the Du Pont merger represented a kind of baptism of fire for them: some of the biggest investment bankers, including Morgan Stanley and Salomon Brothers, went head-to-head in one of the most dramatic takeovers of the early 1980s. In August 1981 Du Pont purchased Conoco for $7.2 billion, until then the largest amount paid for a takeover in American business history—double the previous amount, which was the $3.65 billion paid in late 1979 by Shell Oil Co. for Belridge Oil Co. Du Pont paid First Boston's team $15 million. Recalls Perella: "That was a real achievement and I think it sort of said to the whole world, 'Hey, these guys have really arrived.'"[12]

First Boston's fees from M&A for that year—triple those of 1980—were $75 million, considered a record on Wall Street. Its earnings were $93 million in 1982. Profits kept growing. In the early 1980s First Boston helped in the Bache Group's successful effort to evade the Belzberg brothers of Canada by introducing the Prudential Insurance Company of America to the deal. It aided in the St. Joe Minerals Corporation's fight to escape the clutches of Joseph E. Seagram & Sons, selling off a Canadian oil subsidiary and then introducing the Fluor Corporation as a White Knight. Under Perella and Wasserstein's supervision, First Boston helped to orchestrate Marathon Oil's $6.2 billion merger with U.S. Steel. Wasserstein helped Marathon stave off Mobil Oil's hostile bid by bringing in U.S. Steel as a white knight. First Boston received a $17 million fee for that deal. In 1982,

First Boston participated in four of the five top deals. Its fee for helping Bendix into the hands of Allied that fall was over $5 million.

By 1985, First Boston had corraled the most deals (seventy-five) of over $100 million each. Its fees were over $150 million, up sharply from 1984 and double the 1982 figure. And in 1985 it had been involved in seven of the ten largest deals. In 1985, it represented Phillip Morris in its $5.7 billion buyout of General Foods; it advised Texas Oil & Gas on its $3.8 billion sale to U.S. Steel; and it handled the $3.5 billion merger of American Broadcasting Co. with Capital Cities Communications. In announced transactions of $100 million or more, it had done $51.2 billion worth of deals. (Only Goldman Sachs was higher at $53.1 billion; but it had done two more deals than Goldman, sixty-one to Goldman's fifty-nine.)

All of this boosted Perella and Wasserstein immeasurably. *Fortune* magazine put them on its cover in early February of 1986 for a story about those "Mind-bending Merger Fees." Then shortly afterward First Boston announced that it was reorganizing its investment banking department and putting the two merger stars in charge of it. Mergers and acquisitions, which had brought in $200 million in fees in 1984, almost one-fourth of the firm's total revenue of $883.3 million, would be subsumed under the broader investment banking department. Perella and Wasserstein would continue to run the M&A operation as well. And they would now be in charge of all First Boston contacts with clients.

Undeniably, First Boston's continued preeminence in the mid-1980s was due in no small measure to a new type of financing which had created a major revolution in the takeover field—the use of "junk bonds." These are unsecured, high-interest securities which receive low ratings from credit-rating agencies and are thus called "junk." Their first use came in early 1985 when Coastal Corp. bought American Natural Resources Co. for $2.46 billion. Junk bonds were used in six deals valued at over $1 billion each during 1985. The investment banking house of Drexel Burnham Lambert pioneered their use for hostile takeovers beginning in the mid-1980s. Perella and Wasserstein to date have stayed away from the junk bond raiders. They were being used to aid corporate raiders in their campaigns against the major firms, many of whom were already clients of First Boston. It made no sense to the First Boston duo to engage in the obviously contradictory practice of representing raiders and the big firms which were their targets in takeovers. "Pretty soon," noted Perella, "you're going to run out of clients on the big company side."[13]

Even without employing junk bonds, First Boston gained from their growing use. "The junk bonds being there created more business for us," acknowledged Joe Perella. "Some firms may not admit that. I freely do. Drexel helped create business for us just by being there, expanding the market; because on every merger transaction there's always two sides or more."[14] He pointed to the Revlon-Pantry Pride deal in which Pantry Pride, a Florida-based retail chain, bought Revlon in 1985. First Boston worked for Beecham and Rorer, purchasing the pieces from Pantry Pride that it didn't want once it took over Revlon. "Had (Ron) Perelman at Pantry Pride not had the junk bond offering that he did before he raided Revlon, there never would have been that whole series of transactions. That's what I meant when I said they expanded the market for a lot of people."

And so they did.

The story of how Drexel Burnham Lambert used junk-bond financing to fuel hostile takeovers begins in November 1983 at a three-day barnstorming session in the Beverly Wilshire Hotel in Beverly Hills. Drexel's corporate finance group had come together, led by two men who were searching for a way to use Drexel's increasing financing capabilities to advantage in the M&A business dominated then by Morgan Stanley, Goldman Sachs, Lazard, Salomon Brothers, and First Boston. One of the two men was Frederick H. Joseph, then the chief of corporate finance in New York for Drexel. The other was Michael Milken, then 39 years old. While an MBA student at the University of Pennsylvania's Wharton School, Milken had done research on junk bonds. He knew that they were generally issued by firms in financial trouble. But during the 1970s firms which were not in trouble sought ways of gaining high yields; these firms did not qualify for investment-grade ratings. They were ripe for a more risky proposition. Milken had done his research and unearthed one single fact that convinced him junk bonds might be suitable for these firms. The junk bonds defaulted only a bit more frequently than the certificates considered less risky. What was more, they were paying interest rates that were 3 to 4 percent higher than the less risky paper. Milken had been laboring during the 1970s to convince some of the large, established investors such as the pension funds and the banks that the junk bonds were safe. Drexel began issuing large amounts of them.

At that Beverly Hills conclave Drexel hatched the idea that would shake the takeover world. It would combine junk-bond financing with hostile takeover bids. For corporate raiders such financing was a fortuituous discovery. Until the junk bonds came along, it would have been unheard of for anyone but the corporate giants to come up with a few billion dollars. But now, junk-bond financing brought with it a set of advantages that widened the range of businesses which could enter the takeover game. Purchasers of junk bonds didn't have to put up the customary 50 percent in cash. The purchasers were not dependent upon the banks for additional financing. Financing with junk bonds could be arranged prior to the takeover bid, allowing the corporate raider to act with the swiftness that was a sine qua non in a hostile takeover.

How does junk financing work? A potential buyer sets up a shell company—a company with no real assets—which then issues new junk bonds. Drexel's list of 400 corporate and individual investors are then approached by the shell company and presented with letters of commitment to purchase the new junk bonds that will aid in the financing of the takeover after the shell company acquires control. If the shell company should win control via the junk bonds, corporate raiders can then use the target firm's assets as collateral to obtain additional bank loans. One classic example occurred when Drexel helped Saul Steinberg, the New York investor, to come up with a $1.3 billion fund so his shell company called MM Acquisition Corp. could make its takeover bid for Disney.

High-yield financing, as Drexel prefers to call junk-bond use, opened up the floodgates to the new band of corporate raiders. Without such help, the plan put forward by T. Boone Pickens in December 1984 to purchase a major portion of Phillips Petroleum would have been out of the question. He sought 20.6 percent of Phillips at a cost of $1.38 billion. Drexel was the engine in most of the junk-bond financing arrangements. Early in 1984, it won commitments from investors for a $1.7 billion takeover bid by Pickens' Mesa Petroleum to acquire Gulf. Under that kind of pressure, Gulf turned to white knight Chevron. These attempts—Steinberg's bid for Disney, Pickens' for Gulf, and others—did not succeed, but the raiders walked away with impressive profits. The raiders were delighted. As David Batchelder, Mesa Petroleum's chief financial officer, was quoted as saying in the *Wall Street Journal* on December 7, 1985, "Their fees are high, but who else can raise $3 billion in a week?"

It is that reputation for being able to raise lots of money quickly that has made Michael Milken such an investment banking star. He doesn't like publicity and so not a lot is known about him. But others speak of him with awe, as does T. Boone Pickens, who said, "When he tells you he can get you the money, he can get you the money."[15] Milken profited from this enormously. He was reported to have earned $15 million in 1984. And he had persuaded his bosses at Drexel to let him work in California. He moved there in 1978, as he told friends, so that he could get in a 14-hour day and still have time for his family. To do that he would rise at 4 A.M. and get to his office an hour later. His schedule included occasional "lunches" at 10 A.M. in the trading room as well as 6 A.M. meetings on Sundays.

By May 1985 Drexel controlled three-quarters of the junk bond market. It had gone from ninth in total underwriting in 1981 to third in 1984. Among underwriters of corporate securities it had gone from fifteenth in 1973 to third by the first half of 1984, bypassing such major houses as Goldman Sachs and Morgan Stanley, trailing only Salomon Brothers and First Boston. Profiting from all this were the investment bankers. Others got into the act, following Drexel's cue. They liked the concept, and they especially liked the fatter fees. Drexel was earning, according to the *Wall*

Street Journal of December 6, 1984, advisory fees of 2.5 to 4 percent for junk-bond sales—compared to a 0.65 percent fee for selling investment-grade securities. The sale of junk bonds in 1985 had gone over $14 billion, and $11 billion of that total was sold by Drexel Burnham Lambert.

The critics were out there, and they would not go away. Takeover attorney Marty Lipton was one. In late 1984 he had said that junk bonds threatened the "destruction of the fabric of American industry."[16] Nonetheless, for a while Drexel and the raiders had a field day. Undervalued corporations were knocked off, threatened by takeover and then forced to buy back the raiders' stock. There seemed little that anyone could do about it. It took a while before corporate defenses were thought up and became effective enough to create barriers against the raiders. By 1985, the corporations—and the advisers at their side—had had enough. While the anti-raider campaign was winning support from the courts (via the Delaware Unocal decision against T. Boone Pickens) it was in parallel fashion finding new friends in Washington, D.C.

And it needed them.

By May 1985 the politicians were once again trying to arrest the takeover mania. New Mexico Republican Pete Domenici introduced a bill in the U.S. Senate that would impose a moratorium until the end of 1985 on almost all takeovers that were financed by junk bonds. That would have meant that such deals as the one T. Boone Pickens was working on at the time to acquire Unocal with some $3 billion in junk bonds—one of the largest junk-bond issues yet proposed—would have been stopped in its tracks. Domenici's bill would have prohibited banks and savings and loans from buying junk bonds. (The largest category on Drexel's list of investors is that of savings and loan associations.) The bill went nowhere.

The real blow to junk bonds came early the following year (1986). By the end of 1985 the Federal Reserve Board was discussing a new measure that aimed at ending the junk-bond craze. Naturally, the protakeover Reagan administration was against the new step. So was T. Boone Pickens. In their view, the Fed was just trying to hurt the stockholder, that was all. It wouldn't stop raids. Pickens acknowledged that it might make a $5 billion raid impossible, but it wouldn't stop $2 billion ones. Neither the Reagan adminstration nor T. Boone Pickens had much influence on the Fed. In January 1986 the Federal Reserve Board voted 3-2 to apply Federal margin rules to the purchase of junk bonds issued by shell companies to finance takeovers. The new rule would subject the low-grade bonds to the 50 percent margin requirement that had been in effect for purchases of common stock. This meant that a shell company would have to come up with a lot more cash than had been required in takeover bids. Margin rules had forbade investors from financing over 50 percent of a stock purchase with loans secured by stock. While shell firms had escaped those rules before, the Fed was now insisting that these firms were subject to the margin rules.

So the Federal Reserve Board's new ruling cut into the raiders' abilities to come up with the kind of financing to go after the big corporations. Would the raiders be stopped entirely, or could they find alternative financing? The question weighed heavily on Wall Street in the early part of 1986. The conclusion was that the raiders would find other avenues. Drexel protested that the rule "will cause disruption in the capital markets for corporate control, because a substantial number of transactions will be subject to uncertainty." The step was "unwise and unwarranted." In a statement, Drexel noted that less than one-fifth of the $18 billion of junk bonds issued in 1985 helped to finance takeovers.

Players in the game predicted that hostile takeovers would continue, though it would be more difficult for a small company to grab a bigger one via junk financing. Still, a raider could keep going. If he had enough resources, he could guarantee the debts being incurred by the shell company or he might even put some of his assets into the shell company.

The investment banking community has added one more important feature to the takeover game, the leveraged buyout, resurrecting a defensive tactic that once was called "bootstrap financing." By the mid-1980s LBOs, as they were called, had taken corporate America by storm: the LBO had become the most common of the schemes for taking a business private to avoid hostile takeover. In an LBO, a company (or a division of a company) was purchased from public stockholders by a group of investors, the purchase financed largely by borrowing against the assets of the company. Usually used to finance the deal were a combination of bank loans and junk bonds. The group doing the leveraged buyout routinely included the investment banking firm that designed the deal, the company's management, and financial institutions, among which might be insurance firms, pension funds, and endowments.

While the concept had been around for years, LBOs played an especially crucial role in the 1980s in helping companies to deal with potentially hostile merger situations. More and more companies found that the conventional defensive measures were just not working. Executives searched for a way to save their jobs: LBOs had the great advantage of doing just that—and at the same time making executives wealthy in the process. Executives who had once owned nothing or very little of the firm suddenly found that they could increase their stake dramatically, perhaps to as much as a 30 percent ownership.

LBOs became increasingly fashionable in the early 1980s: the number of companies which adopted the technique tripled from thirteen in 1980 to thirty-six in 1983. Four years earlier, in 1979, there had been only $636 million worth of leveraged buyouts, but by 1983 the figure had risen to $7 billion: then the following year to a record $10.8 billion. Of the two hundred firms doing LBOs, the leader in the field was the investment banking house of Kohlberg, Kravis, Roberts & Co.—known as KKR. It differed from other investment banking houses in one important sense: rather than simply acting as an agent in dealmaking, KKR might wind up owning a large portion of the company for whom it was doing the LBO.

Between 1977 and 1984 KKR had completed eighteen LBOs, six for over $300 million each—$3.5 billion in all. By the spring of 1986, KKR had arranged twenty-four LBOs—for a total of $18 billion (that included the Beatrice buyout). Of the fifteen largest takeovers in 1985, three were LBOs, and two had been carried out by Kohlberg, Kravis, Roberts & Co.: the $6.2 billion purchase of Beatrice Co., and the $2.5 billion deal involving Storer Communications.[17] The large minus in the LBO schemes was that companies had to go into huge debt to finance the deals. Eventually, Washington would step in, hoping to control that corporate debt to some extent: the regulators chose to limit one of the main means of financing the LBOs, junk bonds.

Given the pressures on management from stockholders and potential raiders, taking a company private did not seem like a bad idea at all in the early 1980s. It was not hard for a senior executive to convince himself of the advantages of liberating himself from nagging investors and the board of directors. Once the company was no longer public, it did not have to worry about short-term earnings, filing documents with the SEC, or the many other burdensome tasks associated with a public firm. Relieved of these concerns, the newly private firm could concentrate on long-term growth. Proponents of LBOs argued persuasively that executives, once they acquired a stake in the business, would be far more likely to concern themselves with making the company more efficient and getting rid of corporate fat. If managements thought they could get dispense with all burdens, however, they were sadly mistaken: gone were the stockholders and the board of directors, but watching over them just as closely were the banks, which wanted to assure that their loans would be paid back in time, and suppliers and clients, who were equally concerned that the company could function effectively carrying so large a debt.

KKR began business in May 1976, though its three founding partners had already been doing LBOs for several years. The founding partners were Jerome Kohlberg Jr., 60, Henry Kravis, 42, and George Roberts, 42, three of the most secretive men in the American business community. Kravis and Roberts, who work out of San Francisco, are first cousins. They handle acquisitions for the firm. Individually, the three men were said to be worth between $150 million and $500 million. Rarely do any of the trio speak to the press; Kohlberg's distaste for public exposure was legendary:

he would average thirty seconds before answering a newsman's question. A native New Yorker who had both a law degree and an MBA, he had worked at Bear Stearns since 1955, becoming head of its investment banking department. All three KKR founders had been partners at Bear Stearns & Co.

Kohlberg did his first LBO in 1965, though at the time that term was rarely employed. Realizing they were a good device, he did three more LBOs in 1966. In 1969 he did another, this time aided by Kravis and Roberts, new to the firm. Of the three, Henry Kravis has become the most public figure. His father, Raymond F. Kravis, was a successful petroleum engineer. Henry went directly to Wall Street. A collector of nineteenth-century British oil paintings, Henry Kravis was on the board of the New York City Ballet, to which he contributed generously.

Until 1980, apart from KKR, only a few other medium-sized investment banking houses had been doing LBOs. In time the large houses, such as First Boston, Merrill Lynch, and Morgan Stanley, took the plunge. Once LBOs had been used as part of what was called the deconglomeration of the United States; by the mid-1980s they were first and foremost anti-takeover weapons: a corporate raider might well find that his bid for a company would be matched by one from KKR.

By showing that large-sized leveraged buyouts were possible, KKR acquired a name for the first time in the LBO field. Until 1979 no one did leveraged buyouts of more than $100 million. But after that date, major firms were undervalued and under attack from corporate raiders: the combination made them likely candidates for LBOs. In the spring of 1979, KKR made a $355 million purchase of Houdaille Industries, a Fort Lauderdale, Florida, firm which made pumps, machine tools, and automotive products. Other deals were large as well: in 1981 KKR and its partners bought three firms, one for $381 million and three for more than $400 million each. LBOs had indeed become popular devices to avoid hostile takeovers in the 1980s. Storer Communications, the fifth biggest cable-television firm in the United States, turned down a bid of $95 to $96 a share from Comcast Corp., a smaller cable company, in July of 1985. Instead, it agreed to a $2.51 billion LBO offer—or $93.50 a share—from KKR. Also, Dan River Mills Inc., which had been the target of aggressive action by Carl Icahn in 1983, went private via an LBO: largely financing the measure was the firm's employee-stock-ownership plan.

In a number of ways, the KKR buyout of Beatrice Co., completed in the spring of 1986, was a milestone for the investment banking firm. First of all, it was the largest LBO in American corporate history—valued at $6.2 billion. Second, the $45 million which KKR was to receive for handling it was the top investment advisory fee to date. KKR had avoided hostile takeovers, but its bid for Beatrice was the closest it had come to hostility. At first, when KKR bid $4.9 billion for the company, the Beatrice board said

Revlon, the cosmetics firm, ordered up a $1.8 billion LBO to keep from being taken over by the Florida firm of Pantry Pride. The courts, however, ruled against Revlon's plan to sell two divisions for a bargain price of $525 million as part of the proposed deal; Pantry Pride was free to continue its takeover bid, which was eventually completed. Blue Bell, a North Carolina jeans maker, managed to stave off a hostile bid from Allegheny Ludlum Industries in 1981; it then became the target of another unfriendly takeover from the Bass Brothers of Texas, who managed to get a 23 percent stake in the company. Blue Bell paid $144 million in greenmail to keep the Bass Brothers away; when the Belzbergs, a group of Canadian investors, made a takeover bid for the company, Blue Bell went private in an LBO. Carl Icahn was the cause for Uniroyal's LBO: Icahn had appeared at the annual meeting in the spring of 1985 owning 10 percent of the tiremaker's stock. After making a hostile tender offer, he watched as Uniroyal sought unsuccessfully to come up with a white knight; when it could not, the firm went private quickly with the help of Clayton & Dubilier.

no. Neither the price nor the concept of an LBO appealed to it. Kravis brought the opposition around. The buyout of Beatrice was particularly satisfying to KKR: in 1983 it had lost out in the bidding contest for Esmark Inc.—to Beatrice. The Beatrice LBO generated comment from critics who wondered whether the Chicago-based conglomerate would be taking on too much debt: it was already carrying long-term debt of $1.8 billion or 64 percent of its total capital; the LBO would increase that by nearly $4 billion. Beatrice's annual interest payment was estimated at $480 million, which was equivalent to its entire earnings in 1985 debts. It was assumed that Beatrice would have to be largely dismembered in order to retire the huge debt. Donald P. Kelly, the former Chairman of Esmark Inc., was to run Beatrice for KKR. He was expected to rebuild the company around what was left.

Debate developed over whether all this leveraging was good for the American economy. To many, LBOs provided a way to stay on the job, and to get rich: there was little incentive to worry about whether the economy was being adversely affected. For those who were distressed at the amount of corporate debt created by LBOs, advocates of LBOs were quick to point out that Americans had done a lot of leverage in other fields, mortgaging their homes being the most prominent example.

Whatever the fate of junk bonds and leveraged buyouts, one thing was clear. Investment bankers remained in the mid-1980s the great focus of the takeover game. Some would argue that the bankers were too much of a focus, that they were too active in urging takeovers. But as long as the rules permitted the merging of corporations, big and small, as long as the money was available, and as long as the investment bankers brought in those large fees, in all likelihood they would not move off center stage.

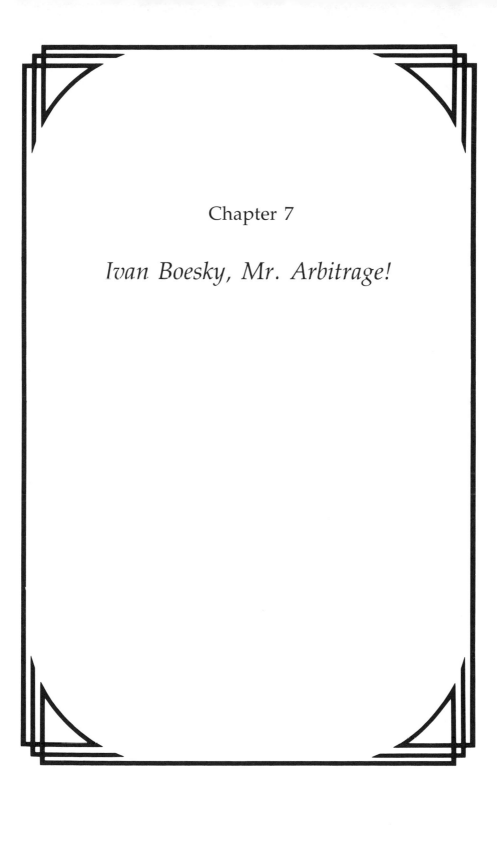

Chapter 7

Ivan Boesky, Mr. Arbitrage!

Ivan F. Boesky. Courtesy Steven Borns.

The Gulf takeover of 1983 and 1984 was tailor-made for Ivan Boesky: lots of available stock to buy up and the lure of a happily large arbitrage spread. Once T. Boone Pickens had started to acquire stock in Gulf, Boesky did the same, not to compete with Boone, but rather to profit from the corporate raider's entry, from his putting Gulf into play. The average arbitrager wouldn't touch Gulf stock this early in the takeover game—before Pickens actually made a tender offer. But Ivan Boesky is not your average arbitrager. In fact, no one is better at it. He has, according to published accounts, created a net worth of over $150 million in the past decade. But don't ask Mr. Boesky how much cash he has in the bank. You would be wasting your time. And don't ask him how he knew that Pickens had begun his foray against Gulf. He won't tell you. In fact, he will not tell you very much at all about how he operates. He is as secretive as a CIA agent. He is not even sure he needs all that covertness any more, but keeping his financial moves hidden from the public view has become as much a part of Boesky's day as putting his shoes on in the morning.

He is a major player in the takeover game. He can make or break a takeover deal. That perhaps explains why many Wall Street people won't talk about Ivan Boesky. Investment bankers curry his favor. So do attorneys. So do many others. He is respected, and feared, and watched, and studied. And why not? His word has been golden for two decades. Not always. But golden enough. Anyone on Wall Street trying to make a buck will try to track his maneuvers. When the rumors hit the Street that Boesky is buying, they are like a current of electricity. "Ivan's buying." The Street springs to life. If he is buying, he must know something. After all, he has the best research team in the field. No one has as many sources or as many resources as Ivan Boesky. Who are they? How did he find them? That is like asking the FBI to reveal the names of its informers or asking Woodward and Bernstein to discuss the identity of "Deep Throat."

It will take the Street a while to discover what Boesky is up to. He has got that "13D" cushion, for one thing. Only when he owns 5 percent of a company's total shares does he have to divulge what he is buying. Boesky can stake out a position in a company quickly, as he did in the case of Gulf, keeping the rest of the Street in the dark. Why the speed? According to one Boesky aide, quicker is safer. "If you perceive the pregnancy early," Lance Lessman observed, mixing his metaphors but making a point anyway, "then you don't get beat up too badly if you're wrong, and you make a fortune if you're right."[1]

Boesky knew T. Boone Pickens, knew his style, knew that he wanted to take Big Oil by storm during that fall of 1983. He detected pregnancy early all right. So, when Pickens announced his 8.75 percent stake in Gulf in late September, Boesky started to accumulate Gulf stock at roughly $42 a share. Exactly how much he bought is a closely guarded secret. Not a great deal, is all he would say. Through that fall he continued to purchase Gulf stock. Although some thought he would have been deterred in December, when Gulf won a proxy fight preventing Pickens from gaining a seat on the Gulf board, Boesky sensed that Boone had not decided to give up the fight. At that point the stock reached the high 40s.

By early February, Boesky had a stake in Gulf that was worth hundreds of millions of dollars. Then came Pickens' partial tender for Gulf stock on February 23, and finally on March 5 Gulf's acceptance of a tender offer from white knight Chevron to be purchased for $13.2 billion. The next day, Gulf's shares opened at $72.50. Chevron had agreed to pay $80 a share. Boesky was elated, calculating the expectedly large returns. But by the end of the day Gulf closed at 69 ¼, and at 64 ¾ the next day. Stockholders had panicked at the news that Louisiana Senator J. Bennett Johnston was pushing a new antitakeover bill aimed in part at the Gulf-Chevron deal, and it had a 60 percent chance of passing. Reading the tea leaves, Boesky began to sell his Gulf stock.

That pressure-cooker environment, which the "arbs," as Boesky and his crowd are called on the Street, seem to thrive on, now took over. If the Gulf-Chevron takeover, the biggest corporate merger ever, were to go through at the $80 price, Boesky and his pals would make $15 a share. But if Johnston's legislation threw a spoke in the wheel, the stock would almost certainly return to its pre-tender-offer level, and Boesky et co. would confront a $20-a-share loss. He put a team of researchers to work on the Johnston bill, fearing that the Gulf-Chevron deal might be jeopardized. His researchers concluded that, though the bill might pass, the Gulf-Chevron deal would not be affected by the legislation (which in fact was not adopted). The merger went through and Boesky supposedly earned $80 million.

That is what makes arbitrage so attractive. The very word "arbitrage" has long been considered arcane. Arbitragers were little known outside of Wall Street. They are the men who once sat in the back rooms of the prestigious investment houses and practiced their trade as a mere sideline. There might have been money to be made from it but no one had come up with the magic formula. As late as the 1960s the field was little known to the public. Only in the 1980s did newspapermen begin to write about the subject, after discovering that Ivan Boesky and others had been making such large sums.

Risk arbitrage, the game Boesky has mastered, has to do with betting on the outcome of business transactions. A risk arbitrager puts his money into securities which are the focus of a tender offer, a merger, or a liquidation; if he plays the game correctly, he will earn a profit from the spread between his purchase price and the selling price at the time the deal is finalized. Boesky insists that risk arbitrage is far removed from the gambling practiced by the simple, unsophisticated investor who does no homework and simply relies on his stock broker. For the latter investor, prayer is his only recourse once he buys shares. The past two decades have shown, Boesky says, "that buying 'safe end' may have been the reckless and hair-raising kind of way to spend one's hard-earned money and perhaps arbitrage was the most scientific, carefully calculable, conservative form of investment technique."[2] He took great joy in the report that in early 1986 the Chemical Bank was considering opening up an arbitrage department, a step that would have been unheard of until the 1980s. "This is twenty years after I began the business," boasted Boesky.

Arbitrage made big news in the wake of the merger wave of the 1980s. The "arbs" were attracted to the takeover game, with its huge stock price spreads and its opportunity for making heady profits. And as they learned how to play with some sophistication, their influence grew and so did their numbers. In the mid-1970s only a dozen or so big-time arbs were in the field, but by the mid-1980s at least fifty major-leaguers and another hundred lesser lights were involved. Beyond that, wealthy investors, realizing that huge profits were possible in arbitrage, became less shy about engaging in this practice.

In the takeover game, the arbitrager in effect bets on the outcome of corporate transactions. When a tender offer is announced, the arbitrager must decide first of all whether he wants to involve himself. Does the deal stand a good chance of going through? If it does, he should gain, as the value of the stock ought to go up by the time the merger is sealed. But risks exist, and he must weigh them as well: there may be hidden obstacles that have doomed the merger from the start—antitrust violations, the inability of the acquiring company to finance the deal, or whatever. If the arbitrager thinks it wise to invest at the time of a tender offer, he will offer to buy that stock from holders at a price higher than the one just offered in the tender offer.

Why would someone sell to an arbitrager, knowing that the tender offer has been made, and that waiting may well result in getting an even higher price? The reason is this: all sorts of things can happen. The tender offer may not lead to a deal after all; then the stock will drop dramatically. If stockholders take the arbitrager's offer, they walk away with a quick profit. As Ivan Boesky has written, "A retired couple who has held three hundred shares of Getty Oil for twenty years will welcome an opportunity to sell shares at a large profit and not worry whether Texaco will ultimately buy the company. So too will many a sophisticated financial institution."[3]

Meanwhile, the arbitrager is busy collecting shares. And collecting. And collecting. He is banking on the deal's going through. If and when it does, he will resell his shares to the acquiring firm and walk away with a huge profit.

Often the arbs might hold as much as 30 percent of a takeover target's shares. That could give them the balance of power, and they could determine the nature of the outcome. All of this is heady stuff. As one arb put it:

> There's no fun like being an arbitrager . . . in a contested takeover situation. The bankers and lawyers on all sides are courting your favor, and you can develop a nearly perfect understanding of what's going on behind the scenes. These guys don't just come out and tell you everything they're doing, but there are plenty of hints, and unless some idiotic board of directors screws up the deal you have to be a fool not to make money.[4]

For a number of years, the arbs were not fools, they were making a lot of money, and they knew they had a good thing going. Other than perhaps missing out on a chance to see their names quoted on the front page of the *Wall Street Journal* or having their picture appear on the cover of *Business Week* or *Fortune,* they appeared quite happy in their splendid anonymity. They did not consciously avoid the press or hide. It was just that no one seemed to care that much about them or understand what they were doing enough to care.

Then, along came Ivan Boesky.

The conventional wisdom on Wall Street suggests that he alone was responsible for bringing arbitrage out of the closet, so to speak. He became arbitrage's first public crusader, not only defending the practice, but also becoming its Number One Philosopher, its spokesman, its advocate. In doing so, he punctured holes in the myths, arguing that arbitrage was not a mysterious exercise practiced by voodoo experts with secret incantations. Rather, it had its scientific side. You could calculate the risks, look at the problems rationally. He was the first to perform arbitrage exclusively and he was the first to bring investors into his arbitrage business, pioneering efforts which, because he was so successful, made Wall Street stand up and take notice. Boesky never disguised the single greatest reason to leap into arbitrage: making lots of money. The rest of the arbitrage community might well have preferred that Ivan keep its little secret. But he chose not to. He deserves the credit for opening arbitrage to the rest of the world. According to one major participant in the takeover game, "Ivan is a relentless, extraordinarily courageous high-risk player who has brought the arbitrage function to its highest point in terms of visibility, prominence and power. He didn't invent arbitrage by a long shot but he pushed arbitrage deals to an outer limit so the arbitrage function itself becomes increasingly important."

Boesky has explained that he "saw no particular merit in guarding that secret for its own sake, because I felt that it's a legitimate, recognized activity for investors and that it is good for the investing public and it's good for the stock market and good for industry. It provides a better marketplace and therefore I see no reason for not making it available for those who care to know."[5] It is also true, and he acknowledges this, that once he turned to the public for financial support for his arbitrage trade, he was in fact required to divulge what he was doing. But, says Boesky, he would have been open about his field in any case. The evidence of his real sincerity, he says, is that he now has substantial capital but he still teaches a course in arbitrage at two universities, NYU and Columbia, and writes books about the field; and he still continues to disclose. "So," he insists, "it wasn't because I just wanted the money that I was willing to talk about it."[6]

In truth, he is careful to reveal only the tip of the iceberg of the arbitrage business. He titled his 1985 book *Merger Mania; Arbitrage: Wall Street's Best Kept Money-Making Secret,* suggesting that readers would learn for the first time just how Ivan Boesky worked, what financial positions he had taken in his various deals, what calculations he had made that led to his making $150 million. But the critics noted with much disappointment that, in producing a marvelous how-to manual for corporation executives, raiders, corporate defenders, investment bankers, and attorneys, Boesky had stopped short and refused to provide the first inside look at the nature of the decisions an arbitrager makes day by day. "I'm a paranoid person," he explained at the end of 1984. "I won't show trading records, won't show financial records—I'm the kind of person who looks at his address book like this" (he held it close to his chest and opened it a crack).[7]

He can perhaps be forgiven all that paranoia. Finding out what Ivan Boesky is up to might make some people very wealthy. It might also do damage to Boesky's own investment plans. Unquestionably he is the pre-eminent actor in the arbitrage game, "The Pied Piper of Arbitrage" in the colorful phrase employed by *Business Week* in its October 21, 1985, piece on Boesky. One of the by-products of his success is the respect he's gained within the corporate world. "Ivan," said one colleague, "could get any CEO in the country off the toilet to talk to him at 7 o'clock in the morning."[8] He controls seven operations, including Ivan F. Boesky Corporation, a private investment bank which has assets of about $1 billion. Boesky can feel flattered at the number of Ivan Boesky imitation efforts popping up of late. Not only do the major investment banking houses on Wall Street practice arbitrage, but lots of independent firms, called "boutiques," now do so as well, started by Ivan Boesky clones. He has done so well that *Forbes* magazine, which each year tracks America's 400 wealthiest people, had him on its list. Someone once figured out that his earnings in the past decade made his time worth about $1,700 an hour. From 1975, when he established his own arbitrage operation, he has earned profits every year. Investors have reason to love him: one dollar invested with him in April 1975 would have been worth $20.65 on March 31, 1985.

Boesky's reported profits from arbitrage have been substantial: $100 million when Texaco purchased Getty Oil in January 1984, his biggest gain ever; $80 million when Chevron bought out Gulf in March 1984; $40 million when Du Pont acquired Conoco in the summer of 1981. There were huge losses as well: $70 million in the Pickens fight with Phillips Petroleum in the winter of 1985, supposedly his biggest loss ever; $12 million in 1981 when he apparently sold shares in Delhi International Oil Corp. prematurely; Delhi then agreed to be acquired by CSR Ltd.

There have been other unhappy moments. During the summer of 1982, Gulf, which had made a $63-a-share bid to buy Cities Service, suddenly pulled out. Boesky and his partners had a reported $1 billion investment riding on the outcome of that deal. Boesky spent time calming down his partners. He was able to cut his losses when Occidental Petroleum came along three weeks later and offered $52 a share for Cities Service. Even so, Boesky reportedly lost between $25 and $50 million. In the 1984 Disneyland buy-back of Saul Steinberg's shares, Boesky and other investors were forced to sell at $48 a share. Steinberg had sold his stock at $77 a share. One of Boesky's happier efforts involved the Ted Turner takeover attempt of CBS in the spring of 1985. Buying shares in the American TV network when the stock was only $60 a share, Boesky put down $270 million for an 8.7 percent stake at the time Turner was making his takeover bid. Turner failed, but the struggle caused the stock to soar to $115 and brought Boesky a $16.7 million profit.

Needless to say, these figures are almost incomprehensibly large to the average person. Boesky will risk millions of dollars with the seeming casualness of someone betting $50 or $100 on a horse. "The fact of the matter is," Boesky observes, "that when you are a person responsible for the administration of money, one has the ability to run substantial sums with some degree of comfort. The amount of money that he stands ready to lose or not is all relative as long as it fits into the scheme of a total portfolio." Relative? "I suppose the fellow who runs his drugstore with five employees considers it a weighty responsibility to move the parts of the drugstore around and the people around to perform services. We find the President of the United States who can move nations around and treasuries around and so on. . . . Some people are more or less able to do that. So I guess that in terms of handling substantial sums of money, it has just been evolutionary with me and I've grown into the ability to do that."[9]

As with the other men of megawealth profiled in this book, one searches for some clue as to why an Ivan Boesky feels compelled to work 20-hour days in pursuit of ever more wealth. One answer came from a former associate, who recalled that Boesky had a T-shirt which he never wore but would sometimes show to others. On it was inscribed, "He who owns the most when he dies, wins."[10] Clearly, he is a driven man who admits that his preoccupation with money and earning more and more of it are something of a disease. Yet, as he observed, he doesn't see much of an alternative to continuing: "Well, I sometimes say casually that I was given the God-given gift of being a horse that's kind of good at running around a track. I don't know any other way. I don't know how to be a milk horse and I don't know how to go to pasture, so I just keep doing what I was allowed to have the good fortune to do well and try to do it better and better and better."[11]

Boesky, to his credit, seems always aware that missteps in the future could bring his empire crumbling. Because he has had luck in the past does not guarantee a golden future. "It's quite possible," he said, "that tomorrow you'll see my epitaph and it will be something like "News Pending Stop Trading."[12] Still, the man's appetite is voracious, and his mind is singular. One evening he was walking with his wife down the Champs Elysees in Paris. "Ivan," Seema said, "It's a beautiful evening. Just look at the moon. Isn't it gorgeous?" Boesky thought a moment, looked up at the white object in the sky, and observed, "What good is the moon if you can't buy it or sell it."

Money was not a great object in Ivan Boesky's childhood home. His father had reached America from Russia, a poor boy of 12. In time he would purchase three restaurants in Detroit, one on the corner of Farnsworth and Hastings. Later, Ivan would name a subsidiary of an English trust which he controlled after that intersection. Some thought he did so because it had an English-sounding name; perhaps he was just nostalgic. The enterprising spirit struck Ivan at age 13. That was when he purchased a 1937 Chevrolet panel truck; after painting it white, he drove to Detroit's parks and sold ice cream. The fact that he did not have a driver's license must have added to the adventure not to mention the $150 a week he made, collecting those nickels and dimes. He eventually abandoned the job when it was discovered that he was too young to drive.

Education was the highest value in the Boesky home. But Ivan's main interests as a youngster were extracurricular. At age 15 he unloaded box cars to stay in shape. He became a wrestler in ninth grade, and in time became obsessed with the sport. Every minute was devoted to either thinking about wrestling or engaging in the sport. If he had a 15-minute recess, he had it timed so that he could practice for eight of those minutes, using the other seven to change in and out of his gym clothes. By tenth grade he was the best member of the wrestling team. Sensing that he had no real natural ability, Ivan had proven to himself that other factors could compensate for that, most of all the will to succeed. He would never forget the sport. He would draw from his experiences on the mat comfort and solace later when the going was tough in arbitrage. He liked to say later that both wrestling and arbitrage left the individual dependent on his own wits and talents. Wrestling offered the added value of teaching one not to quit even when the odds appeared stacked against you.

Most of Ivan's undergraduate work was done at Wayne State in Detroit. He transferred to the University of Michigan for two semesters, then switched again to Eastern Michigan College, but did not receive a college degree. Between college and law school he joined the United States Information Agency and taught English literature and language in Teheran to Iranians. In September 1959 Detroit College of Law accepted him, not requiring a college degree. Though he left the school twice, he returned in 1962 and two years later obtained a law degree. Detroit's better law firms wouldn't hire him, so he clerked for Federal District Court Judge Theodore Levin. In 1962 he married Seema Silberstein, whose father owned the Beverly Hills Hotel. Armed with his clerking background, Boesky reapplied to the same law firms which had rejected him; he was once again turned down. He joined the Detroit accounting firm of Touche Ross, only to find that this did not work out either. At the age of 27, he compared himself unfavorably with his more successful friends. There was little relief in that.

But his luck changed when an old wrestling teammate, Marvin Davidson, explained risk arbitrage to him. Eager to get into the arbitrage trade, Boesky came to New York in 1966. He discovered that the practice had a bad name on Wall Street. That tiny, exclusive elite who engaged in it would accept only sponsored members into their "club." Boesky, as a novice, had no sponsors. At first he had little chance to practice arbitrage. When finally in 1972, while employed at the firm of Kalb Voorhis, he managed to get into a deal, he lost $20,000; he was fired the next day. Although he appeared intent on proving that he could make it in arbitrage, he had difficulty finding another job. Friends from that time would comment that Boesky was intent on showing his father-in-law, Ben Silberstein, that his daughter had married the right man. Several months passed, and eventually Boesky was hired by the brokerage firm of Edwards & Hanly, where he was put in charge of its arbitrage department. It was a major break for him, and he was determined to make the most of it.

Boesky had always been a loner and an iconoclast; he behaved no differently once at Edwards & Hanly. Other major arbs had found it convenient to cooperate with one another, to instruct a broker to buy stock on behalf of all the arbs. But that was not for Boesky: he purchased stock for himself. And rather than spread it around, he put all of his money in one company. Few would understand his reason for doing that. It was not that he was conservative; he understood as well as anyone, after his experience at Kalb Voorhis, the importance of being cautious. He genuinely felt that stocks were like food: a person had preferences in food, and so there was nothing wrong with him having preferences in stock. And, if he had a favorite stock, why not put large amounts of money on it, and forget the others? Needless to say, Boesky was a rule breaker. He was also sharp-witted: he realized that by becoming a specialist on regional exchanges he could increase his borrowing power on stocks from 50 to 90 percent. In that way, he was able to take positions of a couple of million dollars, then considered giant-sized.

Edwards & Hanly was not able to support an Ivan Boesky. By 1975 it went bankrupt; Boesky decided he would be best off starting his own company. Becoming the first person to set up a business devoted purely to arbitrage, he reportedly accepted $700,000 from his in-laws to open Ivan F. Boesky & Co., located in two small rooms that had been Edwards & Hanly's trading area. He decided to split his profits with his investors so that he would receive 55 percent of the profits while his investors would have to absorb 95 percent of the losses. That remains the case until today. Boesky and his family hold almost all the stock in his corporation while the investors hold only preferred stock (for which they receive dividends). The minimum investment has been raised from $75,000 to between $5 and $10 million.

For a long time the arbs had made sure that only a few played the arbitrage game—to maximize profits. The less capital there was, the larger the spreads. To go to the public for capital at that time was unthinkable. The arbs simply used the money available from their firms' capital. But Boesky needed investors. As his mortified colleagues watched, he placed ads in the *Wall Street Journal* and hired a public relations man. He managed to get quoted in the newspapers. One arb with whom I spoke expressed red-hot anger at Boesky for exposing arbitrage to the public so nakedly. "There was a time when all you saw was his name quoted about cake recipes. The son of a bitch would get quoted for something that had nothing to do with arbitrage just to get his name in print. To the point where people would say, 'Who is Ivan Boesky? What the hell does he do that he's in the newspapers, in the (*New York Times*) Living Section, the Finance section, he's everywhere.'" And in being "everywhere," he offered the public a chance to learn what arbitrage was all about—and to judge whether it was a good thing. "He sure made it harder for us," the disgruntled arb went on. "It was a nice, cushy little deal. You know, who needs this turkey to come along and start trouble? It was neat. It's possible somebody else would have done it if not him, but a lot of people don't like him."

Like him or not, Boesky has been enormously successful. His first large triumph came in 1977 when he earned an estimated $7 million in the takeover struggle for Babcock & Wilcox Co. Boesky guessed that Babcock & Wilcox would not be able to avoid a takeover. He purchased the firm's shares in large number. A wild contest ensued in August of that year and Babcock's common stock rose skyward. By early 1980 Boesky had turned his $700,000 stake in his firm into $90 million of capital. But 1980 would prove a bad year for him. He lost $10 million in one day and $45 million in the first quarter. By May he had decided to sell his interest in the firm to his six senior employees. He brought in Stephen A. Royce, head of the arbitrage department at Morgan Stanley, to run the firm in his place. He kept $7.25 million of his wife Seema's cash in the company, by now renamed Bedford Partners. Two years later, when Bedford suffered big losses, Seema Boesky took her money out, finally severing the Boesky family's ties with the company. To Boesky's employees it appeared that he wanted out in order to avoid the liability that came with limited partnerships and to gain a tax advantage: once out of the limited partnership he could pay deferred taxes on capital gains instead of on ordinary income, making for a large savings.

Declaring that he was going to pursue new investment opportunities, Boesky began a new corporation. In May 1981 he started the Ivan F. Boesky Corporation and shortly thereafter was earning large sums. In the first ten months he earned $12.4 million in pretax income. By the time the corporation was two years old—in the summer of 1982—Boesky had assets of $300 million. But in the fiscal year ending March 1983 Boesky lost $13.7 million. It was during that year that Gulf pulled out of the Cities Service deal. For the year that ended March 1984 Boesky brought in $76.5 million in pretax income. With his successes he had been able to diversify into other businesses, including real estate, financial services, and London merchant banking. He acquired a 52 percent of the Beverly Hills Hotel Corp. and San Diego's Vagabond Hotels Inc. In time, Boesky turned the corporation into a limited partnership and called it Ivan F. Boesky & Company, L.P.

Just how does Ivan Boesky work? Secretly, of course. He knows full well that his every movement is watched by other arbs who would love to purchase when he does, sell when he does. So Boesky works through subterfuges, asking one broker to inform a second to purchase for him through a third. His 13D forms, the SEC forms which he must submit when he has 5 percent of a company, are scrutinized once they are printed. Then the guesswork begins. Why did Boesky buy into this company? Is he certain it will become the target of a takeover? Is he just investing? What does he know that I don't? Boesky may be trying to throw people off the track, but he insists that it's impossible to watch him buy or sell something and then draw a conclusion about what he is going to do. When asked by a reporter what it was like being so closely watched, he replied, "I want to throw up a caution light to all those who follow everything I do. I am the same person who owned some Phillips stock on the wrong date (and reportedly suffered heavy losses). So not everything I do is right."[13]

Not everything, but enough for the crowds to want to know his every move.

With so much interest in his activities, it is little wonder that he guards his private life jealously. As a result, few details have emerged. He lives on a 188-acre estate in upstate New York that was purchased from John Revson of the Revlon cosmetics family. He will not talk about his wife or family for publication.

The Ivan Boesky whom the public does get to see is in seemingly perpetual motion, though never very far from access to the stock market—and that means never very far from a telephone. Boesky knows the value of the telephone and calls it his umbilical cord. He will routinely have three in action at once, one on each ear, one resting in his lap. Inside his chauffer-driven car are three telephones. He has 300 telephone lines in his office so that he can be within reach of his research teams and informants. If he ever gets too far afield from the market and from his sources, he becomes slightly neurotic. Once, while on a fishing expedition on the Salmon River in Idaho, he suddenly changed course and headed back up the rapids in a speedboat. The thought that he had been out of touch with the market for four entire hours unnerved him; he had to race to a telephone.

Boesky keeps up the frenetic pace during busy workdays. He will use the hour-long drive into the city for paperwork and listening to his favorite tapes. His day can begin as early as 6 A.M. with a meeting. At 7:30 A.M. he will see his arbitrage staff to plan the day and the fifty to sixty transactions with which he is routinely involved. During that day he will be in continuous contact with his researchers and traders via an elaborate audiovisual system that he claims is like NASA's. Using screens, he can see his staff and they can see him. He dresses like the archetype of the New York financier, with his three-piece blue suit and a gold watch chain fashioned after one Winston Churchill wore. He employs anyone and everyone to serve as his eyes and ears as deals progress. He will ask someone to sit in a courtroom or a legislative hearing in Washington and then rush to a phone to call him with information that could be vital. Boesky's eyes are never far from the computer terminal, always ready to tap out a few key letters to get the latest stock quotation, check the latest news, put in bids for a block of shares. He is never far from the microphone on his desk through which he barks orders in his low voice to staff, near and far. By the time the market opens at 10 A.M. he is at his desk watching computer screens and tapes, checking stock transactions. Instead of lunch he drinks black coffee. He may hold some afternoon meetings at the Harvard Club in mid-Manhattan. Dinners are meager as well. He is trim and obviously intends to stay that way. He often returns home at 1 A.M., works until 2:30 A.M. and then sleeps for two hours.

It is almost impossible to get a sense of how Boesky decides to invest. Still, many are convinced they know how he does it. One popular theory has it that brokers automatically pamper him with tips, since Boesky provides millions of dollars in brokerage commissions through his arbitrage trade. If a broker hears something, he will call Boesky first with the news. The phone call can win quick, handsome rewards, since Boesky can make major decisions without resort to committees or boards of directors. Able to make snap decisions, Boesky offers the brokers the lure of quick commission fees. The more he triumphs, the more people become convinced that Boesky relies on insiders' knowledge. Boesky denies this, saying that he uses public information and that he doesn't take rumors about companies seriously. One close observer of the takeover game noted that nine out of ten rumors about takeovers are false, suggesting that Boesky is right to stear clear of them.

Boesky's network of informants is legendary. One oft-repeated tale suggests that he has someone watching for any unusual corporate jet travel. By sifting through Federal Aviation Agency data on the movements of nearly all corporate jet aircraft in the United States, the watcher might be able to provide an early-warning system to Boesky about an upcoming deal.

When asked if it was possible to educate oneself to become a successful arbitrager, Boesky replied, "There's no myth, no history, no mystery. There's just a lot of hard work, technical skill and artistic sense that either one has or doesn't have."[14]

Though Boesky admires the raiders, he hates the word "raider" and dislikes the concept of greenmail. The raiders seek to control companies, he told me in our interview, whereas he is an impartial stock market operator who is essentially interested in a spread on a stock, not control of a firm. Still he finds some benefit in what Pickens, Icahn, Jacobs, Goldsmith, and the rest are doing: "I think their influence in the stock market has been extremely valuable and has prompted the industry to relook at itself and reassess what one of their main obligations is: which is to find ways to administer companies that helped to serve the interest not only of themselves, but of stockholders, their owners."[15] One day he himself might make an offer for a company. He won't rule that out. But he insists that it would be a friendly one; he is not interested in greenmailing, not interested in hostile takeovers. Meanwhile, when a raider makes a move on a company, it is a sure bet Ivan Boesky will be watching and thinking carefully about when and how to get in on the action.

After the CBS deal fell through in the summer of 1985, cynics thought takeovers would slow down. Not Ivan Boesky. He predicted an explosion of mergers and acquisitions in the next five years even greater than that of the early 1980s. To get ready for that explosion, Boesky was busy putting together a new $1 billion treasure chest that he could use to exploit more takeovers. One Boesky dream is a plunge into politics. Boesky has been lining himself up with the Republicans: in the mid-1980s he was serving as Jewish adviser to the National Republican Committee. He does not disguise an interest in joining the government at some time, maybe as an ambassador, maybe even a cabinet post. I half-jokingly suggested that he might become the first Jewish Republican president.

"I don't know," he said. "But I'll tell you I'll be one of the most ardently Republican supportive Jews in the United States. I don't think that I will be that Republican Jewish President." Without a second's hesitation he added, "But I don't think it unthinkable that someday there shall be one."[16]

It is that artistic sense that has some critics of the power of the arbitrage community deeply worried. As one major participant notes:

> In the last several years you see in every deal that the ownership moves to "hot hands" very early. That company is then sold: it's no longer owned by the stockholders. It's owned by a half dozen Ivan Boeskys. . . . Management has the job of getting a higher price out of someone who has made an offer or from someone else. Every once in a while the management doesn't do it and the arbitragers get burned, and they don't like it. Arbitrage has, in my opinion, a huge, huge influence, maybe an undue influence in shaping all of these transactions. There is a big breakdown in the logic of the free market system. The investors have invested their money in this company. The managers are now supposed to be performing for them. Now they've sold it all to arbitragers who by definition are gamblers, not investors. And they're in it for twenty-four hours, not twenty-four months, or twenty-four years. Now the decisions have to be made to suit them.

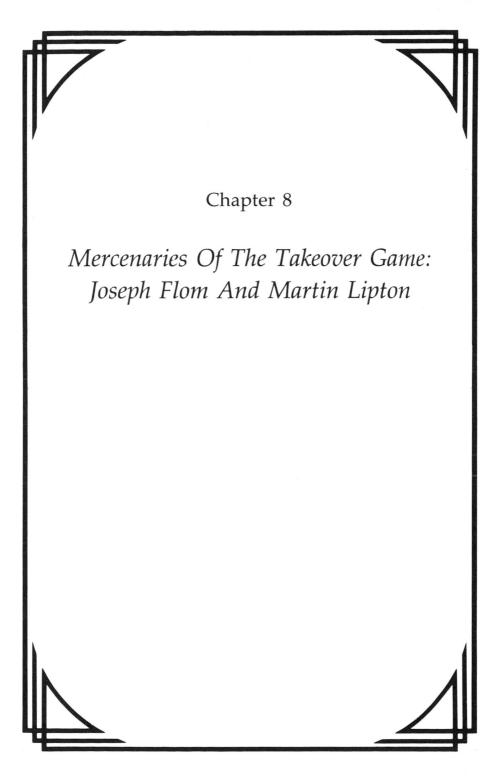

Chapter 8

Mercenaries Of The Takeover Game:
Joseph Flom And Martin Lipton

Joseph H. Flom. Courtesy Skadden, Arps, Slate, Meagher & Flom.

Martin Lipton. Courtesy Bachrach.

Lawyers were not always a key part of the Takeover Game. There was a time when all they did was to put down on paper what the parties had agreed upon: as long as mergers were friendly, as so many had been in the past, corporations did not need to turn to lawyers for advice in making a deal or preventing one. It was cut-and-dried, unexciting work. All that would change when hostile takeovers became an acceptable form of behavior on the Street. But for the law firms it would be a gradual change. Not all of them would jump immediately and aggressively into the Takeover Game. Some considered themselves too genteel, too gentlemanly, to take part in acts of confrontation. Yet, the very nature of confrontation would require lawyers as it did investment bankers—to become part of the game. Anyone who was prepared to go against the grain, to show a little nerve, would be able to get in on the ground floor.

One man who did just that was Joseph Flom, who would become a giant in the takeover field, perhaps the single most important force in the game during the 1970s and 1980s. A member of Skadden, Arps, Slate, Meagher & Flom, a New York law firm, since the late 1940s, by the mid-1970s Flom was a successful corporate lawyer with a wide-ranging knowledge of proxy contests. He was well positioned to take advantage of the new opportunities emerging in the takeover field. Business executives knew him and were comfortable with him; the investment banking community also got along with him. And why not? Few others knew this part of the law as well as Flom; few also were willing to engage in the burgeoning field of takeover law. Flom did not recoil from being quite alone in this new field: he rather welcomed it.

Flom was mild-mannered and had a quiet approach; there was in him none of the haranguing associated with other lawyers. Small of build, he spoke in a hushed, calm voice, always giving the impression of knowing the field inside and out. The gentility was deceptive; it left the impression of a man with little belligerence welling inside. Yet, he could be as aggressive as any lawyer. So much was he feared that arbitragers were eager to know which side Joe Flom was on whenever a takeover was announced.

As the number of takeover fights increased in the 1970s, it became clear that there was room for more takeover lawyers. Those corporations unable to get Joe Flom on their side sought an alternative: they found him in Martin Lipton. He belonged to the New York law firm of Wachtell, Lipton, Rosen & Katz. Like Flom, he was tough and aggressive. Like Flom, Lipton won friends easily among the corporate crowd.

At first, Flom and Lipton were regarded by the major law firms on Wall Street as mavericks, two unconventional types who had chosen to engage in a field with no real luster and no prospect for drawing big fees. They had even set up their practices in midtown Manhattan far from the mainstream of Wall Street life. Self-respecting lawyers did not fool around with such unimportant trade, it was simply not white-shoe, in Joe Flom's apt phrase.

Flom and Lipton quarreled on the corporate battlefield, but remained good friends for many years—until they had a falling out in the mid-1980s. Photographs in magazines showed them breakfasting at the Regency Hotel, smiling, in animated conversation. There are no photographs of the two men scowling at each other. For years they had the field all to themselves, knowing that they were in the unique position of being able to structure the rules of the game as they saw fit. To their good fortune, no one ever tried to figure out who was the better lawyer, who won more cases. When Flom was on his own, he was considered the best; when Marty Lipton came along, Flom and Lipton were counted the two top takeover attorneys in the field.

Having the field to themselves, the two men automatically found themselves thrown together. As Joe Flom remembers it:

> Naturally, with two guys basically in the field, you had to be working with each other on a fairly intensive basis. And very often since you spoke the same language you could avoid a lot of unnecessary by-play and litigation by just saying, "Look, here's where the chips are, talk to your client and see what it's all about." We also became friends just because shooting at each other on the professional level doesn't mean you can't be friends on a social level. That went on for a number of years. The relationship cooled considerably in the last few years.[1]

Flom doesn't like to talk about why the relationship cooled except to say that it had nothing to do with their being rival lawyers in the takeover game. Lipton was more candid: he pointed to the Household International case of 1985 as the chief cause. More on that in a while. It was generally assumed incorrectly that their rift stemmed from Flom always taking the offensive and Lipton the defensive side. Yet both lawyers worked both sides.

By the 1980s, Joe Flom and Marty Lipton had become the superstars of the Takeover Game, pioneers and workaholics who reaped enormous profit and at the same time appeared to love every minute of their back-breaking schedules. Flom once flew the Atlantic twice in one day; he recalls the "family" vacation he took in Spain when he made seven round trips in two months. For their extra hours, Flom and Lipton were well paid: by 1982, they were reportedly earning at least $1 million a year.[2]

Much of the way the game was played was due to these two men. The very fact that the a takeover team of advisers had to include investment bankers, attorneys, and public relations men was their special contribution to the rules of the game. Marty Lipton admits that devising that structure was fortuitous:

> I certainly didn't realize what I was doing as it was happening. It happened because the necessities of the moment dictated it. . . . Essentially the structure evolved from the decisions we made in the 1975 to 1980 period, and we (he and Flom) were undoubtedly the dominant factors in determining how the deals were done, the people involved in the deals and so on. Even to this day most of the innovations stem from our two firms. In a way it's natural because we have the greatest exposure to the (takeover) activity.[3]

Moreover, it became one of the unspoken verities that Flom and Lipton did not perform exclusively as lawyers in takeover struggles; because of their special acumen and the breadth of their knowledge, they roamed easily into the investment banking and public relations aspects as well. One acquaintance of both men stressed to me that Flom and Lipton were in fact public relations specialists of the highest order; both men virtually dictating the nature of public relations campaigns in takeover contests. Perhaps in self-deprecation, Marty Lipton had written that "corporate takeovers are analogous to feudal wars, and the lawyers are the mercenaries."[4] But when he wrote those words in 1979 there was an element of truth to them: lawyers did do the "mercenary" work in the Takeover Game, engaging in litigation, entering the main arena where the nitty-gritty of the contests were being waged. Seven years later, when I interviewed Lipton, I asked him whether he still thought lawyers were the mercenaries of the Takeover Game. His mind had changed somewhat:

> Today investment bankers are still the clergy. The distinction (in 1979) was that investment bankers created the philosophy of the deal and the lawyers went out and fought out in the trenches, the litigation and so on. It's really different today.[5]

When that was written litigation was crucial to the takeover process, but as antitrust and disclosure issues became less important, the role of the lawyers changed: by the mid-1980s

> it's much more of a team of investment banker, lawyer, public relations adviser. Today the primary focus is what I would call corporate structuring, which is essentially divided between the bankers and the lawyers. It almost melds together, the legal aspects and the financial aspects.

When I suggested to Lipton, half-facetiously, half-seriously, that lawyers were no longer mercenaries, he agreed, and laughingly suggested a new phrase, "mercenary princes!"

As the new "mercenary princes," Flom and Lipton towered over the field. "Everybody seems to take the takeover movement as starting with me," Joe Flom said to me. "That's not true."[6] But it was a sign of how esteemed he and Marty Lipton were, that someone could even think such a thing. By the mid-1970s companies were convinced that they had to have Joe Flom or Marty Lipton on their side to have a serious chance of succeeding in a takeover contest. Flom was so feared for his prowess in helping corporate raiders that companies paid him retainers to guarantee that he would not work against them and to provide that he would be the company attorney in the event of a takeover threat. One report, published in 1984, suggested that as many as 200 firms were paying Joe Flom $50,000 a year—or $10 million in all—in defensive retainers.[7] Of the various figures in the takeover game whom I interviewed for this book, I found Joe Flom one of the most candid. But on this subject he was decidedly tight-lipped. When I asked him whether those figures were true, he would say only that they were wrong "in so many respects."

The "Joe Flom protection policy," as the practice became known, drew critics, but Flom insisted that those critics were merely jealous. Besides, he contended, if the money was not used for takeover cases, the client could always use the retainer for other Skadden Arps services. Flom noted to me that some of the retainers had become burdensome. Keeping companies on retainer cost the firm a good deal of money on occasion: Skadden Arps was kept from engaging in deals in which companies on retainer were involved. Noted Flom:

> We've gotten rid of a number of companies that haven't used up the retainer, because, who the hell needs it? The retainers were great when you could identify the aggressors. And then you'd say, "OK, I'm going to stay away from them." But now there are so many companies that are aggressors that you beat yourself coming and going on occasion.[8]

Flom and Lipton appeared to merge into one in the public's mind— they were the takeover attorneys, plain and simple. They did, of course, possess common traits: both men had razor-sharp minds, both knew the takeover business better than almost anyone around. Both men enjoyed the legal battles and especially enjoyed the creative side to the game. On the surface, Joe Flom was the quieter, the less flashy, but that did not automatically make him meek. Physically they are different: Marty has a more commanding presence than does Joe, partly perhaps because he is well over six feet tall. One acquaintance of both men summed Flom up this way:

> Joe is the kind of guy who in any situation he's in really wants to run the show. He's not very happy if he doesn't. His lawyers defer to him a lot. If Joe hasn't endorsed it, it's no damn good. Joe is a very resourceful person. No matter

what's happened, he always has the ability to look at it as it is and to contrive some way out of if he can. He never gives up. He keeps trying to think, "Now, let's face the facts and try to make the most of them." Joe will be up there by himself, with everyone in the fort gone, he'll be pouring oil when you'd wonder what the point would be.

Lipton was no less energetic, but he was more likely to work as a team player. The acquaintance added: "Marty is an enormously proud person. He is a little bit more mercurial than Joe. He is more apt to yield gracefully in a doomed situation." While Joe is credited with an intuitive kind of genius, Marty is thought to be the more cerebral of the two men. Another professional who knows both men well described these contrasting qualities: "Joe is much more held back. He doesn't come out openly as much as Marty does. He will think to himself and then come up with an idea and put it on the table, maybe after everybody else has thought something through." Lipton's most exceptional quality appears to be an ability to focus almost exclusively on one subject at the expense of all others. As a result he is impressive to watch in action, as one investment banker noted: "Marty can sit and talk to a board of directors meeting, make a presentation, without notes, and it comes out as a brilliant performance. He never misses a cue. He always chooses the right word."

Reading the press in the mid-1980s, one could easily get the mistaken impression that Joe Flom did only aggressive work in the takeover game, and Marty Lipton only defensive work. That, as Joe Flom points out without much excitement in his voice, is just not the case. When I asked Flom why he had acquired a reputation as Mr. Takeover, he shrugged his shoulders and said simply, "Well, I guess we're all captives of the PR aspects of the thing."[9] Oddly enough, Flom has received far less publicity for his defensive work, though he has sided with the defense frequently. Flom emphasizes that he prefers to do defensive work: indeed 75 percent of his takeover caseload has been defensive. The problem, he notes, is that "if you just do defense, you lose some of the thinking capacity that goes with the offense."[10]

Joe Flom was born in Baltimore on December 20, 1923, and grew up in a family of modest means in Brooklyn's Borough Park section. His father was a Russian immigrant, a small manufacturer and union organizer. It was always assumed in the Flom household that Joe would wind up a lawyer. "My mother," recalled Flom in our interview, "was always upset that she didn't have enough money to send me to a Yeshiva (a Jewish religious seminary). Strangely enough, my parents thought that law was a good steppingstone for politics. You go into things very often for the wrong reasons. So, from the age of 5 or 6 I knew I was going to be a lawyer."[11]

In high school Joe did a book report on Edmond's cases on constitutional law. Attending City College of New York at night between 1939 and 1941, he supported himself at a number of jobs: he was a drill press operator as well as a messenger for a law firm. With the war on, he left school and joined the U.S. Army in 1941. Though he did not have an undergraduate degree, he was able to enter Harvard Law School in 1945. In 1947 and 1948 he was an editor of the *Harvard Law Review*. Graduating in 1948, Joe was one of the few members of the *Law Review* unable to land a job in the first wave of interviews. He was not particularly eager to get a job with a large law firm and so was pleased to learn of a small firm just starting up. What would become Skadden, Arps, Slate, Meagher & Flom had been founded in 1948 by four men who had recently broken off from another law firm, Dewey Ballantine. Getting off to a slow start, the four partners were eager for business, any business. The first associate they hired was Joe Flom. "I liked the guys. They spent all their time telling me why I was crazy to join them: they would say, 'Think of all the risks involved.' I just said, 'Look, I'll take a shot at it.'"[12]

He was a great success from the start. In his first two years Flom was on a salary, earning $3,600 a year and making more than all the four founding partners combined. As partners they shared in the profits—but at the outset there were few clients—and thus few profits. For the first five years, the basic income of the firm came from Henry Friendly, general counsel for Pan American and a partner at Cleary Gottlieb. With little else to do, the partners took an interest in Flom and spent a good deal of time training him. He learned taxes from one partner, litigation from another, corporate law from two others. Flom would prepare memos, and the partners would explain how to improve upon them. To make ends meet during 1948 and 1949 some of the partners moonlighted, taking work as counsel to special investigatory commissions. Flom benefited from their absence by being given the brunt of the law firm's work to do.

At one stage around 1955 Flom, with little to do at the time, interested himself in a proxy contest case which another lawyer in the firm was handling. Learning all that he could about the subject, Flom got to handle his first case: "I liked it. It was a multidisciplinary kind of activity, involving public relations, litigation, corporate law, accounting analysis, and a lot of psychology."[13] By his third proxy fight, Wall Street had singled out Flom as a rising attorney in the field. He remembered the case vividly thirty years later: it involved someone who owned one-third of the stock of a company but could not get a seat on the board. During the 1950s and 1960s he developed into one of the master legal strategists in the proxy contest field. He remembers them as free-for-alls. As the merger boom developed in the mid-1960s, Flom realized that opportunities for corporations existed, opportunities arising from the highly unregulated takeover field. Knowing that he was the most experienced proxy contest lawyer around, companies turned to Flom more and more for advice in takeover contests. By 1977, 40 percent of Skadden Arps' work was in the takeover field.

The star attraction at the law firm was Joe Flom. Skadden Arps' business grew in leaps and bounds. From 29 attorneys in 1970, the firm more than doubled in size by 1977 and grew to 350 in the 1980s. Its supremacy in the takeover trade was unquestioned. By the late 1970s Flom (along with Marty Lipton) was involved in 90 percent of all tender struggles. In the early 1980s Skadden Arps had grown to the eleventh-largest legal firm in the country. By 1986, when it was the third largest, it was generating the largest revenues of any American law firm—even more than the two larger law firms. In the fiscal year that ended March 1985 the 429 attorneys on its staff brought in $129 million in gross revenues. That represented, according to *The American Lawyer*, $540,000 profit per partner. By the mid-1980s Skadden Arps was broadening its range, realizing that it would be difficult to dominate the takeover field in a post-Joe Flom era. Flom was still very active in the mid-1980s, but he liked to call himself a head coach, with the other partners his starting lineup.

Marty Lipton was born in Jersey City, N.J., on June 22, 1931, making him eight years younger than Joe Flom. After spending his childhood years in Jersey City and Bradley Beach, N.J., Marty entered the Wharton School of Finance at the University of Pennsylvania in Philadelphia in 1948. Though he would have preferred to study humanities, in particular history, Marty followed the wish of his father, a manufacturer of ladies' lingerie, who had urged Wharton upon him in the hope that he would become an investment banker. The Wharton School bored him. The life of a college student held little appeal for him as well: he did not join a college fraternity and he thought of his four years at Pennsylvania as one large waste of time. During the spring of his senior year he decided that he wanted to become a lawyer and so he took the law school aptitude examination. After graduating from the University of Pennsylvania in 1952 with a bachelor's degree in economics, he entered the New York University Law School that fall.

In contrast to the previous four years, he discovered a whole world of learning in which he took great delight: "It was my thing. The day I arrived I knew it was my thing. I just loved it. I did well. I sort of reveled in it."[14] He was first in his class and editor-in-chief of the *Law Review*. He thought of becoming a law school professor, and the Dean of the NYU Law School, Russell Dennison Niles, who had spotted Lipton early as a promising student, pushed him toward an academic life. During the summer after law school Lipton worked for Charles Seligson, who taught at the NYU

Law School and was a senior partner in the law firm of Seligson & Morris. That fall, encouraged by Niles, Lipton enrolled at Columbia University, where he held a teaching fellowship.

As he neared the end of the fellowship, Lipton sought Niles' advice once again and was told this time that he must get some practical experience in the law before joining the NYU law faculty. And so between 1956 and 1958 Lipton clerked under Judge Edward Weinfeld. When those two years came to an end, Niles proposed that Lipton work for a year for a law firm; Lipton signed on with Seligson & Morris. He was not there more than ten days when he bumped into Niles at an NYU Law School reception. What was Lipton up to in the law firm, Niles asked? Lipton mentioned that he had been working on an SEC registration statement for the sale of a small oil firm's securities. That piece of information clearly stuck in Niles' mind, for a few days later he called Lipton urgently to say that the professor who had taught the course in securities law had suddenly died and there was no one to teach his course the next evening. Lipton agreed to fill in and was somewhat amused when Niles told him in parting, "Don't worry. I'll find someone next week who knows how." Lipton recalls that event as a significant turning point in his career. Rather than find someone "who knew how," Niles prevailed upon Lipton to teach the course the rest of the semester. Combining academic life with the law, Lipton found that the two disciplines served as mutual reinforcement. He became successful at both.

Throughout the early 1960s Lipton worked on friendly acquisitions, most of them in the $5 to $10 million category. "In those days," recalled Lipton, "we thought of a $5 million acquisition as a very big deal."[15] In retrospect those deals seemed far less exciting and glamorous than the ones he would handle later on, but they were interesting and helped his growing reputation. Lipton worked directly for Morris: "I was his bag-carrier."[16] He made his real mark in those days in the securities regulation area, handling new issues of securities by smaller companies and representing clients who were the subjects of SEC enforcement investigations and proceedings. By 1964, the law firm of Seligson & Morris had broken up and Lipton, along with four others, formed a new law firm, which would become Wachtell, Lipton, Rosen & Katz. Jerry Kern was a founding partner but dropped out a few years later to become an investment banker.

There was a streak of idealism among the founders of the new law firm—and a collective desire to avoid some of the problems they had found in Seligson & Morris: in particular, they would steer clear of close connections with their clients' businesses. Noted Lipton: "We decided we would be equal partners. We would run it in a way that would make us happy, not as a business but as a law firm."[16] At the outset the attorneys had no great game plan. The attorneys, Lipton among them, sought business wherever they could: it was their good fortune that the time was ripe for the securities law practice, as new investment banks were popping up left and right in the mid-1960s.

The firm began with five partners and two associates, and from the very beginning decided to keep the place small: it would retain that outlook into the mid-1980s when it would grow, but only to a hundred lawyers. Their practice was mixed: litigation, bankruptcy, and corporate securities. Out of a lack of choice, they adopted the task-force method of work with all seven lawyers digging into a single case. "Later on," noted Lipton, "we realized it was the ideal way to handle tender offers and the hostile acquisitions."[17]

Lipton and the new law firm gained their first publicity when they defended Pepsi Cola General Bottlers, a midwestern bottler of Pepsi Cola, against a series of takeover attempts in the late 1960s. When Edgar Higgins, Pepsi Cola General Bottlers' head, decided to expand, Lipton and his colleagues helped Higgins' firm to merge with Illinois Central Industries. This marked the largest transaction Wachtell, Lipton had negotiated, just under $100 million and it led to more large M&A business as Illinois Central asked Wachtell, Lipton to represent it in a series of major acquisitions, all of them friendly. The experience would prove invaluable in the law firm's later confrontations on the hostile-takeover battlefield. Wall Street began to take notice of the firm.

One crucial turning point for Marty Lipton came in the early 1970s when he began advising Salomon Brothers on their arbitrage activity. Whenever a deal was announced, someone from the investment bank would call him and seek a legal review: What did he think about the antitrust aspects? What did he think about the Williams Act? He became a student of merger and acquisition activity. And he came into contact with Ira Harris, the premier dealmaker of the early 1970s, who was a Salomon Brothers partner. A quick study, highly intelligent, a great salesman and prodigious worker, Harris lacked only one quality: he was not a technician. So, wherever he was, whatever time it was, day or night, he would pick up the phone to Marty Lipton to say that he had just met a potential client, he was interested in doing a deal: Could Ira use preferred stock? Would there be any antitrust problems? "A good part of what I did in that period," remembered Lipton, "was to represent Ira Harris or his clients in these deals."[18] And that was where Marty Lipton got his start in the intense M&A whirl. Those were essentially negotiated, friendly deals, complicated and innovative, but not hostile. It was in 1974, when Loews launched a hostile takeover against CNA, an insurance company, that Lipton won public notice as a rising takeover attorney. Never before had there had been a hostile tender offer against an insurance company, and so the press focused on the battle. Lipton helped Loews take over CNA, and the press attention put him for the first time in the limelight.

As the number of hostile tender offers increased in the mid-1970s, investment bankers looked around for attorneys to represent them other than Joe Flom, who had developed a close relationship with Morgan Stanley. Lipton's handling of the CNA deal left its mark on Wall Street—and soon he became the "other lawyer" to whom one would turn. Goldman Sachs became Wachtell, Lipton's major client, and that inevitably meant the law firm would gravitate toward the side defending against takeovers: Goldman Sachs had a policy of not representing clients who made hostile tender offers. Lipton's law firm was open to handling both aggressive and defensive actions, but its relationship with Goldman Sachs led it more to the defensive side. Marty Lipton noted: "Certainly there was no conscious decision at this point (whether to do only aggressive or defensive work). We still didn't quite realize what we were into."[19] The year 1975 was the watershed for Lipton's firm: that was the year it began to get called regularly on takeover issues, especially from Goldman Sachs; and it was the year that Wachtell, Lipton was asked to serve as Special Counsel for the City of New York in helping to solve the city's fiscal crisis. The latter effort established the law firm in the eyes of the major Wall Street institutions.

Thanks to Marty Lipton, Wachtell, Lipton grew impressively in the late 1970s and early 1980s. The law firm has always been much smaller than Skadden, Arps. Lipton's firm sought not to be overwhelmed by the takeover trade. It did not accept retainers, as Skadden, Arps did. Hostile takeovers accounted for only 30 percent or so of Wachtell's business, though mergers and acquisitions accounted for well over half during the 1970s and into the 1980s.

In 1976 Lipton chaired an American Bar Association National Institute on takeovers and in connection with that prepared what his colleagues would later refer to as "the telephone book" because of its huge size. The "telephone book" was eventually published in 1979 as a two-volume legal treatise, *Takeovers and Freezeouts,* which Lipton coauthored with his second wife, Erica H. Steinberger, a partner at Wachtell, Lipton. *Takeovers* later acquired a reputation as the technical bible of the takeover business.

Flom and Lipton confronted each other in a law case for the first time way back in 1959 in a proxy fight involving the United Industrial Corporation. Flom was on management's side, Lipton on the side of some dissident stockholders. The finale was a standoff: both lawyers won four seats each for their clients on the board. Their first battle involving a tender offer was the $84 million Colt takeover of Garlock in 1975. Flom was Colt's lawyer; Lipton was Garlock's. The Colt raid became part of the lore of takeover history by virtue of the suddenness with which it was announced. To gain the advantage over a target company, an aggressor benefited from announcing his plans over the weekend, as Colt did. This caught the target company off guard and made it far more difficult to mount a suitable defense in time. The Colt raid became known as the

"Saturday Night Special," as did all other sudden, weekend or holiday raids in subsequent years.

Though Lipton was unsuccessful in representing Garlock, he looks back to that episode as pivotal for the takeover game: "It was one of the earliest attempts to use a literary defense against the takeover. It failed. We thought we might scare them away by saying, 'These guys are supplying the guns for muggers. (They) are trying to take over this wonderful company.'"[20] What Marty Lipton calls a "literary" defense—in effect, using a public relations ploy to win support for one's side—would become a standard tactic in the coming years. Beyond the tactics, Colt-Garlock was one of several early deals which forged the close relationships between the lawyers, the investment bankers, and the public relations specialists. At the same time, corporations involved in the Takeover Game simply could not do without Joe Flom or Marty Lipton: by 1977 and 1978 there was hardly a deal in which the two men were not involved—on opposite sides of the fence, of course.

Joe Flom gained fame in 1975 by coming up with a creative strategy known as the "Jewish dentist" defense. In 1975, Sterndent, a manufacturer of dental equipment, had come under attack by Magus Corporation, a foreign-based conglomerate. Searching for a way to keep Sterndent from being taken over, Flom discovered that 10 percent of Magus was owned by the Kuwait Investment Company. Realizing that his own client, Sterndent, sold most of its products to dentists, many of whom were Jewish, Flom decided to press the point that if Sterndent were taken over by a company partially owned by Arabs, those Jewish dentists would take their business elsewhere. "I'll never get over the fact that my client said to me, 'What the hell has that got to do with a takeover contest?' and I said, 'Let's just put it in the statement. Don't make any claims or anything. Just put it in the statement that they should be aware that Arabs own 5 percent of it.'"[21] Representing the Kuwaitis was none other than Marty Lipton. To Flom's good luck, the takeover fight coincided with the annual dentists' convention where orders were placed for new dental equipment. Sterndent did not win a single order. The court decided that Flom's ploy had no legal merit, but it worked very well as a public relations ploy. The takeover battle threatened to get even messier. Meanwhile, Flom managed to recruit a white knight, and Magus backed off.

With the successful conclusion of the "Jewish dentist" case, Flom became a firm believer in waging a broad-based campaign for his client, not merely relying upon legal techniques. This was demonstrated in August 1978 in Occidental Petroleum's takeover bid of Mead Corporation. Mead, represented by Joe Flom, was determined to resist the takeover attempt, using maximum publicity against Occidental Petroleum as a major weapon. Sensing that legal strategy could profitably be combined with good public relations, Flom turned to PR specialist Gershon Kekst, and the two men waged a vigorous battle against Occidental Petroleum. Calling in Stanley Pottinger, a Washington attorney, Flom decided to publicize some alleged misconduct on Occidental's part to weaken the company's public image. Included were illegal campaign contributions to reelect President Nixon; illegal bribes given to foreign officials; and potential liabilities which Occidental's subsidiary, Hooker Chemical, faced for polluting Love Canal. These actions were considered relevant to the tender offer, since Occidental planned to pay Mead stockholders in Occidental stock. The public relations barrage worked: on December 20, Occidental withdrew its tender offer.

Mead's legal and public relations strategy had just been too much. Lipton had not been involved in that deal, but he was impressed that twice in a row Flom had taken the battle beyond the courtroom. "It wasn't just a matter of doing the deal by the law books and by the money," observed a Mead-Occidental participant. And so, by the time American Express made an $880 million offer to buy McGraw-Hill in 1979, Lipton had developed an appreciation for the extralegal tactics that could be employed in takeover struggles. Lipton recognized that public relations would be crucial to the outcome of the McGraw-Hill–American Express battle. He and public relations adviser Kekst managed to convince Harold W. McGraw Jr., head of McGraw-Hill, that his case would be immeasurably enhanced by going public with the outrage he felt toward American Express. In private, Harold McGraw had expressed genuine concern that some McGraw-Hill publications such as *Business Week* might have trouble covering topics objectively in which American Express had an interest. The trick for Lipton and Kekst was to convince McGraw to take this concern public. Only then would it be possible to persuade the stockholders and public that American Express would have a real conflict-of-interest problem if it managed to take over McGraw-Hill. Harold McGraw was finally persuaded: he held a news conference and ran a full-page advertisement in several major newspapers. At the news conference, the McGraw chief told of a letter he had sent to James Robinson, III, Chairman of American Express, in which he had accused American Express of a lack of integrity and corporate morality and in which he had termed the tender offer illegal and improper.

As part of McGraw-Hill's multifaceted tactics, Lipton used more conventional legal tactics as well: he requested the FCC to block the proposed takeover on grounds that American Express should not be permitted to operate McGraw-Hill's four television stations; he asked the New York State Attorney General to investigate the legality of the American Express offer under the state takeover laws; and he filed a complaint in New York State Supreme Court in which he alleged that the takeover bid was illegal. He also requested hundreds of internal documents and the early deposition of senior American Express officials. Lipton also made sure to pass the word that McGraw-Hill writers were unprepared to work for a large financial conglomerate like American Express.

American Express had turned to Joe Flom, hiring him, some said, in part to keep him from working for McGraw-Hill. Flom displayed a certain boldness in bringing a countersuit on grounds of libel. Usually raiders such as American Express did not bring libel suits. They could hardly expect to win much sympathy from the courts after taking such aggressive action. But Flom's tack was ingenious: it sought to put McGraw-Hill on the defensive. The lawsuit charged McGraw-Hill with "publicly disseminating false and misleading statements designed to induce McGraw-Hill shareholders to reject American Express' tender offer." But the lawsuit was not enough to turn the tide. Flom realized that the Lipton game plan was too impressive to challenge. Lipton's "scorched earth" defense would be too embarrassing for American Express. It all seemed terribly familiar to Joe Flom. "You dream up something one day," he noted, "and the next day somebody else is trying to shoot you in the ass with it."[22] James Robinson bowed out without purchasing even one share of McGraw-Hill, giving the victory to McGraw-Hill and Marty Lipton.

While Marty Lipton had great respect for the free market and no fundamental opposition to corporate bigness, he was convinced that serious abuses had occurred within the takeover field in the 1980s, abuses which greatly encouraged and helped the corporate raiders. Greenmail and front-end-loaded two-tiered bust-up tender offers were, in his view, the two chief culprits. Back in the 1970s, he had watched and helped to fashion many of the "industrial" deals, as he called them, deals which were based on a corporate urge to expand or diversify. That urge was OK with him, that was a decent, economically sound, legitimate business motive and he was quite willing to be part of that game. But by the end of 1980 and early 1981, he grew bothered as the character of the deals began to change to the "financial" kind (another Marty Lipton term). These were being fashioned by the raiders, engaging in bootstrap financing and aiming at busting up a company. "I felt I was involved in a process," said Lipton, "that was not good for the economy, not good for the people involved, and I developed a very, very strong bias against doing bust-up deals."[23] Concretely, Wachtell, Lipton decided not to represent what Lipton calls "the takeover entrepreneurs," and so it has never represented T. Boone Pickens, Carl Icahn, Irwin Jacobs, or other similar raiders. It will not represent anyone who wishes to make only a partial bid for a firm; the aggressor company must show Lipton's law firm a plan how it plans to acquire all of the shares of the target company.

If he had his way, Lipton would limit hostile takeovers sharply. He believes that most of them don't work, that putting together two companies with differing cultures is difficult, and that such mergers do not automatically make management more efficient. The heart of the problem, in his view, lies with the raiders and the arbitragers who are "really in a position to topple any major public company that they decide to topple," with $10 to $20 billion of capital at their disposal and an ability to leverage that up two or three times with junk bonds:

> Just the term junk bonds is indicative of what's happened. It is the glorification of highly speculative, high-return investments instead of a focus on soundness and prudence. Our financial institutions have developed this tremendous leverage and tremendous volatility in transactions, which works just fine as long as there are no downturns: it presents a great danger of panic and collapse if there is a downturn. I think the junk bond explosion will turn out to be like the pyramided holding companies of 1929 which did so much to cause the 1929 crash.[24]

He has proposed legislation to restrict junk bonds and takeover activity, meeting with some success at the state level but none at the federal level.

At the same time, Lipton began the search for a tactic that would strengthen the hand of the corporation vis-à-vis the raider. In the past, it had been possible to use antitrust issues as a legal weapon. That would do the trick without resorting to anything fancier. But, once the Reagan Administration took power in January 1981 with its liberal view toward mergers and its relaxed attitude toward antitrust actions, Lipton realized he would have to seek other defenses to keep raiders from moving against corporations. His gem was the "poison pill."

He came up with the idea in 1983; it was a device which corporations could employ to make themselves more expensive, hence too "poisonous" to swallow. The pill could be effectively used against corporate raiders because they routinely did not offer 100 percent cash offers. One hundred percent any-and-all cash offers are difficult, if not impossible, to defend against. But the raiders often bid for a company in two stages, and the pill could be used to make the second step unattractive to the raider.

Without having to turn to the stockholders, a company could, by adopting the pill, radically alter the dynamics of the takeover playing field, making it uneconomic for the aggressor to proceed. At first Lipton had created the Warrant Dividend Plan and circulated it to clients and investment bankers. It was in fact the genesis of the poison pill, but it was to take a couple of years to develop fully. In the meantime, Lipton employed a different kind of poison pill in 1983 when he represented Lenox Inc., then trying to avoid a takeover by Brown-Forman Distillers. Lenox eventually decided to dissolve the pill in order to accept a sweetened offer from Brown-Forman. The pill had not prevented the takeover but had increased the price. Martin Siegel, the investment banker from Kidder, Peabody who represented Lenox, coined the term "poison pill" in remarks he made to the *Wall Street Journal*. But it was Lipton's invention.

In the form used by Lenox, the pill was used only a few more times. Because it entailed issuance of preferred stock, it substantially altered a company's capitalization. Lipton searched for a device that would accomplish the same purpose but have no impact on the company until triggered. He found it in the rights plan first adopted by Crown Zellerbach in the summer of 1984.

The new pill works like this: the company issues a right which enables a stockholder to buy shares in the company at a price designed to reflect the ten-year value of the company's stock. The rights become exercisable if someone acquires 20 percent of the company's stock or whatever other "trigger" figure is set. If someone tries to acquire control of the company through a merger or sale of assets, the stockholders have a right to buy shares in the acquiring company, usually at half price. If the acquirer does not acquire the entire company, but engages in self-dealing transactions, or, in some variations, simply acquires a stated percentage of the company's stock, the stockholders other than the raider have a right to buy shares of the target company's stock at half price. In most cases stockholders are permitted to buy up to three times the value of their shares at that bargain price. The rights thus represent substantial potential dilution to a raider. But, until triggered, the right have no balance-sheet or earnings impact.

Lipton and Flom were quite hostile toward one another over the Household litigation. The source of the hostility was what Lipton called a "gratuitous personal attack" on him. Skadden, Arps had filed a brief which accused Lipton of misrepresenting to the Household Board of Directors what the effect of the poison pill was: Lipton, according to the brief, had not explained the details of the poison-pill plan or the degree to which it would deter takeovers. Essentially, as Lipton recalled to me in our interview, Flom was trying to establish that the Household board did not properly exercise its business judgment in adopting the poison-pill plan. Lipton was furious. When we met in June 1986, months after the case, he was still angry. "One, it wasn't true. Two, it was done in a manner that I thought was grossly unfair, and indeed the court went out of its way, both the Chancery Court and the Delaware Supreme Court, to state that that was not so."

Sir James Goldsmith's acquisition of Crown Zellerbach, the San Francisco forest products firm that first adopted the pill, led some to question the pill's effectiveness. Goldsmith had made a tender offer for Crown Zellerbach in 1985 but was rebuffed; a client of Joe Flom's, Goldsmith was still able to take over his target after the Crown Zellerbach pill had been invoked by purchasing more and more shares on the stock market until he had accumulated enough to control the company. Goldsmith's foray led many to believe that the pill was not unbeatable. After all, they argued, the triggering of the pill had not stopped Goldsmith from taking over Crown

When the pill was first created, there were some who objected to it. One concern was that its introduction would lead to a decline in the company's stock, a concern that proved unfounded. Another concern was the legality of the pill. Indeed, Household International Inc., a consumer finance and manufacturing group, and the second company to adopt Lipton's new pill, was sued by a dissident director, John Moran, challenging the pill's legality. Moran was represented by Joe Flom. Moran and Flom contended in the lawsuit that Household's pill would prevent Household stockholders from deciding on tender offers and would limit proxy contests.

In November 1985, the Delaware Supreme Court upheld the lower court's decision that the pill was legal. The high court noted that "the ultimate response to an actual takeover bid must be judged by the directors' actions at that time, and nothing we say here relieves them of their basic fundamental duties to the corporation and its stockholders." Still, the pill had received its greatest boost to date. Most likely the high court's ruling would be accepted by other courts around the nation, as Delaware's judiciary was so widely respected in this field. Following the Delaware Supreme Court's decision, the pill grew into one of the most popular corporate defenses. By the summer of 1986, over two hundred major corporations had adopted it, most of them in the previous six months. Wachtell, Lipton had advised in fifty of those cases.

Household's pill contained the "flip-over" feature: this entitled stockholders to purchase $200 of an acquirer's stock for $100 in the event of a merger. The pill would be triggered and become nonredeemable when a hostile suitor acquired at least 20 percent in Household or made a tender offer for 30 percent. This was supposed to discourage hostile bids because the cost of doing a second-step merger would rise dramatically. The Delaware Chancery Court upheld the pill, and Flom and Moran appealed the decision.

Zellerbach. Marty Lipton, however, insists that Crown Zellerbach illustrated just the opposite—the effectiveness of the poison pill. Lipton contends that Crown Zellerbach's decision to trigger the pill forced Goldsmith to drop his tender offer of $41 a share, precisely what the pill was designed to do. "It was designed to protect the shareholders of the company in the event that somebody bought control in the open market and then tried to squeeze them out at an unfair price. It performed exactly that function. And indeed the shareholders who did not sell ultimately received $48 or $49 a share which was considerably more than he (Goldsmith) offered in his tender offer."[25] In addition, Goldsmith's experience in dealing with the pill after he triggered it ultimately may have increased the pill's effectiveness by deterring other raiders from repeating the gamble. As of the summer of 1986, Crown Zellerbach was still the only case in which the poison pill had actually been triggered.

An important variation on the pill appeared in the Phillips Petroleum takeover battle against corporate raider Carl Icahn (see Chapter 4), who made his bid in February of 1985. When Boone Pickens had first attacked Phillips, the company had come to Lipton for representation. Lipton had considered the use of the pill, but Phillips had no authorized preferred stock and insufficient authorized but unissued shares of common stock, prerequisites for adopting the pill. Instead, in response to Icahn's bid, Lipton developed a "back-end" pill, which defends against a partial bid by guaranteeing stockholders a back-end price for their shares determined by the board to be a fair price. The Phillips rights would give Phillips stockholders, other than the acquirer, the right to exchange each of their shares for a one-year 15 percent note worth $62; those rights could be exercised only if a Carl Icahn obtained 30 percent of Phillips' shares. The poison pill was never activated; instead Icahn and Phillips came to an agreement which reaped solid financial rewards for him, in return for which he promised not to press on with his takeover bid. The pill had proven its effectiveness: it had deterred Icahn from taking control of Phillips.

The Phillips version of the pill threatens, if invoked, to put the target company in jeopardy of survival. That can trigger a great battle of nerves between the corporation and the raider. After all, the corporation might be merely bluffing, and at the crucial point it might be unwilling to invoke the pill. The raider could not know that, of course. But should the pill be triggered, the raider runs the risk of winning control of a company that is worthless. As a result, the raider must seek ways to pressure the company's board into redeeming the pill. One good example involved Revlon Inc., the cosmetics and health care firm fighting a $1.8 billion takeover offer from Pantry Pride Inc. In August of 1985 Revlon adopted a Phillips-type pill that would permit all stockholders, except for a hostile bidder, such as Pantry Pride, to exchange their shares for debt securities at a premium over the current stock price if a would-be acquirer purchased 30 percent of Revlon's shares. This "suicide pill," as it was dubbed in Revlon's case, would raise Revlon's debt so much that the company's survival seemed in doubt. If the pill were triggered, Revlon would virtually have to be liquidated to retire its huge debt. Pantry Pride was not deterred. Instead, it kept raising its price, responding to competing bids from Forstmann-Little, a leveraged buyout firm. When the price went high enough, Revlon's board redeemed the pill. Thus, the pill failed to prevent Pantry Pride from taking over Revlon. It did, however, succeed in raising the price.

Another variation sought to respond to the fact that the power of the Household-type pill, the flip-over feature, was triggered only when an outsider tried to do a second-step transaction. The problem was this: in Crown Zellerbach's case the flip-over feature did not deter Goldsmith from acquiring a certain percent of the firm and gaining control of the company's board without acquiring the whole company in a second step. Once he gained more than 50 percent of the common stock, Goldsmith was actually able to negotiate a very complicated sale of a number of Crown Zellerbach's assets without triggering the flip-over. This led some to look for a way to put teeth in the pill even if a raider did no more than gobble up shares on the open market, as Goldsmith had done.

A new tactic was devised—not by Marty Lipton, but by others—called the "flip-in" feature. This new device prevents a raider from buying more than a given percentage of the target stock. The flip-over feature takes effect after a stockholder gains a certain amount of stock—usually 20 to 30 percent, but it becomes operative only if the stockholder tries to take over the entire company. The flip-in feature becomes effective not when a tender offer is made, but when a certain amount of stock is accumulated—thus it is considered far more lethal as a deterrent to a raider than the flip-over feature. Different percentages are used, ranging from 25 to 50 percent. The flip-in provision states that if somebody exceeds the threshold, say 25 percent, then all the other stockholders have the right to buy the target company's stock at half price but the acquirer of the 25 percent does not have that right. That causes a very major dilution of the corporate raider's position, making it unlikely that he will exceed the threshold.

The new "flip-in" feature was first tested in December 1985 by Sea-Land Corporation to keep Dallas investor Harold Simmons at bay. The pill, with its flip-in provision, had been put in place after Simmons had acquired 26 percent of the company. He stopped buying shares just before he would have triggered the flip-in provision, which would have occurred if a stockholder acquired 40 percent of the New Jersey shipping concern's common stock. Simmons was still able to acquire a 39.5 percent position, however, making an ultimate sale of the company necessary. Simmons sold his stock to CSX Corporation, which agreed to acquire Sea-Land in a friendly deal for $28 a share or $742 million. By the summer of 1986, over fifty firms had adopted this kind of pill. While the flip-in feature is a potentially effective tool against moves such as Goldsmith's against Crown Zellerbach, Marty Lipton is convinced that it is illegal and that the courts won't uphold it: "It's highly unlikely that the courts will sustain a prohibition on somebody just buying stock in a corporation."[26] And in fact in the early summer of 1986, the Seventh Circuit of Appeals in the *Dynamics Corporation of America v. CTS Corporation* decision said that the flip-in provision was illegal.

But for the time being, managements had a coat of armor that looked like it might last for some time. Marty Lipton was glowing:

> I think the pill has had a major effect in strengthening the target company. It's the only thing that has come along that really gives the board of a target company a voice in the future of the company and a real option as to what should happen.[27]

Corporate raiders appeared impressed with the deterrent value of the pill: they had certainly become less active since its introduction. Whether that was due to the pill or other factors was still not clear. More than likely, if

The impact of the pill and its variations was felt quickly. By the spring of 1986, the advent of the poison pill had clearly slowed up the takeover movement. It had forced managements who wanted to act aggressively to rethink their plans in some cases; it had resulted in a number of friendly mergers that might have been hostile otherwise. The takeover specialists say that the pill can be overcome. They point to Crown Zellerbach. And they point to the General Electric–RCA merger of late 1985, in which General Electric was able to negotiate a friendly transaction with RCA despite the fact that RCA had the pill. Finally, they cite the Revlon case, where Revlon had a pill, but Pantry Pride was still able to take the larger company over though at a far higher price than it had originally proposed. Beyond this, these specialists insist that the real significance of the pill has been to strengthen the backbone of target firms in their negotiations with raiders. In short, the momentum still rests with the raiders. If a raider can come up with an attractive offer, especially one based on cash, he will triumph over all devices, including the pill. So while the pill has made the process more difficult, it has not stopped takeovers. In the words of Joe Flom: "I think you will find that it (the pill) will be about as important psychologically as the Maginot Line was and probably ultimately just as effective."[28]

pills continued to serve as useful deterrents, raiders would look to innovations that would effectively neutralize them. For the time being, the pills were the rage.

Chapter 9

*"Captain Outrageous" And The Fight
For CBS*

Ted Turner. Courtesy Kelly Mills/TBS.

Thomas H. Wyman. Courtesy CBS, Inc.

Ted Turner, the maverick television mogul from Atlanta, had thrown down the gauntlet in 1983, revealing his dreams and ambitions to everyone. "I'd like to get my hands on a network. I'd like to be the big guy for a while."

So Ted Turner wanted to run one of the big American television networks. It was a nice ambition. Ordinarily, however, given Turner's dwarflike size in the industry, such thoughts would have been dismissed without much ado.

But by 1985, large enterprises had already had their share of experiences with raiders—many in the same "dwarf" category as Ted Turner—who wanted to be the "big guy for a while." Those enterprises had increasingly erected solid defenses, learning to use the courts, to make themselves less attractive as takeover targets—in short, to fight.

The battle between Ted Turner and CBS in 1985 was a prominent example of how the major corporations had stopped spinning their wheels, stopped giving in to the raiders, and begun to fight back—no matter how difficult the effort, no matter how large a price had to be paid. If the early 1980s was the era of capitulation, when large companies buckled easily under the pressure of the corporate raiders, by 1985 the watchword had become defense.

Maybe someone should have told Ted Turner about the anger building up in corporate America against the schemes of the raiders. Maybe someone should have advised him that, although the David and Goliath tale might have garnered sympathy for a corporate David a few years ago, in the mid-1980s all that was changing. Little sympathy was left over for the raider after managements had been forced to swallow their pride, after all the greenmailing, and after the courts had started to support managements more decidedly. Sympathy might not be on the side of Goliath, either. But no one warned Turner that in challenging CBS, the great giant of the air waves, he would be moving against a managerial Goliath willing to do almost anything to keep a raider at bay. The word coming from Black Rock, as CBS headquarters was known, was to be as immovable and unshakeable as possible—and to fight to the very end.

One CBS executive expressed it aptly. CBS's plan for anyone who tried to win control was "to make him sorry he ever got up in the morning."[1] Tom Wyman, the Chairman and Chief Executive Officer of CBS and the man who would lead the campaign against Ted Turner, reflected the venom and the new-found aggressiveness in corporate management. What should one do about prospective raiders? he was asked. "You ought to reflexively bite their ankle," he said unhesitatingly.[2]

There would be a lot of "biting of ankles" at CBS as the year 1985 progressed. For suddenly, the huge American television networks, bastions of permanence and strength, were showing signs of the same torpor and vulnerability that other big corporations in America were experiencing. In March, Capital Cities Communications Inc., one-quarter the size of its target, acquired ABC for over $3.5 billion. That marked the first time that one of the three major American networks had changed hands since 1953, when Leonard H. Goldenson's United Paramount Theaters merged with a young network to create the modern ABC. But that had been a friendly merger. The major networks remained immune to the phenomenon of hostile takeovers. With that historical record as seeming proof that the communication giants could not fall against their will, CBS felt safe.

But how long would it last?

In January of 1985, a group calling itself Fairness In Media, endorsed by North Carolina Senator Jesse Helms, declared that it would try to win control of CBS to rid the network of its supposed liberal bias. Political conservatives would be encouraged to buy CBS stock in anticipation of a proxy fight.

Then in February, Ted Turner let on that he had designs on CBS.

Ted Turner.

He was a financial wizard who had done some startling things in Atlanta, taking a run-down local television station and turning it into an impressive money-earner with programming that attracted a national audience. He had also founded Cable News Network and created something of a revolution in television in the 1980s. From his early days he had looked for new worlds to conquer. In time, he would get around to CBS.

It was no wonder that CBS had begun to attract outsiders. There was a common feeling that the large American networks were undervalued— that, whatever troubles they were experiencing, with good management they could be back on their feet. If this was true in general for the networks, it was particularly so at CBS. When Tom Wyman took over the reins at CBS in June 1980, it was a $4 billion conglomerate going through a decline. Into the 1960s the network had been a money-winner, dating back to its inception 50 years earlier. But lately there had been problems with its properties. After paying too high a price to purchase the New York Yankees baseball franchise, CBS lost money on the deal. Fawcett Books was losing millions of dollars; CBS Records showed little sign of breaking out of its downward spin. The same was true of the CBS chain of stores which sold high-fidelity sound equipment. Even CBS-TV, the crown jewel of the conglomerate which accounted for 60 percent of the company's profits, was in the midst of a slide, feeling the new competition from cable television and the independent stations.

Nothing seemed to work at CBS. When Tom Wyman succeeded John Backe as President and Chief Executive Officer, he was the fifth president of the corporation in only nine years, and the third in under four years.

Wyman himself appeared something of an odd choice. By his own acknowledgement, "I haven't had any broadcast experience, or publishing or toy-business experience, and I don't know much about music."[3] If he had no special expertise in CBS enterprises, Wyman did possess good credentials as a generalist, which was what appealed to Bill Paley, the CBS chairman. Even the fact that Wyman had been an English major at Amherst College (Amherst, Massachusetts), and not a Harvard M.B.A., added to his luster. Wyman came to CBS from the Pillsbury Corporation in Minneapolis, where he had been vice-chairman. Prior to that he had been President and Chief Executive Officer of the Jolly Green Giant Corporation, which Pillsbury had acquired in 1979. He had spent ten years at the Polaroid Corporation as well, rising to the number 2 position in the company at age 42. *Time* magazine included him in its list of America's 200 future leaders in 1974. It was right. When the offer from CBS came, it was too good to pass up: he would be paid $800,000 a year for three years plus a $1 million bonus. Some suggested nastily that CBS seemed to be buying a major league baseball star.

Wyman's strategy, in taking over the flagging CBS, was to shed the money-losing parts of the corporation and search for new profitable enterprises: he closed down the CBS record plant in Terre Haute, Indiana, firing 1250 workers; he sold Fawcett Books. The television network, CBS's mainstay, needed beefing up: so he invested $150 million to upgrade news broadcasting and daytime shows; he also moved news shows into prime-time slots. The strategy at CBS-TV worked: prime-time ratings for the 1982–83 seasons rose. In March 1981 Wyman established CBS Theatrical Films, but when that lost $10 million he dropped the project. He spent $58 million to acquire Ideal Toys, the company that produced the famous Rubik's Cube. In the early 1980s CBS's broadcasting income more than made up for the poor performance of the records group. But in 1984 a phenomenon named Michael Jackson struck the country: his hit record "Thriller" on the CBS label brought in $8 million. Wall Street appeared to like what Wyman was doing. CBS stock rose from a low of $33 to $53. When Bill Paley announced that he was retiring as chairman as of April 20, 1983, Tom Wyman was appointed to succeed him.

With its stock low, with the corporation clearly undervalued, with so many small or medium-sized companies going after the Big Guys, CBS looked increasingly like a takeover target. Though never a serious threat, Fairness in Media's bid in early 1985 put the idea on the table: under the right conditions CBS might be a suitable target. If Jesse Helms could not become Dan Rather's boss, he did at least focus attention on CBS's stock price, which was far below the value of the corporation's assets. (CBS had sales in 1984 of $4.9 billion.) The Fairness in Media campaign against CBS did little to push Black Rock into a defensive posture. Indeed in February, the CBS board chose not to introduce antitakeover measures, such as staggering the terms of directors; it feared that stockholders would say no when the annual meeting was held on April 17. And in forcing the stockholders to take a stand, the board was concerned that it would be focusing attention on CBS's potential vulnerability, something Wyman and his colleagues obviously did not want to do. CBS did bring a lawsuit against the Fairness in Media group in March in order to delay its obtaining a list of CBS shareholders—a minor triumph that kept the conservative organization from turning to stockholders in time for the April 17 meeting.

All of this was but a ripple in the water compared to what would happen in the wake of the announcement on March 18 that Capital Cities Communications had acquired ABC. Upon hearing of this deal, Ted Turner sensed that the monoliths in the communications industry were not as immovable as they appeared. He sensed that it might now be possible to turn his long-standing dream of owning a major network into reality. It would not be easy. The very fact that ABC had been acquired meant that one of the major players had been eliminated as a potential takeover target. That left only two others: RCA, the parent of NBC, and CBS. Of the two, RCA seemed far too large to be taken over. That left only CBS.

If the press reports during the spring of 1985 were to be believed, Turner was prowling for financial partners to aid him in his big move. Among the names mentioned as potential Turner allies were William Simon, the former Treasury Secretary, and MCI Communications. Turner was also reported to have turned to Drexel Burnham Lambert as well as Shearson Lehman Brothers, the two important investment banking firms, to arrange financing for a CBS takeover. But no one was talking; no one was confirming the Turner approaches.

The idea that Ted Turner would make a run on CBS appeared laughable to many inside and outside CBS. How could someone entertain such far-fetched thoughts, especially such an outsider as Mr. Turner? Who would bankroll him? How could he do it? Yet Turner had worked miracles before, and that alone was enough to give pause at Black Rock. Nonetheless, it looked on the surface totally preposterous. Turner Broadcasting, the backbone of Ted Turner's empire, had 1984 sales of only $300 million, a dwarf compared to the CBS giant. Still, the rumors persisted. Turner was talking to financiers. Turner was going to make a bid for CBS. The speculation had a way of feeding upon itself. In time, whether it liked it or not, CBS was in play. And all this talk had a positive effect on the company's stock, it rose $4, moving to $88.50.

It was time for the barriers to go up at Black Rock.

Tom Wyman took the Turner threat seriously. He began regular Wednesday strategy meetings. His colleagues were expected to report on everything they heard in order to plan, plot, devise strategy. The point was this: CBS would not give in. It would not allow Ted Turner, or any other corporate raider, to mow down the corporation. The era when the raiders could do their thing, accumulate stock, build up enough of a stake to become a genuine threat, were over, as far as Wyman was concerned. CBS had history going for it, it had size going for it, and it would use those assets if need be. Tom Wyman was on the phone to investment bankers to say that he would appreciate their not lending a hand to Ted Turner's war against CBS. Who was Ted Turner after all? Wyman knew that he was operating from strength: he had Dan Rather and Michael Jackson on his side; and if necessary he would bring them into the act. The whole of America knew Dan Rather's handsome face and friendly, authoritative voice, beamed to millions of Americans on the CBS nightly news at 7 P.M. He was not just an anchorman. He was an American institution. And Michael Jackson? This was a legend. How could CBS lose with an institution and a legend on its side? Wyman would fight. Word was passed quietly that if Mr. Turner or anyone else thought they could just walk in and acquire a Dan Rather or a Michael Jackson, they were wrong; CBS had ways of stopping them. For one, Wyman might rip up the contracts of stars like Rather and Jackson. New ones would be drawn that would contain provisions calling for them to be broken if management changed hands. Try and take us over, Mr. Turner, just try.

The barriers were going up at CBS. In early April the board decided to eliminate a bylaw that had enabled holders of 10 percent of CBS stock to call special stockholders' meetings; after the change only certain board members could call such a meeting. In addition, CBS took a $1.5 billion line of credit that could be used to finance the acquisitions of companies and thus make CBS less attractive to a takeover raider.

As CBS was erecting those barriers, trouble came from an unexpected source. On April 1, just three days after it had stopped the Fairness in Media group in its tracks, CBS learned that the king of Wall Street's arbitragers, Ivan F. Boesky (see Chapter 7), had disclosed that he now owned 8.7 percent of CBS. Incredibly, he had become the largest CBS stockholder without anyone's taking much notice; Bill Paley, whose name had become synonymous with CBS, owned only 6.5 percent. Beginning on February 8, Boesky had paid $247 million for his 2.6 million shares, purchasing them at an average cost of $95 a share. On April 1, the day Boesky ended this round of buying, the stock was selling for $108 a share. The Fairness in Media move had most likely led Boesky to believe that CBS might soon be in play. Occasionally the mere fact that Boesky was expressing interest in a company could be enough to turn a company into ripe pickings for a corporate raider.

Though Boesky insisted that he had no plans to seek control of CBS—and indeed it was not his style to raid corporations—the mere fact that he, an outsider, had become CBS's largest stockholder, meant that Boesky might align himself with some other force, and together they could make a bid for the corporation. Or he could play the greenmail game, though again that was not Boesky's style. As long as Boesky continued to say that he was interested in boosting CBS's stock price, the management would have to assume that he might try to do so by luring another bidder into the game. This would not bode well for CBS. It was time to take action against Ivan Boesky.

CBS filed suit in U.S. District Court in Manhattan against him, hoping perhaps, though it did not say so at the time, that the legal action would force Boesky to leave CBS alone. The network charged Boesky with making false and misleading statements to the Securities and Exchange Commission regarding the way he had financed his CBS stock purchases. Specifically, it charged that his borrowings to purchase the stock went beyond the 50 percent limit set by securities regulations. By exceeding the borrowing maximum, Boesky was taking undue financial risks that might cause CBS's stock to plunge, according to the CBS accusations. Furthermore, CBS accused Boesky of contradicting his avowed claim that his only motive in buying CBS stock was to encourage its upward climb. If that had been the case, why then had Boesky tried on March 27 to sell his stake back to CBS at $105 a share, presumably netting him a handsome profit? And, CBS asked, if Boesky truly supported CBS management, as he said he did, why then did he turn to other investors, checking whether they might be interested in buying his stake? CBS was referring to conversations between Boesky and Ted Turner as well as other unidentified parties. The lawsuit caused a loss of nerve on Wall Street. CBS stock fell nearly 10 points on April 10, the day after the suit was brought.

On April 17 the CBS stockholders met. Tom Wyman was in a fighting mood: "Those who seek to gain control of CBS in order to gain control of CBS News threaten its independence, its integrity—and this country." Strong words. But then again, Wyman may well have known what was in store for him.

Ted Turner was about to make his move. "These networks need to be gotten into the hands of people who care about this country," he had said in 1984 in a speech before the National Conservative Foundation. Yet, was he the man to do it—the man they had called "turbulent Ted" and "Captain Outrageous," the man known unaffectionately in parts of the media as "the mouth of the south"? Unquestionably, he was an underrated figure, especially by those who had not followed his career until then.

"Fame," Ted Turner had once said, "is like love. You can never have too much of it."[4] He seemed driven by a need for popularity and respect, a sense of being recognized. By the time he had made his mark and was on its cover in 1982, *Time* noted that "Ted Turner . . . is a prototypical modern celebrity, famous above all for being famous."[5] Overcoming the obstacles as he did, Ted Turner decided along the way that he would go for it all, whatever that was. In *Time*'s words again, "He is perhaps the most openly ambitious man in America."[6] Turner himself thought the word that explained him best was not ambitious, but rather, tenacious, as one of his yachts was called. He had to be tenacious to achieve what he had and to overcome his difficult childhood.

He was born Robert Edward Turner 3rd in Cincinnati on November 19, 1938. His relationship with his father, Ed Turner, was problematic. It began when Ted was 6 years old: his father had gone off to the Gulf of Mexico on a Navy job during World War II. He took his wife and his daughter, Mary Jane, but, for some unexplained reason, he left Ted behind in a boarding school in Cincinnati. His father moved the family from Cincinnati to Savannah when Ted was 9, part of a game plan to build up his billboard business, the Turner Advertising Company. Ted was sent off to Georgia Military Academy just outside Atlanta. The last entrant in his class, he came six weeks late. He also attended the McCallie School in Chattanooga, Tennessee.

There were some happy moments during childhood. Never much of an athlete, Ted took up sailing. For his twelfth birthday his father presented him with an 11-foot Penguin class catboat. The sport of racing thrilled the boy; he would take great risks, but at this early point in his career as a sailor, he usually found himself among the losers. The Capsize Kid, they called him.

Nowhere is it explained what motivated Ted's father to act as he did, but whatever the reason, he appeared to treat the youngster more like a new recruit to boot camp than a loving son. There was the wire coathanger used to get the boy's "attention," as Ted once recalled; there was the time Ed charged the boy rent for using his parents' home during summer vacations; or the occasion when his father gave him a Lightning-class sailboat, then insisted that Ted share in the cost even though it would mean that the youngster would have to spend every last penny of his savings.

Ted represented McCallie at the Tennessee state high school debating contest when he was 17. He liked history and the classics, and said: "As a kid I was a little bit of an artist and a poet. I painted and sculpted a little, but it was too slow-moving for me to really get into. But the whole idea of grand things always turned me on—the grand idea of building the Parthenon (or) the Pyramids."[7]

Ted hoped to attend the U.S. Naval Academy at Annapolis, but his father rejected the idea: he wanted his son to become an Ivy Leaguer and to study business. But Harvard said no, and so Ted went to Brown University, where he studied the Greek classics, a choice that sent Ed Turner into a rage. "I am appalled, even horrified, that you have adopted classics as a major," he wrote his son. "I am a practical man, and for the life of me I cannot possibly understand why you should wish to speak Greek." The elder Turner, who divorced Ted's mother while Ted was in college, added that he had found Plato and Aristotle mere time-wasters since they deliberated so much. "I think you are rapidly becoming a jackass," he concluded in his letter to his son, "and the sooner you get out of that filthy atmosphere, the better it will suit me."[8] One indication of how strongly Ted felt about that diatribe: he turned the letter over to the Brown University newspaper, which went ahead and published it!

Still, Ed Turner proved persuasive. Ted switched majors—from classics to economics. Meanwhile he did well at sailing and debating. Ted won his first nine regattas on the college dinghy circuit. One summer he had a chance to race in a fleet of Lightning boats when the Noroton (Connecticut) Yacht Club offered him a summer job; his father, however, demanded that he spend his summers working for the family billboard business, which by then was established in several cities in the South. Accepting his father's edict, Ted worked as an account executive with the flagship company in Savannah. Returning to Brown, Turner once again landed in trouble, breaking the rules that disallowed women in the rooms. He was suspended, and then not asked back. A summer cruise with the Coast Guard followed. Then in 1980 he joined his father in his billboard business.

A millionaire by the time Ted was in his 20s, Ed Turner nurtured in his son a desire to succeed. He taught him the business inside out, and all about business in general. Ted worried that he might fail, might not attain the kind of achievements his father had. His younger sister Mary Jane had died after a five-year battle with lupus erythematosus. Ted was 20 years old when she died. He was now the only child. From this point on the spotlight in the family beamed on him exclusively.

Ed Turner grew increasingly despondent. Perhaps the loss of his daughter was a key factor, or perhaps it was his business, which had incurred large debts. He had bought into the General Outdoor Advertising Company, largest in the country, which had a base in Atlanta. But by early 1963, overextended, Ed decided to sell out; he may have been further depressed by Ted's opposition to this step. Whatever the reason, Ed went to his plantation in South Carolina on March 5, 1963, and shot himself.

Ted, now 24 years old, decided that the family billboard business would be better off if he could cancel the sale his father had just put through. He employed every device in the book, luring away workers from the Atlanta division to the Macon, Georgia, division; moving contracts between companies; threatening to destroy financial records. He convinced the purchasers they would be better off canceling the deal in exchange for a $200,000 payment. Ted found the means to make the payment, and the new deal was concluded.

Turner built up the billboard business to greater heights than his father had. This gave him time for his greatest love, world-class sailing. He would be away from home months at a time. He had married, and the marriage would last 20 years, producing two children. He was to have three more children by a second marriage.

At age 30, Ted Turner took up broadcasting. In time he would become a giant in the cable television business. Against the counsel of his financial advisers he traded $2.5 million worth of stock in his billboard firm and bought Atlanta's Channel 17. No wonder his advisers were howling: a UHF station at a time when few viewers could pick up UHF signals, Channel 17 was losing $600,000 a year. Ted began by screening inexpensive reruns, old movies, and sports. But then he had a flash of genius: he would expand the audience many times by beaming the station's signal via satellite to cable-television systems all around the United States. In effect he would be creating a new network that he hoped would appeal to advertisers. In December 1976 the "Superstation" was created; Turner called WTCG-TV "the Super Station that Serves the Nation"; and imitators soon appeared in Chicago (WGN-TV) and New York City (WOR-TV). The station showed mostly reruns and sports; in 1981 it garnered $18 million in profit and it was on its way. Turner's station moved into 34 million homes by 1986.

Turner obtained the right to broadcast the Atlanta Braves games; when this proved exceedingly popular, he decided the only way to keep the profitless Braves in Atlanta was for him to purchase them, which he did in 1976. (In early 1977, Turner appointed himself manager of his last-place team; but the Commissioner, Bowie Kuhn, found this unamusing and kicked him out of uniform after one day.) Also in 1976, Turner bought the Atlanta Hawks basketball team. At the time both teams were the worst in their respective sports. He also put money behind a soccer team, which eventually became defunct; he carried their games on the station that would become WTBS.

In the 1970s television news was not something in which Turner was very interested. He thought that the major networks played up bad news too much and had been outraged at their Vietnam coverage. If he could have, he might have shown the country some good news, but because of his limited news budget, his only news programs were at 3 A.M. That policy changed in 1980 when Turner created Cable News Network (CNN). He became a firm believer in the value of TV news, proclaiming himself someone who would communicate and bring people together by informing them about such issues as disarmament, pollution, and population control. CNN would not make a profit until 1985. Prior to that it weathered some major financial problems: it suffered from competition from the Satellite

News Channel which ABC had begun, as well as from Westinghouse Electric. Turner Broadcasting finally purchased Satellite News for $25 million and took it off the air.

Sailing remained a passion of his. Turner went after the top yachting prize, the America's Cup; he lost it in 1974 but won it three years later. Winning earned him immense popularity. Few seemed bothered when he showed up at his press conference drunk. In August 1979 he entered the Fastnet Race, named for the Fastnet Rock off the south tip of Ireland. Of the 306 boats which began the race only 87 finished, as 40-foot waves, churned up by 65-knot winds, turned the Irish Sea into a whirlwind. Turner won the race which resulted in a major tragedy for other contestants: the storm took 15 lives and caused $4.5 million in damages to yachts. Afterward, Turner remarked to his British hosts that they should be thankful for the bad storms, despite the calamity which had just occurred. Had there been no storms in the sixteenth century, the Spanish Armada might have reached British shores, and everyone in Britain would be speaking Spanish today!

On April 19, 1985, Ted Turner made his bid for CBS. He held a press conference in Manhattan and announced that he would try to take over the network. Turner had combined clever financial maneuvering with raw nerve. CBS stockholders were asked to exchange their shares for some Turner Broadcasting System Inc. stock and high-yield, high-risk junk bonds with a total value of $5.41 billion. Turner said the offer amounted to $175 a share, but others thought it closer to $125. He then walked the twelve blocks to the Madison Avenue office of the law firm he had hired. Taking the walk, rather than driving, was seen as Turner's way of thumbing his nose at those who doubted he could pull off the takeover. Why this was so, no one could explain. But Turner got a lot of publicity out of the stroll.

The news that Turner was about to raid CBS did not exactly delight the people at Black Rock. Turner was an outsider, an upstart. It was true that he had built up his own little television empire, but he had done so far from New York. So his efforts, though impressive, hardly counted to the New York financial community. What was more, Turner's moralizing turned the people in New York off. He sounded all too much like the Fairness in Media people, promising, as he did, to improve the quality and objectivity of CBS's programming, insisting that he would get rid of the sleaze and stupidity and violence, as he had preached. One public relations figure told me that if ever there was someone who needed a public relations campaign to try to change his image, it was Ted Turner.

It was hardly surprising that the stalwarts at CBS would not welcome

Ted with open arms. "I have yet to come across anybody at CBS News who has the slightest desire to work for Turner," said Mike Wallace, the "60 Minutes" correspondent. "No one takes him seriously."[9] Walter Cronkite, the former CBS anchorman, added, "CBS News has achieved the greatest credibility. It would be terrible to change all that."

But how could Turner succeed? Although he had talked about staging a takeover of CBS, no one could figure out where Turner would get the cash, where would he raise the $4 or $5 billion it would take. Certainly not from his Turner Broadcasting. True, the company had earned profits for the past two years, $10 million in 1984 and $7 million in 1983. But its revenues were small compared to the $224.5 million CBS earned in 1983 and the $281.7 million in 1984. Still, some who insisted that the deal could not be done reminded themselves that Ted Turner had been written off in the past—too quickly. Nonetheless, Wall Street appeared to take the Turner offer as some kind of bad joke. Whereas the stock of a targeted company will routinely enjoy a steep rise after a bid is made, CBS's stock went up only $3.25 after the offer—to $107.

At first glance Turner had much going against him. For one thing, the experts thought CBS stock should have been valued at between $220 and $240, so his offer was way too low. For another, he was offering CBS no cash: indeed, stockholders were in effect being asked to pay for the deal with CBS's own money. Turner planned to sell off parts of the company after the takeover, including all thirteen radio stations CBS owned and one of the five CBS-owned TV stations. He was contemplating selling the CBS/Records Group or its publishing division as well.

CBS had chosen not to erect the kind of defense that might have deterred an offer such as Turner's. While other companies would turn increasingly in 1985 to such avowed deterrents as the "poison pill," CBS was not prepared to take such drastic action. But, once the Turner offer was made, CBS was determined to stop him—even at a very heavy price. There were rumors galore that CBS was about to take a white knight into its embrace. Time Inc. was mentioned, as was General Electric. But it soon became manifest that CBS had no plans to sell out to anyone, friend or foe. It would fight Turner in every way that it could to keep the status quo. Three days after Turner's offer was made public, the CBS board of directors turned it down unanimously. "Grossly inadequate," was its angry reply. That was just the start. The board fought Turner in the courts, charging him with materially misstating the earnings of Turner Broadcasting in 1983 and 1984. That was an important ploy, for CBS wanted to show that Turner would not be able to service the debt on the securities that Turner Broadcasting planned to issue in the merger. Tom Wyman employed another ploy: he let on that he thought Turner unfit morally to run the network.

The first important triumph for CBS in its campaign against Turner had to do with Ivan Boesky. The CBS lawsuit against Boesky was still pending, and now CBS realized it had an ace it could play. Perhaps sensing that Ted Turner's offer was going nowhere, Boesky decided to cut his holdings in CBS stock by nearly half to 4.3 percent. Between April 8 and 19, the day Turner made his offer for CBS, Boesky sold 1.3 million CBS shares earning $142.7 million; that gave him a profit of $16.7 million. Negotiating with the arbitrager, the board agreed that it would drop its lawsuit against Boesky if he would pledge in turn not to increase his stake in the company. Boesky, of course, had good reason to come to terms with CBS. By getting the network to drop the lawsuit, he extricated himself from an unpleasant legal tiff and he could claim that he had been exonerated. For its part, CBS was heartened by the knowledge that Boesky could no longer threaten to join forces with anyone, Ted Turner included, to make a serious bid for the network. Wall Street took little notice of the CBS-Boesky settlement when it was announced on May 3: CBS's stock closed at $108.76, up $2.

In keeping with its plan to pull out all the stops to defend itself, CBS rallied 'round the flag a wide assortment of groups, some acting out of affection for CBS, some out of hostility toward Ted Turner. Their motives were of no great interest to the CBS board. The effect was the same. Such organizations as the National Organization for Women and the United Church of Christ expressed sympathy for the network. The Hispanic National Association voiced the view that Turner had "demonstrated an insensitivity for blacks, Hispanics, women and Jews." Some one hundred CBS affiliates rushed in with notice of their support as well.

The battle moved into high gear during the summer months. In June of 1985 CBS petitioned the FCC to stop Turner's bid. By mid-July, Turner himself had filed with the FCC, detailing his plans should he succeed in the takeover bid: he planned to break up CBS, something many suspected for quite some time. He would sell for cash all of the operating parts of the corporation as a way of getting his hands on the network and four television stations: WCBS in New York; KCBS in Los Angeles; WBBM in Chicago; and KMOX in St. Louis. Just as CBS charged, Turner would generate $4.5 billion in debt. Turner had no regrets; CBS called it a "death spiral."

No stockholder wanted to push CBS into that spiral. Had the Turner offer been a better one, say for cash, then a deal might have been possible. While the experts valued the stock at $220 to $240 a share, some said they would take $150 a share—if it were a cash offer. Few gave Turner a fighting chance in early summer. Perhaps another buyer might come along, sniffing the scent of weakness at Black Rock.

CBS's executives could convince themselves that Ted Turner was not the problem, but they could not convince themselves that they did not have a problem, a more fundamental one than Turner presented.

CBS needed something more decisive, more effective. The statements of support were helpful; the attacks on Turner's character surely made it more difficult for him to succeed. Yet, what was missing was the knockout blow. But what could CBS do? It could do what Phillips Petroleum had done: tender for several billion dollars' worth of its own stock, adding so much debt that no one would be attracted to the company. It could sell off a piece of itself to a friendly buyer, again to look much less attractive to a raider. Or, CBS could buy back 40 to 50 percent of its stock from the public, say, at $140 a share; then resell 20 percent of that to a white knight. Add that 20 percent to the 6.7 percent already owned by Bill Paley, and CBS would have a guaranteed safety net to repel any Ted Turner. While the ideas sounded terribly seductive—they were designed to save CBS, nothing less—each one had a catch. The bosses at Black Rock would have gone on record as being interested in adding to CBS's burdens in order to keep management intact, in order to stave off outside forces. There was a great unknown: how would the stockholders react?

The stockholders would have to go along. Tom Wyman realized there was little choice. The alternative would be to invite trouble, not necessarily from Ted Turner—no, he could be handled—but from others, yet unidentified, lurking out there in the corporate night, waiting to see how CBS would react to the man from Atlanta. If the barriers did not go up against Ted Turner, surely they would not go up against other, more sturdy foes. The Ted Turner bid was a test case for CBS. The entire financial world was watching.

A decision was taken at CBS in July to put through a measure that would all but assure the removal of Ted Turner from the battleground. The board would offer to buy 21 percent of CBS's stock at $150 a share. That represented a $955 million total purchase price. Wyman broke the news to stock analysts in the Manhattan studio where "As the World Turns," a daytime soap opera, was once filmed. This was another kind of soap opera, but unlike "World," which went on and on, this might have a quick ending. CBS would pay stockholders $40 a share in cash; plus $110 in ten-year securities that would pay 10.875 percent annual interest. CBS would pay in other ways too: its debt, $386 million in 1984, would rise to $1.3 billion. Wyman declared that CBS would be selling some $300 million in assets, but it would not remove itself from the broadcasting, records, or publishing end of the business. A goal of trimming $20 million in corporate fat was announced as well, the most painful part for CBS employees. The CBS defensive scheme was put into action in midsummer. Naturally, the stockholders were wild about it. Suddenly their shares, which had been valued at just $82.38 the previous March, had zoomed up to $150 a share. Thank you, Ted Turner!

As for Ted, he had plowed $15 million of his own money into the takeover bid, taking profits from his "Superstation" and placing them in the war chest for his latest campaign. Upon hearing the news that CBS had erected its Big Barrier, Turner must have been disheartened. He didn't show it. Instead, all he would say was, "We believe that our offer . . . is far more attractive . . . and we intend to pursue it vigorously."[11] He could pursue it all right, but it would not be easy. By early August he was acknowledging that it had become "very, very difficult, if not impossible" to finalize his takeover offer, and only if he were to win the support of the FCC and the courts did he have a chance.[12] But both institutions said no to Turner: his challenges to block the network's buy-back plan went nowhere. As the summer came to an end, and Turner realized he was no longer in the fight, he talked about staging a proxy fight the following spring at the next annual meeting; or he might try to come up with the financing necessary to make a cash bid for CBS. No one gave these new ideas much chance.

The CBS battle for survival would prove costly, terribly costly to CBS. To finance the 21 percent stock buy-back, CBS would have to nearly double the interest it was paying to borrow money for the fourth quarter of 1985— from $22.2 million to $40.8 million. For all of 1984, its interest payments jumped from $50 million to $117.1 million. There was some maddening lesson to be learned in all this, but executives at Black Rock had little time to undertake any postgame assessments. In early August came word from the upper echelons at CBS that it was time to pay the piper. About 2,000 employees—or fully 7 percent of the workforce, would be given incentives to retire early. Rather than wait for normal retirement at age 62, employees who were at least 55 years old and had 10 years pension credit would qualify for significantly higher pension benefits. CBS figured that this move would save $7 million a year. In November 1985 CBS closed its toy, computer software, and theatrical film businesses. It reported its first quarterly loss—$114.1 million—since the first days of the company in the 1930s.

Sensing that its troubles were not entirely over, even with Ted Turner effectively stymied, CBS took one more precautionary step in the fall. Tom Wyman had had some discussion with Laurence Tisch of Loews Corporation over the summer. Tisch is the billionaire chairman of Loews, the New York-based conglomerate which owns a hotel chain, sells insurance, and manufactures Kent cigarettes as well as Bulova watches. Tisch himself was all New York establishment: Chairman of the New York University Board of Trustees; a leading supporter of the Metropolitan Museum of Art; a major force behind the Federation of Jewish Philanthropies. The Tisch empire began in 1946 when Laurence and his brother Preston, the President of Loews, borrowed money from their parents to buy Laurel-in-the-Pines, a resort hotel in Lakewood, N.J. By 1955 they owned twelve hotels; in 1960 they purchased control of Loews Theaters. They also gained control of CNA Insurance and Lorillard Tobacco. Their company eventually had $12.5 billion in assets. The personal fortune of the two brothers has been estimated at $1.7 billion each.[13]

The offices of Tisch and Wyman were right around the corner from each other in Manhattan. The two men reached a tacit agreement that if CBS really got into trouble from the Turner bid or another one, it could turn to Loews to discuss a friendly deal. Tisch began accumulating CBS stock in July. By the fall Wyman and Tisch had joined forces on a plan. This was not the plan they had discussed during the early part of the summer—a friendly merger. It fell far short of that. Rather, the plan envisaged keeping control in the board's hands without a hostile takeover. CBS decided to place a large block of its stock in friendly hands, asking Laurence Tisch to raise Loews' stake to as much as 25 percent from its current 11.7 percent level. This tactic had an appropriate name: it was dubbed the "white squire" defense. White knights come in and buy companies; white squires do the next best thing, buying up large blocks of stock. Some risks are involved in turning to a white squire: if he should want to buy the entire company, he would have a great advantage; for he might be able to win control without having to pay a premium simply by virtue of his friendship with management. As the *Wall Street Journal* wrote, "Without spending a dime on lawyers or investment bankers, Laurence A. Tisch may have accomplished what Ted Turner and an $18 million roster of takeover advisers couldn't do: de facto control of CBS Inc."[14]

But CBS had no such worries about Larry Tisch. CBS was quite up front about the whole thing. Seeking an alliance with Larry Tisch was, in the words of CBS Vice President William Liley III, "a mutual love affair. We want this guy. We welcome this guy."[15]

Tisch had already benefited from CBS's takeover woes: as a result of the 21 percent buy-back he had sold a fourth of Loews holdings in CBS at what was described as a "nice" profit. Tisch declared that he had no intention of running for the CBS board or of interfering in its operations. Nor would he buy more than 25 percent of CBS stock. He would be glad to lend his advice and expertise to the network, and that was all. So CBS would not become another piece of the Tisch empire. Though he had once vowed that he would not join the CBS board, in November of 1985 Tisch did just that. If he had wanted, he could have joined forces with a corporate raider and given CBS a scare. But he displayed no such intentions.

Immediately after realizing that his bid for CBS was going nowhere, Ted Turner set his eye on the movie business, negotiating to purchase MGM/UA Entertainment Company for $1.5 billion. Unlike CBS, MGM/UA was in need of a rich uncle, and it welcomed Turner's offer. A condition of the sale was that Turner would recoup one-third of the purchase price right away by spinning off United Artists for $490 million; he would sell it back to financier Kirk Kerkorian, who owned 50.1 percent of MGM/UA's stock.

Once it was trimmed, United Artists would have little in assets other than its film library. But MGM, in contrast, would have its film and television production and distribution operations, which included 24 sound stages on its 44-acre Culver City lot; it would also have its library of 2,200 films, among which were *Gone With the Wind*, *The Wizard of Oz*, and *Singin' in the Rain*. By owning his own studio for entertainment programming, Turner would have something that resembled a network, compensation for not getting a hold of CBS. WTBS-TV would have direct access to some programming, thanks to the new acquisition, and it could then avoid expensive bidding competitions.

In the following months—through the winter of 1985 and 1986—CBS continued to be subject to takeover rumors as well as the target of one actual takeover bid. Laurence Tisch's actions with regard to his CBS stock raised speculation every time he made a move. In early February of 1986 Loews had raised its stake in CBS—then at 11.9 percent—to 12.3 percent. CBS's stock rose 20 points during one four-day period on the strength of rumors that Tisch might be readying himself for a takeover of CBS. The only fly in the ointment was CBS itself: Wyman and his colleagues seemed genuinely interested in getting Tisch to raise his stake to the 25 percent level spoken of the previous October.

Also that month came the first overture from Marvin Davis, the 60-year-old Denver oil man and ex-owner of Twentieth Century Fox Film Corporation. He offered Tom Wyman $150 a share for CBS. The answer was no. Davis came back a month later with a second, better offer: an all-cash bid of $160 a share worth $3.75 billion. Once again CBS turned him down. Although this was an all-cash offer, the kind the stockholders might have been hoping to get from Ted Turner the previous summer, CBS's management clearly felt strong enough to rebuff Davis without worrying too much about the distress the stockholders might feel. Davis hoped to reestablish his prestige in Hollywood. He had bought Twentieth Century Fox in 1981 but sold it to Rupert Murdoch, the press magnate, in 1985: Davis earned a $325 million profit from the sale. Davis might have tried for a hostile takeover at this point, but he decided against it, saying that he was too old for that kind of thing. What the Davis bid made clear was that CBS was still in the eyes of Wall Street a most desirable property, the "vanity stock of the decade," in the words of one broadcasting executive.

Not surprisingly, one week after the rejection of Marvin Davis, Loews raised its stake in CBS from 12.3 percent to 16.7 percent. This appeared to remove a takeover threat from another seemingly interested duo, the reclusive Fisher brothers, Lawrence and Zachary. Loews, it was presumed, bought the entire 4.4 percent of CBS stock owned by the Fishers, paying $143.50 a share, or $149.3 million in all.

By late March of 1986 Ted Turner was in a position to finalize the takeover of MGM/UA. Drexel Burnham Lambert, Turner's investment banker, sold $1.4 billion in "junk bonds" to finance a large part of the purchase. In getting MGM/UA, Turner was forced to raise Turner Broadcasting's debt to $2.57 billion. As for CBS, resisting takeovers became more and more costly. It was in the process of selling $300 million in assets, including its two jets. Some six hundred employees had accepted a special early retirement package. And the company was forced to lay off another five hundred people. CBS News itself lost seventy-four staffers.

By the spring of 1986, CBS was still independent, still fighting to be free. Its fight against Ted Turner had demonstrated that it was possible to marshall one's resources and to keep a corporate raider at bay—without resorting to greenmail, without resorting to white knights, without resorting to poison-pill provisions. But, if CBS was feeling heroic in the wake of the Turner battle, its generals knew the truth: it was like the old joke about the operation that had been a success even though the patient had died. CBS had not died. But it was badly wounded. The operation had indeed been a success: Ted Turner had walked away from CBS and had been forced to admit defeat. Yet, the lesson of the Turner exercise appeared to be not that staunch defenses would stop any Ted Turner, but rather that a more aggressive warrior, one who had some real cash in his pockets to offer the CBS stockholders, might win the day.

Turner latched onto a new idea during the summer of 1986: the Goodwill Games. Conceived as he watched the 1984 Olympics in Los Angeles—when Americans and Russians did not compete against one another—the idea was to stage a unique athletic event: an Olympics-style contest with athletes from fifty nations—among them the US and the USSR—engaging in eighteen sports. Turner signed an agreement that gave the Soviets $8.9 million to play host; and he obtained the right to televise the games in the United States. The games were broadcast between July 5 and 20, 1986, giving Turner one more achievement in his long and variegated career.

In September 1986 came the stunning news that CBS' Thomas Wyman has been forced to resign as Chairman and Chief Executive Officer. Larry Tisch, who by now had accumulated 24.9% CBS' stock, was made acting CEO, and the 84-year old William S. Paley, CBS founder and holder of 8.1% of its stock, was chosen as acting chairman. Wyman had sought to convince CBS' board to consider a friendly takeover by Coca-Cola Co. Instead, the board decided to act against him.

And so Tom Wyman had managed to stop Ted Turner—but in the end Wyman paid the ultimate professional price.

Chapter 10

The Texaco-Getty-Pennzoil Marathon

Gordon Getty. Courtesy Oscar Abolafia/*Time* Magazine.

In retrospect, the scene appeared comic, or at least devoid of the seriousness one usually attaches to meetings of such moment. Here was John K. McKinley, the 63-year-old Chairman of Texaco Inc., the third-largest oil company in America, arriving at the elegant Pierre Hotel suite of Gordon Getty, 50, described—as his father, J. Paul Getty, had been before him—as the richest man in America. It was midnight of January 5, 1984. A bevy of Wall Street's major dealmakers congregated in the room waiting to hear what McKinley had to say to Getty, to hear the price Texaco would offer to buy Getty Oil, the major business in the Getty empire.

"I am prepared to offer. . . . ."

"I accept," Gordon shouted out, cutting off McKinley, a Lyndon B. Johnson lookalike, in midsentence. Then, realizing that he had spoken too soon: "Oh! You are supposed to give the price first." Others in the room gave off with a nervous laughter. For three hours they had been racing to reach this point. For three hours they had been wondering if they ever would reach this point.

Cutting away the layers of elegance in that Manhattan suite, putting aside the untidiness of sealing a multibillion-dollar deal in quite this way, the undisputable fact was that Texaco had just bought Getty Oil.

Or had it?

Later, as the 24,000 pages of testimony in the marathon trial were examined to prove this point or another, one compelling moment would be recalled above all others: just two days before this scene in Gordon Getty's suite, another similar scene had taken place. The same Gordon Getty was there. The same Getty Oil had been the subject of takeover negotiations. In that earlier scene, Gordon Getty had uncorked a bottle of champagne to celebrate a deal between Pennzoil Co., the thirty-sixth largest oil company in the nation, and Getty Oil, founded by Gordon's grandfather, Oklahoma oil man George Franklin Getty and built up by his father, J. Paul Getty.

In time, a trial would take place, a trial which Pennzoil's flamboyant lawyer Joseph Jamail would call "the most important case ever brought in the history of America."[1] Trial lawyers were always talking in such bombastic terms. In at least one respect, Jamail would be correct. The trial would go into the history books for producing the largest civil judgment ever. But, more important for the purposes of this narrative, the marathon dealmaking which led to the trial and the subsequent legal maneuvering would raise fresh questions about the mergers and acquisitions game. It had been only two years and three months between the outcome of the Bendix-Martin Marietta-Allied affair and the opening volleys in the Texaco-Getty-Pennzoil exercise. To the surprise of many, the Bendix affair had not produced a reaction against megadollar dealmaking, nor had undue restraints been placed on its exercise. Yes, there had been a lot of shouting, a lot of worried calls for reform. But in the fall of 1982, few wanted to tamper with those wonderful market forces. They had been so good and kind to so many. The Bendix business, in that wonderful term that rationalizes even the greatest disasters, was a mere aberration. Yes, an aberration. And it could not recur. The dealmakers, who had been so critical of Bendix themselves, would not sully their hands in quite this manner ever again.

And then along came Gordon Getty.

Gordon Getty earned $28 million a year in dividends from the Sarah Getty Trust—enough money, in that apt phrase of *Time* magazine, not to worry where his next five-course meal would come from. Gordon Getty, the fourth born of the five sons of J. Paul Getty, was determined to prove something to his father, dead since 1976, and to prove something to himself—namely that he could turn the family fortune into an ever greater family fortune. He had inherited 13 percent of the family business and, until a year or so before our narrative begins in 1983, Gordon seemed to take only a passing interest in Daddy's affairs. Gordon was a great patron of the arts in San Francisco, an amateur anthropologist, eager to support and even perform in opera, a composer of songs, but never a tycoon, never a J. Paul Getty. Never, that is, until 1983. "I'm a businessman because I had to be one," he said in 1983.[2] He was a major benefactor of the San Francisco Opera and each year reportedly provided $250,000 or more to help pay for a new production. He disliked the lavish parties his wife threw at their mansion overlooking San Francisco Bay; he seemed happiest among opera lovers; he liked to sing, and sometimes joined cast members or guests, among whom had been Placido Domingo, Luciano Pavarotti, and Leontyne Price. He wrote some music, among which was a song cycle called *The White Election* that was meant to accompany a series of Emily Dickinson poems.

Gordon Getty was convinced that Getty Oil should be doing better, that it was worth far more than its present market value. Once Gordon became sufficiently interested, he had the authority to try to shake things up. Not that he wouldn't encounter resistance within Getty Oil. There was no love lost between the company's management and the Getty family. Gordon could try to persuade the management to take the kind of steps that might boost its financial value. Or he could go for the Big One—in this case, an outside buyer. Getty's management labored to find ways that would dilute the power of the Getty family. It was hardly in a receptive mood to listen to Gordon's proposals for change. So, Gordon Getty opted for the Big One.

In shopping around for someone to buy Getty Oil, Gordon Getty unleashed a series of forces that, like the Bendix case, rocked Wall Street. Once more, as with Bendix, but with significantly more money in play and a drama afoot that would last far longer, the cast of characters appeared quite willing to stretch the rules of the takeover game to their limit—and even beyond. When Bendix thought it was unfair for Martin Marietta to play Pac-Man in defense against a takeover attempt, what Bendix was really saying was: you are not playing by the rules as I understand them. So, too, when Pennzoil told Texaco that it could not simply snatch a take-over agreement away by making a higher bid, Pennzoil saw the rules, as it had come to understand them in American business, as coming unstuck. While there had been plenty of rules and regulations laid down in Washington, none took into account the kinds of situations that occurred in both the Bendix and Getty Oil cases. Perhaps most crucially, the Texaco-Getty-Pennzoil marathon threatened to leave an ugly scar on the takeover game by calling into question the razzle-dazzle, frenetically paced derring-do of the Wall Street dealmakers. As more and more attention was focused on the size of the fees investment bankers were receiving and as increasing interest was shown toward the role of the takeover attorneys, the last thing the Wall Street crowd would have wanted was the kind of adverse publicity that was to grow out of the Getty affair.

Yet, it all seemed terribly inevitable. The takeover targets were there; the money was waiting to be picked off the ground; the protagonists had no trouble justifying the whole exercise. Only when it was over would there be time to think about what really had happened. And whether things had gotten out of hand. In the meantime there was a game to be played—and the stakes were very, very high. No one seemed interested in asking what it was all about.

Our story begins with a 50-year-old man who as a young man had wanted to please his father and thought that doing a good job in the family business was the best way. Yet, Gordon Getty could not hack it, and eventually he turned away from Getty Oil to pursue his favorite pastimes, patronizing the arts, opera, and anthropology. The youngest of the three surviving sons of J. Paul Getty, Gordon grew up first in Los Angeles and then in the Pacific Heights area of San Francisco; he lived with his mother, Ann Rork Light, fourth of the five Getty wives. She was married to the billionaire between 1932 and 1935, but by the time Gordon came along, his mother and father were planning a divorce. Gordon's relationship with his father was almost nonexistent: they saw each other only once a year on Christmas; the only other contact was a gift he received on his birthday.

Wealth and its advantages came only later to Gordon Getty. In grade school his allowance was 25 cents a week, raised to $5 a week in high school. Only when he was 24 years old did he learn that his father was the richest man in the United States. After Gordon graduated from the University of San Francisco in 1956 with a bachelor's degree in literature, he served four months in the U.S. Army, becoming a second lieutenant. He then worked as a $500-a-month management trainee at Tidewater, a Getty Oil subsidiary. He pumped gas and worked in a tire and battery plant. In

1958 and 1959 he worked as a consultant to the Getty Oil Company in the neutral zone between Saudi Arabia and Kuwait. When a Getty oil truck crashed into a pipeline, causing damage, Gordon was held responsible and kept under house arrest for ten days. That incident sent him packing. Twice more he took on assignments in the family business, once in the mid-1960s, the second time in the early 1970s, but associates who knew him believed that his heart was not in the work. Trying to please his father, Gordon earned only harsh letters from the tycoon. Nor could the son console himself with large sums from Getty interests: until the early 1960s Gordon's income from those interests amounted to only $15,000 a year. But things did improve: in 1963 his income had risen to $50,000 a year. In 1967 he was receiving half a million dollars a year.

Though he had little musical training—a few piano lessons as a child and some courses in music theory—Gordon Getty's main interest was music. He started composing early in his life and dreamed of becoming a composer. One strong reason for Gordon's long-standing indifference toward the family business was J. Paul Getty's decision to let an older son, George F. Getty, carry on the family name in the oil business. He had been Executive Vice President and Chief Operations Officer of Getty Oil. But, after George's unexpected death in 1973, and his father's death three years later at the age of 83, Gordon went back to the business. Although he took his father's chair as Getty director in 1976, it was only in 1982 that he took an active role in the company, after the death of C. Lansing Hayes Jr., who had been a cotrustee of the Sarah C. Getty Trust, a fund that controlled 40 percent of the oil company. Gordon had always deferred to Hayes, a major ally of his father. After Hayes' death, Gordon found himself sole trustee of the family trust, which was named after his grandmother.

Sensing that Getty Oil's management could have worked harder to boost the market value of the company, Gordon had always adopted a low profile as long as Hayes was around. But, after becoming sole trustee, he looked for ways with investment bankers to improve the company's record. In 1980 the stock had sold for a high of $108, but by 1983 it had dropped to $48.50. Much to Gordon's chagrin, Getty Oil's management, led by Sidney R. Petersen, Chairman and Chief Executive, had diversified the company. In 1979 it had acquired an interest in the money-losing Entertainment and Sports Programming Network (ESPN); in 1980 Getty Oil had purchased the Kansas-based ERC insurance group. In early 1983 Gordon began to fight with Petersen, peppering the board with proposals. One of them called for an equity restructuring in which the board would repurchase enough stock to bring the stock price up. Just by coincidence that would give Gordon Getty a majority of the stock in the company. More proposals were made, and more rejected. In July 1983 Goldman Sachs, the investment banking firm, working on the company's behalf, recommended a $500 million-a-year stock-repurchase plan as a vehicle for boosting the company's market price. Petersen managed to convince the Getty board to knock the idea down, perhaps, some speculated, because it meant that the Getty family's stake would have jumped to 53 percent. Petersen proposed a stock-repurchase plan but one in which Gordon Getty would have 51 percent of the stock but stockholder votes equivalent to only 40 percent. Naturally, Gordon rejected that one.

Cutting the Getty family down to size was constantly on Petersen's mind: in October the board decided to issue new shares that would dilute the Getty influence. Petersen and the Getty Oil board worried that Gordon would seek ways of bolstering his influence in the company. One sure way of doing that was to enter into alliance with the J. Paul Getty Museum. The Museum, one of the richest in the world, had been run since 1981 by Harold Williams, former Norton Simon chairman, former chairman of the SEC. Located in Malibu, California, the Museum not only housed one of the world's greatest private art collections but also owned 11.8 percent of Getty Oil. In the struggle between Gordon and Getty Oil, Harold Williams was a key figure. He was the pivot who could give control of the company to either Petersen or Gordon Getty. If he linked forces with Gordon, Gordon and the Museum together would have a 52 percent controlling interest that would entitle them to pick a new board. Harold Williams had no desire to be a minority stockholder in a Gordon Getty-controlled company. Toward the end of the summer of 1983 he retained his friend, takeover attorney Martin Lipton, as an adviser.

In late September, upon hearing that Gordon Getty planned to align himself with the Museum in an effort to win control of Getty Oil, Petersen decided to act. At a board meeting on October 2, 1983, in Philadelphia, the board issued another nine million shares to an employee stock ownership program, effectively diluting Gordon Getty's and the museum's shares to less than 50 percent. At that same meeting the board spoke of diminishing Gordon's status as sole trustee of the Getty family trust. A lawsuit was mentioned as a possible weapon. Before proceeding with the suit, Petersen sought a last-minute deal with Gordon. Authorizing the shares would have the desired effect of bringing Gordon to his knees, but it would also tell the world of the controversies within Getty Oil. Armed with this information, someone else could perhaps buy up enough shares, then join forces with Gordon, or with Gordon and the Museum—and take over.

In a certain frantic air, meetings were held with and without Gordon Getty present. Marty Lipton and Harold Williams met in London with Getty on October 3. Getty Oil representatives met with him as well. Gordon would not agree to any deals. The next day, October 4, Marty Lipton met with Petersen and his advisers. Petersen acknowledged his fear of a possible alliance between the Museum and Gordon Getty; he hinted that the board would put into force an as-yet unspecified plan—the stock issuance plan—that would keep Gordon Getty from taking control. At that point Marty Lipton proposed a three-way "standstill" agreement. The accord would last eighteen months, during which all parties would cease all hostilities: all plans for changing various stock interests would be shelved. It was the corporate version of Henry Kissinger trying to obtain a cease-fire among warring Lebanese factions. One difference was that Marty Lipton, unlike the real Kissinger, represented one of the warring factions, the Getty Museum. Lipton further suggested that Gordon Getty be allowed to add one of his own people to the board; Harold Williams would go on the board as the Museum's representative as well. Getty Oil's management seemed to go for the Lipton plan. At first negative, Gordon agreed finally to consider it. Lipton left with him a handwritten draft of the accord.

Two weeks later, Martin Siegel, Gordon Getty's investment banker, won Lipton's agreement to have Gordon get four new board members instead of one. This was the same Marty Siegel who had been an adviser to Martin Marietta during its tumultous fight to resist the takeover bid from Bendix. One of those four Getty Oil board members would be Laurence Tisch, founder and Chairman of the Loews Corporation (a friend and client of Lipton's, as it turned out). In San Francisco during the third week of October, Gordon Getty and Petersen continued to negotiate as Lipton shuttled back and forth between the two men, who remained in separate rooms. Lipton's draft in the hands of Petersen's lawyers had grown into a 16-page, single-spaced document. Gordon Getty wanted two things: to deal only with Lipton's original draft, and to reduce the standstill period to twelve months. Getty was not pleased at the prospect of signing a piece of paper that commited him to yielding in the battle to win control of Getty Oil for eighteen months, or for that matter, even one year. But Lipton pressed him that it was the wisest course, and he signed it. Lipton took the signed document to Petersen's people, who signed it as well.

Three weeks later, on November 11, the Getty Oil board met in Houston to ratify the agreement. Gordon was asked to leave the room so the board could vote on the standstill agreement. But as he was shown out of one door, in through another walked Getty Oil's attorneys—Barton Winokur of Philadelphia's Dechert Price & Rhoads law firm and Herbert Galant of New York's Fried, Frank, Harris, Shriver & Jacobson law firm. During this now-famous "back door" board meeting, the board went ahead and ratified the truce. Gordon was called back into the room and given the impression that he had kept the board from doing anything damaging to his interests for another twelve months. But it transpired that while Gordon had been out of the meeting, the Getty Oil board decided to join a lawsuit that challenged his position as the sole head of the Sarah C. Getty Trust. The lawsuit was brought on behalf of Gordon's 15-year-old nephew, Tara Gabriel Galaxy Gramaphone Getty (yes, that is his name!), a grandchild of J. Paul Getty. The suit was initiated by the teen-ager's father,

J. Paul Getty Jr., 51, Gordon's older brother who rarely got along with his younger sibling.

Four days later, when Gordon was told by his investment banker, Marty Siegel, what the board had done during his absence, he was shocked, hurt, and embarrassed. On second thought, he realized that the board had acted unwisely. It had given him the proof he needed that neither he nor the Museum could do business with Getty Oil.

Realizing that Getty would be enraged, Petersen nonetheless moved ahead with the suit. He didn't realize, however, how angry another actor in the drama would be. Incensed, Marty Lipton felt betrayed by his colleagues at Fried, Frank. He had taken the document to Gordon to sign, and then instead of getting a standstill agreement, the board decided to sue Gordon Getty. It was as if one Lebanese faction had moved in its heavy artillery on the sly while the peacemakers were signing the pact and then, as the ink was drying, unleashed a lethal volley. Petersen came under pressure to call another board meeting to rescind the lawsuit, but he demurred. His own lawyers, after all, thought there was no contradiction between the suit and the standstill agreement.

On December 5, the alliance between Gordon Getty and the Museum was forged: they signed a consent action which permitted a majority of stockholders to change the company's bylaws. They then revised the bylaws so that a vote of fourteen of sixteen directors was needed to undertake any of the steps forbidden under the standstill agreement: such as issuing new stock, or proposing the sale of stock, or beginning any action or proceeding that related to the control or voting power of more than 5 percent of the stock. The motion to intervene in the trustee litigation was withdrawn as well.

With the standstill agreement no longer a possibility and the new Getty-Museum pact a reality, Getty Oil was now ripe for a takeover offer. A number of companies were thought to be interested, among them Phillips Petroleum, Atlantic Richfield, and Chevron. Meanwhile, Hugh Liedtke, the Chairman of Pennzoil Co., had been clipping newspaper accounts of the Getty Oil feuds that winter of 1983, sensing that morale in the company was breaking down and that this breakdown would make Getty ripe for a takeover.

By the time he entered the Getty Oil Fray, Hugh Liedtke had acquired a reputation as one of the tougher and shrewder businessmen around. In 1965 he had engineered one of the earliest of the modern hostile takeovers when he bought United Gas Corp., a large pipeline company that was ten times Pennzoil's size. So he had some experience in picking on businesses bigger than Pennzoil.

To avoid serving in the Prussian army, Hugh's grandfather had emigrated to Texas—where he was eventually drafted into the Confederate army! Hugh's father became a teacher, an attorney, and a judge in Indian Territory; he was also the youngest delegate to the Oklahoma constitutional convention and a regional general counsel for Gulf Oil Corp. Hugh was born in 1922 in Tulsa, then the number one petroleum city in the world.

During his teen-age years Hugh worked summers in the oil fields. He was popular for his card tricks. One hobby of his was to take lead soldiers and reenact the Battle of Waterloo. At Amherst College in Massachusetts his major was philosophy; he studied one year at the Harvard Business School before shipping out on an aircraft carrier in 1943 to the Pacific. After the war he and his brother attended the University of Texas Law School (where they met Lyndon B. Johnson, then a young congressman, and John Connally, future Governor of Texas). The two brothers began practicing law in Midland, Texas. At that juncture they met an oil field equipment salesman for Dress Industries Inc. named George Bush: he would later become Vice President of the United States.

In 1953 the Liedtke brothers and Bush formed Zapata Petroleum Corp, borrowing $1 million for the venture and purchasing several thousand acres of desert in West Texas. They began drilling at six wells, striking oil, lots of it. Within two years Zapata was drilling 137 oil wells in what was later called the Jameson field. Its revenues were $86 million; its earnings $12 million. J. Paul Getty's Tidewater Oil Co. pretty much controlled South Penn Oil Co., a remnant of the Standard Oil trust that had been controlled by J. Paul Getty. Gaining the support of Getty, Liedtke won a showdown with the South Penn management and in 1962 was made president. Under his leadership South Penn's shares rose from $28 to $70. Liedtke a year later bought out Getty, merging South Penn with Zapata Petroleum to form Pennzoil Co. In 1965 Liedtke made his most audacious move—before taking on Getty Oil. Taking $130 million in borrowed cash, he offered to buy 10 percent of United Gas, a pipeline and mining firm; his offer was 20 percent over the market price. Cash offers like this one were almost unthinkable in the United States, though common in Great Britain. Three years later, Pennzoil was able to finalize the merger with a stock swap.

Hugh Liedtke, at 63, still had one career goal: to purchase more and more oil. Getty Oil was selling at $80 a share. On December 28 Pennzoil made a $1.6 billion tender offer for 20 percent of the stock of Getty Oil—at $100 per share. Liedtke obviously was hoping that Gordon Getty would team up with him and the two would then have a majority. Liedtke met Gordon Getty on New Year's Eve at the Pierre Hotel. The two men talked of Liedtke's earlier deals with Gordon's father. Things looked rosy. But the bid, needless to say, unnerved the key players. Most unnerved were Marty

Lipton and Harold Williams. Pennzoil might wind up with everything—the Getty Trust and the Museum's shares, and control of Getty Oil. Once again, a Solomonlike alternative proposal was in order, and Marty Lipton thought he had a good one. Under Lipton's plan, Getty Oil would tender for the 20 percent of the shares—at $110 a share. Since that would remove 20 percent of the shares from circulation, it would automatically mean that Gordon Getty would now have a majority interest in Getty Oil. But, as part of the Lipton plan, Gordon Getty would agree not to exercise control for three months, during which time a sale at some higher price, or some different solution, could be sought. On December 31, Gordon Getty and Getty Oil's management appeared favorably disposed to the Lipton plan.

But the next day (January 1) the plan came unstuck, as Gordon Getty balked. Most likely he was afraid that during those three months when he could not act, Petersen might, and if he did, it would surely be to coax Gordon out of the picture. Fearing that Pennzoil might take all the marbles if no one thought of something else, Marty Siegel, Gordon Getty's investment banker, came up with his own plan, which Liedtke and Gordon Getty liked: for $110 a share, Pennzoil and Gordon Getty would enter into alliance and undertake a leveraged buyout of all public shares of Getty Oil and the Museum's shares. In this new Getty Oil company; Gordon would own four-sevenths and Pennzoil three-sevenths. Gordon would be President and Chairman of the company, Liedtke the Chief Operating Officer. On the basis of Siegel's proposal, the two men struck this new deal. Gordon was optimistic that the Museum would go along with the Siegel proposal, delighted to take a price of $100 or more a share.

The Pennzoil bid put everyone on the defensive. It was as if some hostile alien had landed on the planet and was seeking control of the Earth. At a meeting of the Getty Oil board the next day, January 2, in the Hotel Inter-Continental in New York, a meeting originally called to consider the old $110 self-tender for 20 percent of the Getty Oil shares, the board met for eight and a half hours before rejecting the latest Pennzoil-Gordon Getty bid. Had Pennzoil sweetened the deal, the board might have been more receptive. Twelve hours later—it was now January 3—the Getty Oil board met once more. Pennzoil had in fact sweetened the deal by another $1.50 a share, but the board again said no. One option, pressed by Pennzoil, would have had Harold Williams sign another majority consent with Gordon Getty, remove the board, and put in their own team to approve the sale to Pennzoil. Lipton and Williams thought that unfair and inappropriate. The Museum rejected joining with Pennzoil and Gordon Getty and insisted that all stockholders be treated equally.

By 6:30 P.M. January 3, Pennzoil's advisers were suggesting that they might be willing to raise the price by $2.50 a share—to $115. That would give Pennzoil three-sevenths of Getty's reserves—some 1 billion barrels—in exchange for $3.6 billion, a true bargain. With that, the board approved the new offer by a vote of 15-1. Liedtke was now convinced that he had increased the size of Pennzoil by a factor of four. He went off to celebrate at the "21" Club in New York that night. Yet one overriding question was whether the board had voted to approve the price or the whole offer. Beyond that, a number of important issues appeared left for the lawyers to resolve, among them who would buy the Museum's shares and when; and how the deal would actually be structured. The Getty Oil board directors were tired, as were the lawyers. There was apparent agreement to meet early the next afternoon to look at a document that could be ratified and signed. For that, the lawyers would have to have one ready by 10 A.M.

For another five hours lawyers met and argued; it was apparent that some did not even know what they were supposed to do or, for that matter, what had really been agreed. It was decided around midnight that Pennzoil's lawyers would draft a proposed merger agreement for the others to look at the next morning. With everyone seemingly in agreement on the latest proposal, there was a round of congratulatory handshakes, and Gordon Getty opened a bottle of champagne in his suite at the Pierre Hotel.

It is worth dwelling for a moment on these handshakes. Later, they would become one of the main controversies. Does a handshake consummate the deal? Or does a deal go into effect only upon the actual signing of a contract? Debate on this point would be heated and extensive.

The next morning, Wednesday, January 4, Getty Oil issued a press release announcing its "agreement in principle" to enter into a $5.2 billion merger with Pennzoil. The release noted that the agreement was "subject to execution of a definitive merger agreement." That kind of an announcement was used only in friendly deals; otherwise it could trigger new bidders, which is precisely what happened. One investment banker remarked that when he saw the press release, he knew Getty was up for sale to anyone who could top the Pennzoil offer. Predictably, there is considerable dispute about who was responsible for the press release. If the papers were to be ready for signature by that morning, the timing of the press release was not that premature. But, for reasons that are in dispute among the parties, the Pennzoil-Getty merger contract was not sent for distribution until 6 P.M. that day (Wednesday). Marty Lipton received his package at 8:25 P.M. almost ten and a half hours after the 10 A.M. target. This had all become moot: at 4 P.M. a California state judge signed a temporary restraining order initiated by Claire Getty, a niece of Gordon Getty, who wanted the deal blocked until there was full disclosure of the terms to the beneficiaries of the family trust. This "TRO," as it is known by lawyers, enjoined Gordon Getty from finalizing the Pennzoil merger for at least twenty-four hours. Hence, the deal could not be completed until at least 7 P.M. January 5. The effect was to open the game to new bidders.

At 4 A.M. Thursday morning, January 5, Wasserstein was in White Plains, New York, talking with Texaco's Chairman John McKinley. Later that morning Wasserstein was telling Lipton on the phone that Texaco was preparing a better offer for Getty Oil. Lipton's response was encouraging: by now he had seen the Getty-Pennzoil papers and found them wanting in a number of areas. He passed this observation on to Wasserstein. At 12 noon, as the Texaco board was ready to meet, Chairman McKinley phoned Lipton to say that he wanted a chance to put in Texaco's bid. Lipton said that no deal had yet been reached with Pennzoil and there was doubt that one would be reached that day. At 5 P.M., as the Texaco team was heading for New York to meet with Marty Lipton and, hopefully, Gordon Getty, Pennzoil and Getty Oil lawyers were getting together to work on the final draft of their merger agreement. Lipton sent his comments to the meeting, but he and his associates stayed in their office for a meeting with Texaco representatives. One strong indication of how the wind was blowing came when Getty Oil attorney Barton Winokur showed up at Lipton's office for the meeting with the Texaco people and said that there was no agreement between Getty Oil and Pennzoil, and Getty Oil was anxious to make a deal with Texaco. Meanwhile, the California judge that evening continued the restraining order, keeping Texaco's chances alive. During Thursday evening, McKinley, his key officers and general counsel, met with Gordon Getty, Marty Siegel, Larry Tisch, and Gordon Getty's lawyers. The meeting did not go well, and Gordon's advisers asked Marty Lipton, acting for the Museum, to join the meeting. (Harold Williams was celebrating his 56th birthday with his children; Lipton had been empowered to do the bargaining for him.) Lipton met with the Gordon Getty group, then with the Texaco group. McKinley said that Texaco would offer $122.50 per share if Gordon Getty would acknowledge that he had no agreement with Pennzoil and would sign a letter committing to sell to Texaco. Lipton replied that he thought Gordon Getty wanted $125 a share—a $200 million increase for Texaco. That might be possible, the Texaco chairman intimated, but only if Gordon Getty would agree that evening—and thus prevent others from coming in with a higher bid.

One man who heard about the press release and regarded it as an invitation to enter the bidding was Bruce Wasserstein, who along with Joe Perella was codirector of the M&A department at First Boston. Wasserstein phoned Geoffrey Boisi of Goldman Sachs, representing Getty Oil, to find out how much time was left to find a new buyer. Boisi said there had been no papers drafted yet. Marty Lipton confirmed that a deal had not been signed. That was all the encouragement the First Boston banker needed. He was on the phone to Texaco soon afterward.

Getty looked very good indeed to Texaco which had been looking eagerly for new supplies of crude oil. Texaco's petroleum pool had diminished 25 percent between 1979 and 1982. If Texaco could add Getty Oil's supply, its reserves would double. Texaco and its partners had some time before gone through an expensive and fruitless exploration in Alaska's Mukluk Field, one more in a long string of exploration failures that had put Texaco at the bottom of the oil industry.

It would be one of Gordon Getty's toughest decisions. He had already committed himself to buying Getty Oil—or at least sharing in the purchase of it. McKinley, Lipton, and the others who marched over to the Pierre Hotel that evening would try to persuade him to sell the company for $125 a share—and thus give up his long-standing dream of running Getty Oil. The choice was obviously made that much more difficult by the cracking open of the champagne the other night, signaling to Pennzoil that Gordon Getty was going ahead with their arrangement.

McKinley waited in the lobby of the Pierre Hotel while Lipton and Laurence A. Tisch, a Getty Oil board member for the past two months, went upstairs to Gordon Getty's apartment. Lipton and Tisch talked for two hours with Gordon Getty and his investment banker, Marty Siegel. Lipton then went downstairs and told McKinley there could be a deal at $125 a share. McKinley tried to lower it to $122.50 but gave in on condition that Gordon Getty sign the papers that evening. There was still the problem of the California restraining order. Lipton had a solution for this as well. He drafted a letter for Gordon to sign declaring that he would sign a deal with Texaco save for the restraining order, and he planned to do so once the TRO was lifted. Getty signed the letter at 1 A.M. Five hours later, Marty Lipton, on authorization from Harold Williams, affixed his signature to a definitive agreement on behalf of the Museum; and six hours later Getty Oil held a telephone board meeting to ratify the deal. Gordon Getty would later explain that he had decided to sell to Texaco after learning that the Museum planned to sell its 11.8 percent stake in Getty Oil to McKinley's company (no such agreement was in reality contemplated by the Museum or Texaco, and in fact Texaco was unwilling to proceed at all without Gordon Getty); not to enter into a deal with Texaco at that point would have made him just a minority stockholder in Getty Oil without real power.

For John K. McKinley, it was the high point in a long career, dating back to the days when he was a top-notch high school student who would enter the University of Alabama at the age of 17. McKinley had graduated in three years after studying chemical engineering; he stayed on for a fourth and picked up a master's degree in organic chemistry in 1941. Immediately thereafter, he began working for Texaco: his first job was doing grease research at Texaco's Port Arthur, Texas, refinery at $2100 a year. Three months later the Army grabbed him, and he served until the end of the war. McKinley landed on Omaha Beach soon after D-Day at the head of an artillery unit.

With the war over, McKinley returned to the study of grease. In time he would win thirteen patents, among them one for a gasoline additive which inhibited corrosion. For fifteen years he did research, rising to Assistant Vice President. In 1960 McKinley became general manager of a Texaco petrochemicals unit. His eye for turning a profit smoothed the path up the ranks, until in 1971 he was made President. He became Chairman of Texaco in 1980.

Once in the senior job, McKinley sought to improve the company's position. He got rid of half of Texaco's American gas stations; he closed six of the fourteen American refineries; and he refurbished four others. Some $6 billion went into exploration, but by the mid-1980s there were still no major discoveries. The acquisition of Getty Oil was the highlight of McKinley's career: he had managed, so it appeared, to double Texaco's reserves in one fell swoop.

The Texaco-Getty Oil merger was announced on Friday, January 6. The Texaco offer to purchase Getty Oil for some $9.9 billion would make it the largest merger ever, much larger than Du Pont's $7.2 billion merger with Conoco in 1981, until then the largest takeover. The newly merged company would replace Mobil Corporation as the second-biggest oil firm in the United States, behind Exxon. Mobil sales in 1982 had been $60 billion; Texaco and Getty Oil's together would be nearly $60.3 billion. Texaco was the third-largest oil firm in America with $48 billion; Getty Oil was ranked fourteenth with 1982 sales of $12.3 billion. Pennzoil's sales in 1982 were far smaller at only $2.3 billion. It was ranked thirty-sixth. For the Getty heirs, the Texaco deal was a personal bonanza, bringing them almost $4 billion, whereas just a month earlier their shares had had a market value of about $2.3 billion. No matter what happened—and plenty would—Gordon Getty had fulfilled his dream of driving up the price of the family stock. His company holdings, which had been valued at $500 million a year before, were worth about $1.3 billion in January 1984.

Meanwhile, the biggest merger in American history was making some Getty stockholders very happy—and wealthy—overnight. Clifford Smith, a Getty stockholder from East Chicago, Indiana, went out and bought a used Oldsmobile. Kenneth Herman's family found that the shares they had held for more than fifteen years were suddenly worth $125,000. Arthur Knifton, a retired service-station owner in Seattle, collected $459,000 on Getty shares purchased in 1957. "I thought that man (John Paul Getty) had the Midas touch in the oil business," he would say after hearing about his good fortune.[3]

The merger also pleased the investment bankers, who stood to gain a great deal. First Boston was a big winner, earning an estimated $12.5 million in fees for advising Texaco. Goldman Sachs was to collect between

$15 and $20 million for aiding Getty Oil; Kidder, Peabody, Marty Siegel's firm, stood to collect a similar amount for aiding Gordon Getty.

It was only through the press announcement that Hugh Liedtke of Pennzoil learned what had been transpiring. When he found out, he was livid. For one thing, he could not understand how Texaco's McKinley, a man he thought of as a friend, had not given him the courtesy of a phone call: Liedtke was supposed to have gone quail hunting but canceled the trip to spend the weekend at the Waldorf Astoria. He watched football on television and thought about how to respond to the Texaco gambit. Believing that he still had a deal to buy Getty Oil in partnership with Gordon Getty, Liedtke telexed Getty's board of directors. "If you fail to keep your agreement, we intend to commence actions for damages . . . against Getty Oil Company, your individual board members, the Getty Trust, the Getty Museum, and all others who have participated in or induced the breach of your agreement with us." He also insisted that he would exercise his stock-purchase clause that entitled Pennzoil to purchase 7 million Getty shares at $110 each—a move that would net Pennzoil $120 million. That same day (January 6) Getty Oil took the initiative and sued in Delaware to win a declaratory judgment that it had not entered into a binding agreement with Liedtke's firm. Delaware was chosen to assure Getty Oil a friendly venue. Four days later, on January 10, Pennzoil filed its own suit in Delaware against Getty Oil, Gordon Getty, his Trust, and the Museum, for allegedly getting out of the deal. Texaco, which had been represented by Joe Flom's firm in the merger with Getty Oil, was also represented in the Delaware litigation by the Skadden, Arps Wilmington office. Though Chancery Judge Brown would not allow Pennzoil to enjoin Texaco, he did say that "Pennzoil has demonstrated a likelihood that it will be able to establish . . . that a contract came into being."

That, of course, was what the whole dispute was about.

Then Texaco blundered: it missed the deadline for answering the Pennzoil suit. That gave Pennzoil the chance to withdraw its action in the Delaware court and to introduce another one in Houston, where it would have the hometown advantage. Texaco seemed passive about the whole affair, but Hugh Liedtke could think of little but the Pennzoil suit. He went on a fishing trip to his cabin in Arkansas with a long-time friend, Joe Jamail, an eminently successful personal-injury lawyer who had won verdicts of $55-million and over. Shocked and dismayed at what Getty Oil had done, Liedtke asked Jamail to represent Pennzoil. At first hesitant, Jamail thought about it and finally acquiesced. "By the time I got back to Houston, I figured that if he was willing to stand up to those SOBs, I would sure as hell stand with him."[4]

Joe Jamail proved to be one of the more colorful personalities in the Texaco-Getty-Pennzoil drama. He had flunked torts at the University of Texas Law School but had become so successful later on that he was dubbed the "King of Torts." Though the Pennzoil-Getty-Texaco trial would give him singular fame, he had already made the Guiness Book of World Records for triumphing in one of the biggest individual settlements of all time: a $6.8 million personal-injury suit he had won against the Remington Arms Co. over the issue of a defective gun. Jamail's family emigrated from Lebanon to the United States at the turn of the twentieth century. In fact the family name was spelled "Gemayel"—the same way the Lebanon President, Amin Gemayel, spells it—until American immigration officials phonetecized it for the family. Joe claims that Amin Gemayel is a fourth cousin of his.

Joe was a Marine in the Pacific during World War II and then graduated from the University of Texas, where he majored in history. He earned his law degree at the same school. His first personal-injury suit was a personal one: he and some fellow students learned that a waitress at one of their favorite bars had cut her thumb while opening a beer bottle; they sued the beer company. When offered an out-of-court settlement of $750 they took the money and ran—straight to the bar to drink it all up; they had the last laugh, sensing how weak their case was. Though he has counted among his clients some well-known people, among them country music star Willie Nelson and football player Earl Campbell, Jamail seems proudest of the ordinary people he has helped.

The trial was to be great legal drama. It opened July 9. The main issue was whether any binding merger agreement had been made between Pennzoil and Getty Oil.

From the start Texaco thought it had a strong case. But many believed that Pennzoil had the upper hand, if only because the case was tried in Houston: a Texas jury would likely concur that Pennzoil and Getty Oil had in fact concluded a deal, and that Texaco had snatched that deal away from Pennzoil. Pennzoil's chief attorney, Joe Jamail, would call it "the most important case ever brought in the history of America." Clearly, this was hyperbole. But, by assigning it such grand dimensions, Jamail apparently hoped to dramatize what he saw as the wild and frenetic dealmaking on Wall Street. Texaco's attorney, Richard Miller, sought to derail that line quickly by deflating such grandiose claims: "I tried a case two months ago where a father was trying to get his children back. I consider that case considerably more important than I consider this case. This is a suit over money. . . . The idea that money turns this into the most important case that's ever been filed I think tells you something about the company that's bringing this case."

Texaco would argue that it did not act like a thief in the night. In fact, according to Miller, Getty Oil investment banker Geoffrey Boisi had invited Texaco to make a bid. "We didn't crash this party," he insisted. Miller's main point was that the agreement in principle reached between Pennzoil and Getty Oil was not a binding contract, if only because the two companies planned all along for a final document to be drafted and signed before anyone was committed. What the Getty Oil board approved was not a final deal but the price, a price at which negotiation would begin. "Just as the oil patch has certain expressions, just as the legal profession has legal expressions, (in) the financial community that's made up of New York City . . . the word(s) agreement in principle is always recognized as a statement that you do not have a contract."

Though Pennzoil's evidence was not simply that Gordon Getty and Pennzoil had committed themselves via the uncorking of the champagne and the handshakes and the congratulatory words, the Pennzoil legal team would insist that a man's word was supposed to be his bond—even on Wall Street. One crucial witness for Pennzoil was Arthur Liman, a partner in the New York law firm of Paul, Weiss, Rifkind, Wharton & Garrison. He had negotiated the Pennzoil-Getty deal on behalf of Pennzoil's investment bankers, Lazard Freres & Co. Liman told the jury that the Getty Oil board of directors had indeed given its assent to the essential terms of the agreement on January 3, 1984: the Getty Oil board and the dealmakers truly understood that they had a binding contract. Just after the Getty Oil board meeting broke up, Liman described a key few moments:

> Within a few minutes, Marty Lipton and Marty Siegel came out (of the board meeting), the door opened and they said, "Congratulations, Arthur. You got a deal." . . . I said: "I'd like to ask for permission to go into the board meeting and to shake hands with all of the directors because they've been at it for so many hours and I'd like to just shake hands with all of them." . . . I went around the room and I introduced myself and I shook hands with everyone I could. I said, "Congratulations." They said, "Congratulations to you."

None of the Getty Oil directors remembered shaking hands with Liman, and Lipton testified that he did not say, "You got a deal." There for the jury was the controversy.

It was left to Pennzoil's Hugh Liedtke to put the icing on the cake. Joe Jamail was questioning his old friend. Would a company like Pennzoil have any interest or incentive, he asked, to enter into an agreement that could become the starting point for Getty Oil to shop around for a higher bidder? "Of course not," Liedtke answered. "At some point, the trading stopped. And when you have a deal, when you've agreed to something, which we had done, we had met the requirement. We'd done what they asked us to do. The shopping stopped. You have a deal. That's the end of it."

But Pennzoil did not stop there. It sought to turn the trial into something of a moral crusade. "We think," observed John Jeffers of the Pennzoil team, "that one of the things that has to be done in this case, that ought to be in this case, is to bring the circle of people (he meant the investment bankers and lawyers in New York) square with the law." The issue, Jamail said at one point, was "what a promise is worth, what your word is worth, what a handshake is worth, what a contract is worth."

More damaging testimony came when Texaco witnesses, under cross-examination, acknowledged that Pennzoil would have acquired Getty Oil if Texaco had not weighed in with its higher bid. This appeared to bolster Pennzoil's contention that Texaco had indeed wrongfully interefered with the Pennzoil bid. Furthermore, when Jamail pointed out that the Getty Oil board had demanded indemnification from Texaco before agreeing to merge, the Pennzoil lawyer was able to show that Getty and Texaco understood from the start that their accord might be open to legal question.

Marty Lipton, a Texaco witness, became the symbol for Pennzoil of all that was evil about New York dealmaking. When viewed objectively, Lipton's testimony is a straightforward account of the events and clearly supported Texaco's position. However, Jamail was able to obfuscate the issues. At one point in his cross-examination, by showing Lipton only part of a document, Jamail was able to create the appearance that Lipton was acknowledging that one of his clients had been bound to a deal before signing a definitive merger agreement. Though on redirect examination Lipton later would explain the difference between that case and the one involved in the lawsuit, the jury had probably forgotten the point and therefore came to see the lawyer as lacking credibility. One juror thought he was pompous. A second juror later called Lipton a "fast-talking double-dealer."[5] Yet another thought he was "just in it for the money."[6] At one key moment in the trial Lipton was asked whether there was a difference between the sanctity of contracts involving small or astronomical sums. Lipton testified that large deals were always the subject of definitive written agreements.

Pennzoil's attorney Joe Jemail asked, "You have some distinction between just us ordinary people making contracts with each other and whether or not it's a $10 billion deal?"

"Yes, indeed," Lipton replied calmly.

At that point, one juror, Jim Shannon, recalled, "My jaw just dropped." Arrogance was the only word for it, he thought.[7] "Marty Lipton," added Texaco's chief counsel, Richard B. Miller, "is an outstanding lawyer, but there's no way he is going to look like a good ol' boy."[8] Jury foreman Richard Lawler noted: "Texaco should have left Marty Lipton in New York." Compounding the damage of the Lipton testimony was Texaco's decision not to bring in expert witnesses to make the point that an agreement in principle is understood not to be binding and that it must always be followed by a signed contract.

The trial itself became something of a bore. A number of witnesses gave their testimony on videotape, turning the courtroom into a darkened theater. To make a point, lawyers often had to drone on and on about technical details that could not possibly have been clear or even mattered very much to the jury. Then the original trial judge, Anthony J. P. Farris, took ill three-quarters of the way through and had to be replaced by Solomon Casseb. The latter quickly imposed his personality on the courtroom, banning the reading of newspapers, eating, and smoking. At one point he apologized to the jury for not bringing more clothes with him. It really mattered to him: in 1978 a women's group had voted him the best-dressed man in San Antonio. He also imposed a new efficiency on the trial, cutting lunches from ninety to sixty minutes, insisting that jurors work on Monday and Friday afternoons, and forcing lawyers to keep their remarks short and to the point. Still it took until the late fall for a decision.

The jury made its verdict known on November 19, 1985. It awarded Pennzoil the largest civil judgment in American history, $10.53 billion, upon finding that Texaco had improperly seized ownership of Getty Oil from Liedtke's company. The amount of the judgment left many astounded. The second-largest sum awarded in a corporate court fight had come in 1980 when MCI won $1.8 billion in a suit against AT&T. That dwarfed what had been decided in Texas. No one quite believed that the size of the Pennzoil judgment would stand. One major investment banker recommended getting rid of Pennzoil shares the day after the jury verdict, so certain was he that it would be overruled. But seven days later, it began to dawn on many that the verdict just might stick: Pennzoil was up about $5 a share and nobody was running to dump the stock.

In retrospect many would say that Texaco had made some devastating errors. But, to give the Pennzoil side credit, Jamail's strategy proved quite adept. Three of the most prominent Texaco errors cited were: (1) the failure to check into the family background of one of the jurors, James Shannon, whose wife, it turned out, had lost her job as the result of a merger—between Du Pont and Conoco. Shannon was one of Pennzoil's most vocal advocates. (2) Texaco's decision to bring Chairman McKinley to Houston at an early stage in the trial to show him off as human; that gave Pennzoil the chance to subpoena him to appear as a witness. When Pennzoil finished with him, he might have preferred to have stayed in New York. (3) The failure to challenge the amount of damages sought by Pennzoil. That omission has been cited as strong evidence that Texaco was unreasonably overconfident about the case.

The Texaco side was stunned at the outcome. No wonder. If the verdict was upheld, it could spell the end for the giant oil firm. One of the few professional subjects about which Joe Perella, the First Boston investment banker, showed emotion during our interview was the Texaco-Getty affair. "My own personal view," he said, "is that Texaco was victimized. I have never seen a man try harder to be right than John McKinley did in the twenty-four to forty-eight hours that he bought control of Getty. He was encouraged to come in by the CEO of Getty and the investment banker of Getty. We were told by numerous people on the Getty side that there was no signed contract and we had twenty-four to forty-eight hours before there would be one. It was with all that encouragement that he called his board together and tried to do the deal."[9]

The size of the Texas verdict shocked Perella, as did the claims of Pennzoil and the jury that they would teach businessmen a lesson in ethics through the harsh verdict. "That's a lot of crap, pure bull. If any of those people had a handshake to sell—had what Pennzoil had to sell their house for $200,000 and somebody came along and said, 'Here, let's go to contract, $250,000 right now,' every one of them (by now his voice was rising, and he was pounding his fist on the table) would have taken the 250. So all this blaming it on big business, that is no basis for deciding a $12 billion judgment. . . . It seems to be an emotional verdict, not based on facts. I mean who cares whether Marty Lipton is a likeable guy or not? That's not why Texaco should pay $12 billion. Or (Barton) Winokur, the lawyer for Getty, never looked at them in the face. So what?"[10]

Why such a large judgment? Pennzoil had argued that it deserved $7.53 billion in damages, as that was the amount it would have had to spend to locate and develop the 1 billion barrels of oil reserves it would have gained by doing the deal with Getty for $2.3 billion. It then sought $7.53 billion in punitive damages. The jury awarded the full $7.53 billion for actual damages, but it could not see itself going all the way on punitive damages, cutting that sum to $3 billion. Texas law was unkinder still to Texaco: it would have to pay interest at a rate of $1.2 billion a year starting January 4, 1984, the date on which Getty Oil had agreed to sell a 43 percent stake to Pennzoil.

The size of the judgment shocked some attorneys, who thought it almost unheard of that a company could come away with ten times its previous net worth from a suit. These attorneys pointed to contract law which had as one of its cardinal doctrines that a company could not enrich itself from a lawsuit; it should only emerge whole. Pennzoil, predictably, argued that this was no mere contract case but involved tort claims, since Texaco had maliciously induced the breach of the contract. That made Texaco liable for punitive damages as well, which the jury went ahead and awarded.

The verdict was a remarkable setback for dealmaking, just as the Bendix case in 1982 had been. Whatever the final disposition of the case, the court ruling might well make firms and raiders more hesitant about rushing to make a deal—particularly when a third firm appeared on the threshold of wrapping one up with the target company. When I asked a member of the Texaco team whether he thought the case would affect the way mergers were handled, he shrugged his shoulders and said no. Yet, like the Bendix case before it, the Texaco-Getty verdict earned huge headlines and gave mergers and dealmakers a bad name. It also appeared to be putting a damper on certain practices in the merger movement that had been viewed as acceptable in the past.

The very notion of what constituted an enforceable agreement was now in question. The Texaco verdict was having a chilling effect on such time-honored practices as the handshake. After Texaco, someone could insist that the handshake constituted an agreement when the other party might not agree. The verdict was also having an effect on bidding competition. Rather than run the risk of being sued for breach of contract by some bitter bidder, boards of directors were now forced to accept lower bids for their companies' assets. The very nature of dealmaking was being altered due to the November 19 verdict in Houston. "Letters of intent" and "agreements in principle" were becoming increasingly less common: investment bankers and attorneys labored hard to sew up deals quickly before anyone could come along with a higher bid. Whereas in the past the financial men would seal a deal with a handshake, then have the lawyers take a week or even longer to put the finishing touches on the arrangements, they were dispensing with all that now and trying to finalize matters at once.

The legal aspects of the Texaco case continued to plague the business community well after the verdict. It was not at all clear that other courts would rush in with supporting verdicts in cases that resembled the Texaco-Getty-Pennzoil issues. For instance, in March of 1986 the Nebraska Supreme Court rejected the idea that a merger agreement could be employed to keep interlopers out of the game. That was in striking contrast to the Houston judgment, namely that an interloper, Texas, could not interfere if there was an already existing merger agreement, as there had been between Getty Oil and Pennzoil. In a 4–3 decision, the Nebraska high court overturned a lower-court judgment against Cargill Inc., the Minneapolis-based commodities giant, for preventing a merger agreement between its rival, ConAgra Inc. of Omaha, and MBPXL Corp., a meat-packer from Wichita. The high court ruled that the directors of MBPLX had acted in keeping with their fiduciary responsibility by saying no to the ConAgra agreement in favor of Cargill's higher bid. The court's majority wrote that boards of directors cannot use agreements to "infringe on the voting rights of shareholders or chill the bidding process."

That seemed consistent with a major decision taken in January 1985 by the Delaware Supreme Court, which ruled then that directors can be held personally liable if they agree to a takeover agreement at an undervalued price. The decision, taken in the case of *Smith v. Van Gorkam*, appeared to mean that a board's obligation to stockholders should override an agreement with a suitor. Most likely this issue—whether a director's fiduciary responsibility to obtain the highest price has precedence over contract law—would be tested in the courts fairly soon. Only then would companies feel at ease in entering into bidding wars once again.

With the bad publicity surrounding dealmaking and with the new legal entanglements arising from the Texaco judgment, there was some concern on Wall Street that the merger mania of the past few years would cool off considerably. The evidence suggests, however, that the mania continues despite the bad press from Houston.

Reaction to the verdict ranged from red-hot anger on the part of Getty Oil and Texaco to signs of joyous relief on the part of Pennzoil. "This is an absolute miscarriage of justice," asserted a Getty family lawyer. "It's like the maniacs are running the asylum."[11] Hugh Liedtke was jubilant. "Their milestone verdict," he pronounced, "says the public demands integrity and morality from the entire business community."[12] Agreeing, jury foreman Richard Lawler observed, "We won't tolerate this sort of thing in corporate America."[13] Joe Jamail was naturally thrilled. Asked to cite the most important factor in the judgment, he said simply, "I was." When he returned to his law office, he found a banner that read, "Welcome home, $10.5 billion man." Precisely how much Jamail made from the case no one has divulged; the sum was probably astronomical. He was still the crusader to the end. "The message to the country," Jamail would say, "is that mergers-and-acquisitions people can't deal secretly and duplicitously."

The lawsuit had become known as the "case with all the zeroes." In fact there were no zeroes at all—$11,792,232,783.83. That was what Texaco was ordered to pay in damages plus interest charges. Texaco, soon after the verdict, passed word that it might have to file for bankruptcy if it was forced to put up a $12 billion bond, as Texas law required, to appeal. Hugh Liedtke thought Texaco should have no trouble with such a bond; after all, he noted, its liquidation value was $22 billion (though its market value was only $8.1 billion). As the lawyers wrestled with the distressing options brought on by the verdict, various scenarios were mentioned: Texaco would buy Pennzoil. Pennzoil would buy Texaco. Texaco would go bankrupt. Pennzoil would replace Texaco as a major oil company. With the megaverdict in place, nothing seemed outlandish anymore.

Attention now focused on a hearing scheduled for December 5, 1985, to determine whether the November 19 verdict should be upheld, modified, or tossed out. The hearing was held in a crowded fifth-floor room in the Harris County Civil Courts Building in Houston. A circus atmosphere prevailed. Since the day before the jury verdict of November 19, Pennzoil's stock had climbed $627 million while Texaco's had dropped $1.78 billion. Many people, other than the principals, had a stake in the outcome of the hearing. One stockbroker came in from San Antonio. To save important seconds he prepared both buy orders and sell orders for Pennzoil stock and instructed an assistant in San Antonio to execute them as soon as she got his phone call. By tipping a clerk $10 he had secured one of the rare courthouse phones. Others had the same idea. A dozen traders were carrying cellular mobile phones to be in touch with home offices or the stock market. One New York investment bank had hired a local lawyer to report on everything that happened in court, including the facial expression of the judge!

During the hearing Texaco attacked the judgment, insisting that it would destroy the company. It was, in Texaco lawyer Gibson Gayle Jr.'s words, "the most devastating specter of disaster in all of legal history." Again, hyperbole. Texaco wanted to have the case moved for appeal to the New York Court of Appeals, instead of a higher Texas court. At one point, the proceedings were thrown into disarray when Texaco announced that it had entered into settlement talks with Pennzoil. Pennzoil's Joe Jamail was furious and asked the judge to ignore the announcement. Nonetheless, the judge immediately recessed and called the parties into a private room of the courthouse. Meanwhile, traders, arbitragers and other speculators wondered what was going on.

Finally, on December 10, Judge Casseb upheld the jury verdict. Texaco would have to pay $10.53 billion in damages plus interest—$11.1 billion in all. It was a grave setback for Texaco, which said it would appeal. Later in December Texaco won a temporary Federal Court order barring Pennzoil from attaching Texaco's assets before other issues were settled in the suit.

Meanwhile, negotiators for both firms were meeting in Tulsa, Oklahoma, where they exchanged proposals for an out-of-court settlement. They would meet once again that month in Nashville. Pennzoil was apparently looking for a settlement of around $3 billion, while Texaco wanted to keep it under $1 billion. Though Texaco's John McKinley said he was open to a reasonable settlement, he remained convinced that Texaco had done nothing wrong; some thought he really preferred to stick it out in the courts and seek final vindication. The Texaco chief was spending three-quarters of his time on the Pennzoil problem. He tried to put a good face on things. This was not the most anxiety-ridden time in his life, he insisted. Others, however, thought the problem was having a devastating effect on him personally.

By early January 1986 the two sides had suspended their talks. Mention of a possible settlement sent Pennzoil's stock soaring by $20.50 a share to $83.75. Again, there was talk that Texaco was proposing a merger with

Pennzoil in exchange for which Pennzoil would drop its suit. But that came to nothing.

On January 10, U.S. District Court Judge Charles Brieant extended his order restraining Pennzoil from seizing Texaco's assets. He also ruled that Texaco should not have to put up more than $1 billion in security while it appealed the suit. Suddenly Texaco's hand was strengthened, particularly since the judge had said that the Texas requirement to post a $12 billion bond was "just so absurd, so impractical and so expensive that it hardly bears discussion." Texaco was now in a better position legally and, perhaps more important in a better position to negotiate an out-of-court settlement.

Pennzoil filed an appeal in the 2nd U.S. Circuit Court of Appeals in New York against the January 10 ruling. Once again the courtroom was crowded; this time—in February 1986—the scene was the U.S. Courthouse in Foley Square. The Pennzoil appeal was turned down. Hours before that ruling, a state court in Houston had effectively denied Texaco's motion for a new trial in the case. As of March 1986 Pennzoil was planning to take its appeal to the U.S. Supreme Court in the hope of forcing Texaco to post a $12 billion bond in pursuit of its own appeal of the November 19 verdict. Meanwhile, by late March, negotiations between Texaco and Pennzoil had resumed. On March 25 Liedtke and McKinley met for two hours at an undisclosed location in New York City. They agreed to keep talking. No other details from the meeting were made known at the time. Joe Jamail was in a feisty mood. He noted that the last Texaco offer, before the talks had been broken off in January, wasn't an offer, it was an insult. Texaco, he hinted, had not come in with the right price yet. "Nothing is going to happen until Texaco takes some reality pills and says, 'Here is X dollars.'"[14]

The appeals process moved slowly during the summer of 1986. In June the Supreme Court had agreed to decide whether a federal court could suspend Texas law, which required Texaco to post the $11.1 billion bond while appealing the Pennzoil judgment. But even before the Supreme Court actually did hear the case, a settlement was always a possibility.

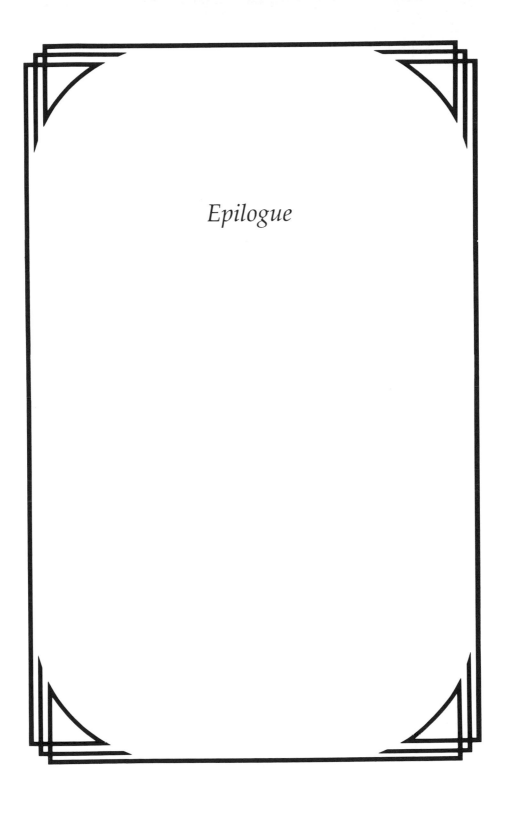

Epilogue

No matter how many pitfalls there were, no matter how many obstacles were placed in its way, by the spring of 1986 the modern takeover movement still had a full head of steam. Merger activity had cooled to some extent during the first part of the year, the main culprit being a rising stock market that had reduced the number of bargains available for takeovers. By the end of April the Dow Jones Industrial Average had jumped more than three hundred points to 1856. A similar gain had taken place during the last few months of 1985. While there had been 1,129 takeovers during the fourth quarter of 1985, that figure had dropped to 943 in the first quarter of 1986. The number of billion-dollar deals had dropped from nine to five during that period. The leveraged-buyout wave appeared to be cooling somewhat as well. By March 15 of 1986 some $533 million of LBOs had been completed, less than one-ninth of the $4.3 billion of 1985. No one had to look very far for the underlying reasons.

While the recent curbs by the Federal Reserve Board on the use of junk bonds were not affecting hostile takeovers and leveraged buyouts, the improved defenses being utilized by numerous corporations were slowing down the merger movement. Add to that the increasing uncertainty about a number of federal tax laws that could make takeovers more difficult to do. Nevertheless, there was plenty of work for investment bankers. Anyone who thought that takeovers would diminish as a result of the heightened Dow Jones average had been proven wrong. One factor kept the takeover business alive and well: the elevated stock prices had been accompanied by diminishing interest rates, which reduced the cost of borrowing money and made takeovers easier to accomplish.

Merger departments in the investment banking firms were expanding as a result of the booming business done in 1985. First Boston now had 110 people on its M&A staff. If there were to be lower revenues for 1986, that did not signal the demise of the takeover raider. Even with the formidable set of defenses and the new regulatory air coming out of Washington, hostile suitors were still expected to do as well as they had been doing in the past few years. Indeed, in the early part of 1986 90 percent of all unfriendly takeover offers above $250 million had been successful. The courts had recently ruled that boards of directors had a responsibility to sell to the highest bidder in a takeover fight, and that appeared to be helping raiders.

The new phenomenon of Megadeals appeared to have a life of its own. Certainly there seemed limits as to how far the merger movement could expand: some industries such as oil had already reached a saturation point, or so it seemed. Yet there was plenty of territory left to conquer along the American business landscape. New warriors who had discovered the monetary advantages of taking part in the takeover game were proliferating and growing increasingly aggressive.

The year 1985 had proven the great watershed for American corporations as they rushed to the barricades in droves, erecting defenses of varying quality and type in pursuit of survival. The verdict was still out on the effectiveness of the new defenses. All one could say by the spring of 1986 was that corporate America appeared to be finally digging in its heels. A whole series of defensive tactics were being employed, ranging from the poison pill to the highly popular leveraged buyout. But the raiders seemed to know better. While the defenses were obviously designed to deter, the raiders seemed to regard them more as challenges than anything else. Those who understood the takeover game insisted that, no matter how complicated and seemingly lethal the defense, a raider who made a cash offer with an enticing premium would almost automatically win the day. Stockholders, in other words, were not going to let a board of directors get in the way of making good money.

Washington continued to play an ambiguous, uncertain role in the takeover game. Passive in the past, willing to let the takeover players alone, the politicians began to sense in 1985 that something ought to be done to curb some of the activities which bothered the public the most. Few wanted regulation of the takeover movement. And so the men in Washington largely went through the motions. Forty-two bills were proposed in Congress to restrict hostile tender offers in 1985—but none was enacted. The Business Roundtable, a group of chief executives of more than two hundred of the major American firms, continued to lobby for new regulations against hostile takeovers. Their effort was unsuccessful. Only the Federal Reserve Board had taken fresh action—to curb junk bonds. But even that step appeared less related to a fear of takeovers than to sensitivities about rising corporate debt.

The courts added to the ambiguity. They had dealt some setbacks to the raiders in 1985 and early 1986. The Delaware court had allowed discriminatory tender offers in the Unocal case and it had condoned poison pills in the Household International Corp. case. Management seemed to be winning increasing powers to deal with unfriendly takeovers. An ever greater legal impediment to dealmaking arose in the Texaco-Pennzoil judgment in November of 1985. There the court had signaled to dealmakers that they would have to behave in more orderly fashion, they would have to think twice before making an offer for a company which had already been locked up in agreement with another. But in other court decisions the raiders were being encouraged. For instance, a Delaware court ruled in 1985 that the long-established "business judgment" rule was not an automatic escape from financial liability if a board of directors did not consider merger proposals fully.

For the first time in 1986 the practice of inside trading was exposed as a part of the takeover game, but just how large a part was not entirely clear. The spotlight fell in the spring of that year on Dennis Levine, who at the time had been one of Wall Street's bright and up-and-coming investment bankers. Just before trouble hit him, he had advised Pantry Pride Inc. on its takeover of Revlon Inc. Taking home an estimated $3 million in salary and bonuses a year, Levine was one of Drexel Burnham Lambert's biggest stars.

Until May of 1986. At that time he was charged with using confidential information to gain $12.6 million in illicit profits for trading the securities of fifty-four companies. In early June Levine admitted to four counts of securities fraud, perjury, and tax evasion and he signed a consent order that settled a civil suit brought by the Securities and Exchange Commission: he agreed to forfeit $11.5 million in profits. But Levine's guilty pleas did not relieve Wall Street of its new anxieties: clearly, now that the degree of insider trading among investment bankers and arbitragers had been revealed, it was probable that the SEC would take an even tougher stand.

And so there were mounting fears that the increasingly cozy relationships between arbitragers and investment bankers might come under new scrutiny. Although it was widely known that investment bankers and arbitragers talked over deals before they had been completed, no one—until now—had raised the idea that those discussions might be unethical, or perhaps even illegal. But that was the main effect of the Dennis Levine case, as it threatened to bring some or all of the coziness out into the open. By the summer of 1986 the arbs were saying little to the press and apparently wondering how serious their new problems were.

One takeover player not fazed by the inside trading disclosures was T. Boone Pickens. He examines potential takeover deals without help from investment bankers or other outsiders—so, as he has noted, he has no reason to worry about leaks. Only two or three trusted colleagues are apprised of his takeover plans, and only one file, under a 24-hour armed guard, is kept.

There was some good news coming out of Washington for the merger movement. President Ronald Reagan had unveiled plans to rewrite the antitrust laws to make mergers easier. This was in keeping with the liberal antitrust atmosphere pervading the Administration since it came to office in 1981. Commerce Secretary Malcolm Baldridge asserted that "We are living in an era of intense worldwide competition, and we think American companies should merge if it is going to increase their competitiveness."[1]

If the major corporate raiders portrayed on these pages appeared by 1986 to be quiescent, few believed that their raiding days were over. In some cases the raiders were trying to shrug off the old images brought to life from their predatory days. Little was heard from Bill Agee and Mary Cunningham except that they had become parents in the fall of 1985. T. Boone Pickens had taken on the role of white knight in a 1986 deal. Saul Steinberg had been approached to play a similar role in the TWA takeover fight (but he had declined). As for Carl Icahn, he was running an airline, not thinking (as far as one knows) of conducting any more raids, at least until he could put TWA into shape. Ted Turner had been, so it seems, chastened by the CBS fight: he had no further plans to go after that target. He was consoling himself with his friendly takeover of MGM/UA. Hugh Liedtke and John McKinley were still locked in the same legal battle over Texaco and Pennzoil. No one would have been surprised to learn that an out-of-court settlement had been reached. The two parties continued to talk even as their lawyers prepared for the next round in court.

References

References

CHAPTER 1

1 *Time,* August 3, 1981.
2 Interview with Joseph Flom, April 29, 1986.
3 *Fortune,* November 12, 1985.
4 Interview with Jay Higgins, February 6, 1986.
5 *Ibid.*
6 *Ibid.*
7 *New York Times,* July 18, 1982.
8 Poll quoted in *Business Week,* August 27, 1984.
9 *Wall Street Transcript,* November 2, 1981.
10 Survey results quoted in the *Wall Street Journal,* January 21, 1985.
11 *Business Week,* December 6, 1982.

CHAPTER 2

1 *Time,* October 4, 1982.
2 *Time,* February 8, 1982.
3 *People,* January 3, 1983.
4 *Detroit Free Press,* September 25, 1980.
5 Quoted in *Current Biography Yearbook,* 1984.
6 *New York Times,* September 25, 1982.
7 *Fortune,* October 18, 1982.
8 Peter F. Hartz, *Merger* (New York: William Morrow & Co., 1985), p. 409.

CHAPTER 3

1 *New York Times,* October 10, 1982.
2 *Fortune,* December 26, 1983.
3 *INC.,* July 1985.
4 *Time,* March 4, 1985.
5 *Current Biography,* July 1985.
6 *New York Times,* March 10, 1984.
7 *Esquire,* September 1985.
8 *New York Times,* February 25, 1985.
9 *People,* June 17, 1985.
10 *Ibid.*

CHAPTER 4

1 *Wall Street Journal,* December 22, 1982.
2 *The MacNeil/Lehrer News Hour,* January 6, 1986.
3 Interview with Al Kingsley, February 12, 1986.
4 *Manhattan, Inc.,* October 1984.
5 Interview with Carl Icahn, February 13, 1986.
6 *Fortune,* March 22, 1982.
7 *Business Week,* May 5, 1980.
8 Interview with Carl Icahn, February 13, 1986.
9 *People,* June 17, 1985.
10 Interview with Carl Icahn, February 13, 1986.
11 *Ibid.*
12 Interview with Al Kingsley, February 12, 1986.
13 Interview with Carl Icahn, February 13, 1986.

14 *Fortune,* March 18, 1985.
15 Interview with Carl Icahn, February 13, 1986.
16 *Business Week,* December 12, 1983.
17 Interview with Carl Icahn, February 13, 1986.
18 *Ibid.*
19 *The MacNeil/Lehrer News Hour,* January 6, 1986.
20 *Fortune,* March 18, 1985.
21 *Business Week,* December 12, 1983.
22 *Time,* March 18, 1985.
23 *Princeton Alumni Weekly,* February 26, 1986.

CHAPTER 5

1 *Fortune,* December 15, 1980.
2 *Manhattan, Inc.,* November 1984.
3 Quoted in the *New York Times,* April 15, 1984.
4 Quoted in *Time,* June 25, 1984.

CHAPTER 6

1 Interview with Joe Perella, February 11, 1986.
2 *Ibid.*
3 *Ibid.*
4 *Ibid.*
5 *Ibid.*
6 *Ibid.*
7 *American Lawyer,* January 1983.
8 *Forbes,* September 19, 1980.
9 *Ibid.*
10 *Ibid.*
11 *Wall Street Journal,* April 4, 1986.
12 Interview with Joseph Perella, February 19, 1986.
13 *Ibid.*
14 *Ibid.*
15 *New York Times,* December 29, 1985.
16 *Wall Street Journal,* December 6, 1984.
17 Figures quoted in the *Wall Street Journal,* April 14, 1986.

CHAPTER 7

1 *Atlantic Monthly,* December 1984.
2 Interview with Ivan Boesky, February 18, 1986.
3 Ivan F. Boesky, *Merger Mania* (New York: Holt, Rinehart & Winston, 1985).
4 Quoted in the *Wall Street Journal,* March 21, 1984.
5 Interview with Ivan Boesky, February 18, 1986.
6 *Ibid.*
7 *Atlantic Monthly,* December 1984.
8 *Wall Street Journal,* June 20, 1985.
9 Interview with Ivan Boesky, February 18, 1986.
10 Cited in *Atlantic Monthly,* December 1984.
11 *Washington Post,* June 23, 1985.
12 *Ibid.*

13 *Washington Post,* June 23, 1985.
14 Interview with Ivan Boesky, February 18, 1986.
15 *Ibid.*
16 *Ibid.*

CHAPTER 8

1 Interview with Joseph Flom, April 29, 1986.
2 *Fortune,* April 19, 1982.
3 Interview with Martin Lipton, June 6, 1986.
4 Quoted in Martin Lipton and Erica H. Steinberger, *Takeovers & Freezeouts* (New York: Law Journal Seminars Press, 1979).
5 Interview with Martin Lipton, June 6, 1986.
6 Interview with Joseph Flom, April 29, 1986.
7 *Time,* February 6, 1984.
8 Interview with Joseph Flom, April 29, 1986.
9 *Ibid.*
10 *Ibid.*
11 *Ibid.*
12 *Ibid.*
13 *Ibid.*
14 Interview with Martin Lipton, June 6, 1986.
15 *Ibid.*
16 *Ibid.*
17 *Ibid.*
18 *Ibid.*
19 *Ibid.*
20 *Ibid.*
21 Interview with Joseph Flom, April 29, 1986.
22 Richard Phelon, *The Takeover Barons of Wall Street* (New York: Putnam, 1981), p. 175.
23 Interview with Martin Lipton, June 6, 1986.
24 *Ibid.*
25 *Ibid.*
26 *Ibid.*
27 Interview with Martin Lipton, June 6, 1986.
28 Interview with Joseph Flom, April 29, 1986.

CHAPTER 9

1 Quoted in *Wall Street Journal,* April 12, 1985.
2 *Ibid.*
3 Quoted in 1983 *Current Biography.*
4 Quoted in *People,* September 12, 1977.
5 *Time,* August 19, 1982.
6 *Ibid.*
7 *Playboy,* August 1978.
8 Letter quoted in *Time,* August 9, 1982.
9 *Time,* April 29, 1985.
10 *Ibid.*
11 *Time,* July 15, 1985.

References

12 *Fortune,* August 5, 1985.
13 *Time,* October 28, 1985.
14 *Wall Street Journal,* October 2, 1985.
15 *Time,* October 28, 1985.
16 Quoted in the *Wall Street Journal,* March 26, 1986.

CHAPTER 10

1 *American Lawyer,* January/February 1986.
2 Quoted in *Forbes,* October 1, 1983.
3 Quoted in the *Wall Street Journal,* April 25, 1984.
4 Quoted in the *New York Times,* December 20, 1985.
5 *American Lawyer,* January/February, 1986.
6 *Ibid.*
7 *New York Times,* December 12, 1985.
8 *Ibid.*
9 Interview with Joe Perella, February 19, 1986.
10 *Ibid.*
11 Quoted in the *Wall Street Journal,* November 20, 1985.
12 *Ibid.*
13 *Ibid.*
14 Quoted in the *Washington Post,* March 27, 1986.

CHAPTER 11

1 *Time,* January 27, 1986.

Index